COLORADO

COLORADO STATE CAPITOL

COLORADO

The Story of
A Western Commonwealth

By
LeRoy R. Hafen

AMS PRESS
NEW YORK

Reprinted from the edition of 1933, Denver
First AMS EDITION published 1970
Manufactured in the United States of America

International Standard Book Number: 0-404-00604-3

Library of Congress Card Catalog Number: 78-100528

AMS PRESS, INC.
NEW YORK, N.Y. 10003

PREFACE

"Long memories make great peoples."

The story of Colorado's past embodies pictures of the life of prehistoric cliffdwellers and nomad Indians, the romance of Spanish and French explorers, the achievements and hardihood of American pioneers—of fur trader, miner, farmer, builder of industries and institutions.

This volume does not purport to give an exhaustive treatment of Colorado history. It aims to present the story of the state in a readable yet authoritative form. Though much of the material here presented is derived from research in original sources, the text is not burdened with detailed notes and citations. A selected list of references at the end of each chapter indicates source material and more extended treatments on particular subjects.

A number of persons have given valuable aid in the preparation of this volume. Dr. George B. Grinnell of New York offered suggestions and approved the chapter on the Indians. Drs. Paul S. Martin and George Woodbury, archaeologists, read the chapter on prehistoric peoples. The following persons have kindly read part or all of the manuscript: Senator C. S. Thomas, Ernest Morris, Henry A. Dubbs, E. B. Morgan, Henry Swan, Theron Field, Caldwell Martin, Frank Gove, Chauncey Thomas, Lee T. Casey, E. C. McMechen, Mrs. Inez Johnson Lewis, A. K. Loomis, and C. L. Cushman. These persons are, of course, in no way responsible for any errors that may have crept into the work. The assistance of my wife has been especially helpful. Most of the illustrations are used through courtesy of the State Historical Society.

The writer wishes to express special appreciation for access, during the past eight years, to the invaluable collections of rare manuscripts and pamphlets, early newspapers, and extensive Western Americana which have been built up through the years by devoted officers, members and friends of the State Historical Society of Colorado. The Society and the State have wisely made these treasures available to the public and are preserving this valued heritage for future generations of Coloradans.

TABLE OF CONTENTS

LIST OF ILLUSTRATIONS

CHAPTER I

THE LAND OF COLORADO

Physical Features and Natural Resources
Affect the History

ASTRIDE the continental divide, in the geographical center of the far West is Colorado. One of the newest states of the Union in point of settlement, she is one of the oldest in the field of exploration and Indian occupation. Many forces have had a hand in shaping her destiny. The interplay of these forces forms the basis for the fascinating story of Colorado's development.

History is concerned with the activities of men, but inasmuch as topography and natural resources largely determine the activity of a region's inhabitants, it may be well at the beginning to take a general view of the physical stage upon which the drama of Colorado history is enacted.

Three topographic zones—*Mountains, Plains* and *Plateaus*—with their rich plant, animal and mineral resources form the physical basis of Colorado.

The *Mountains* are the dominating feature of the state. They gather the snow to feed the rivers that irrigate the lands; they hold the gold and silver veins that attracted the first settlers; their majesty influences the aesthetic attitude of the inhabitants and draws thousands of visitors to the "Nation's Playground" for refreshment.

Colorado has been aptly called the Mountain State of the Union. Here it is that the famous Rocky Mountains assume their greatest height and grandest proportions in the United States. Fifty-one named peaks rise above 14,000

feet; over a thousand reach above 10,000 feet; and the
mean elevation of the state is well over a mile above the
level of the sea. Winding roads lace upward through scenic
canyons and parks to the mountain passes and peaks of the
continental divide and the pleasure resorts of the mountain
area. In summer the Rockies, even the highest ranges, can
be crossed almost anywhere on foot and in most places on
horseback.

The mountain zone, running north and south through
the middle of the state, is a rather complex system of ranges
and cross spurs. The Front Range, running from Wyoming
to Pikes Peak, is continued on to New Mexico as the Sangre
de Cristo and the Culebra ranges. Longs Peak, Mount
Evans, Pikes Peak, and Mount Blanca are the outstanding
sentinels along this chain. West of the Front is the Park
Range, extending from near Wyoming to the head of the
Arkansas River. West of the upper Arkansas is the
Sawatch Range, containing Mount Elbert and Mount Massive (the highest peaks in the state), the Mount of the Holy
Cross, and the Collegiate group— Mounts Harvard, Yale,
and Princeton. West of the Sawatch Range and southwest
of the Roaring Fork River are the Elk Mountains, from
which rise Maroon and Snow-mass peaks. The San Juan
Mountains are a massive, rugged group in the southwest portion of the state. They contain many high and precipitous
peaks, among which are Uncompahgre, Mount Sneffels, and
Mount Wilson.

The *Plains* stretch eastward from the base of the
Rockies. This region for centuries had been a treeless, grass-
covered plain, dotted here and there with isolated buttes
and ribboned with the white, sandy beds of intermittent
streams. The shallow valleys of the Platte and the Arkansas and the broad flat divide between them are the most

prominent features. This area is a part of the land once known as the "Great American Desert," where vast, black herds of shaggy buffalo and tribes of nomad Indians claimed the land. Today six lines of railroads and hundreds of miles of excellent highways cross and checker the region. Thin threads of irrigation ditches wind out from the river channels onto the uplands, inclosing irrigated areas rich with sugar beets and alfalfa, while scientific dry-farming has made a checkerboard of wheat and corn fields on large areas of the higher plains. The section is now dotted with cities, farms, and ranches. Intensive agriculture is reaping an inexhaustible wealth from the fertile soil.

The *Plateau* region of western Colorado consists of a series of mesas or plateaus that decline gradually by step-like intervals toward the western border of the state. The White River, Yampa, Roan (or Book), and Uncompahgre plateaus; the Grand and the Battlement mesas, and the Danforth Hills are the most notable elevations of the region. "If we conceive," says James Grafton Rogers, "of the portion of Colorado west of the Rockies proper as an elevated and much dissected layer cake we need only add that the cake has been disturbed somewhat by mischievous hands." The San Juan and the Elk mountains are the bad boy intruders. The plateau region is cut by numerous deep valleys and canyons, and only a comparatively small area, located in the broader valleys, is capable of agricultural development. But these valleys are peculiarly adapted to fruit growing, and horticulture therefore ranks high among the industries of the district. Large areas of the stratified plateau region consist of vast oil shale deposits, portions of which have been set aside as an oil reserve for future needs of the United States navy.

Colorado is the mother of rivers. From high mountain

parks, from perennial snow-banks of the continental divide
great streams radiate like the spokes of a wheel. One system of streams ultimately reaches the Mississippi, another
courses southward through the Rio Grande to the Gulf,
while a third flows westward through the mighty Colorado
to the waters of the Pacific. The principal rivers of the
eastern slope are the North Platte, South Platte, Arkansas,
and Rio Grande (with the Republican and the Smoky Hill
rising on the plains east of the mountains); those of the
western slope are the Colorado and its tributaries—the
Yampa, White, Gunnison, Dolores, and San Juan. Practically all of these streams, in the mountainous region near
their sources, have cut deep and rugged canyons through
upland ranges or spurs. The Royal Gorge of the Arkansas,
now spanned by the highest bridge in the world, is the most
notable of these. Though none of the rivers are navigable,
they have fixed the routes of land transportation, the areas of
irrigated agriculture, and the location of cities and towns.

The diverse topography of Colorado results in great
variations in climate and rainfall. In general, Colorado is
an arid state, the average precipitation being about $17\frac{1}{2}$
inches, but there is a wide variation in different sections,
ranging from 7 to 60 inches. The winter snowfall varies
almost directly with the altitude, five times as much snow
falling on the 14,000-foot peaks as descends on the 5,000-foot
plains. There are active glaciers and permanent snowbeds in
the north-central part of the state. The precipitation is
rather evenly distributed throughout the year, but the snowfall is usually greatest in February and March, while violent
afternoon thunderstorms generally occur in July and August.

Colorado is characterized by a clear blue sky and consistent sunshine. The night sky is brilliant with stars. As a
result of the high altitude and dry air, there is a great range

MOUNT OF THE HOLY CROSS

TOPOGRAPHIC MAP OF COLORADO

of temperature. In summer a marked contrast is noticeable between the temperature in the sun and in the shade, and the nights are always cool.

The seasons in Colorado do not run true to traditional form. Spring, as the season of gradual awakening of nature, scarcely occurs here. Winter seems suddenly to turn into summer. Colorado may be said to have three seasons: an open, chilly winter that lasts from December to April, with one or two short spells of extreme cold; a summer that continues into September; and an autumn with a gorgeous Indian summer that usually lingers through November. But the variations of altitude alter this for different localities and permit no generalization to be entirely true in all parts of the state.

The geography and climate of Colorado have not always been as we find them today. Through the uncounted years of past geological ages mighty changes have transformed the climate and the land surface of this Rocky Mountain area. In certain past ages this region has been completely covered by the sea. Fossils of many marine animals may be found in the rocks of Colorado; and the limestone and marble of the state have been formed from the lime carbonate of the shells and bones of sea animals which accumulated at the bottom of the sea through innumerable years, and in subsequent ages turned to stone.

The rock layers on the earth's surface form the great record book of geological history. Some pages are badly crumpled and others are missing, but this great book of stone, imperfect as it is, is the only document revealing the history of the earth's past. From its pages the discerning scientist is able to read the general history of the region— the successive rising and submergings of the land, the varied forms of life that flourished in succeeding epochs.

In the remotest geological ages the forms of plant and
animal life were simple and primitive, but through the millions of years a gradual evolution took place which produced higher forms. The record of these plants and animals
is preserved as fossils in the rocks, and it is these fossil im-
prints and remains that reveal life as it existed on the earth
at given periods. It is only in comparatively late geological
time that the plants and animals with which we are now
familiar began to appear.

One of the early geological periods is known as the
Devonian, or "Age of Fishes," because at that period fishes
were the predominant form of animal life. In a subsequent
period, the Jurassic, reptiles ruled, with giant dinosaurs as
the kings of creation. In the Cretaceous (Chalk) period
immediately following, a luxuriant plant growth flourished;
in the widespread swamps and lagoons the dying plants
fell into the water and the accumulation in time was transformed into the great coal beds of Colorado.

It was in late Cretaceous time that the great upheaval
occurred which produced the Rocky Mountains and converted the region of Colorado from a low plain to a high
plateau and mountainous region. It was this upheaval which
produced the conditions for oremaking in Colorado. Says
Professor R. D. George: "The rise of lavas and other igneous
rocks to the surface is accompanied by vapors, gases and
highly heated mineral-charged waters. The folding, fault-
ing and crushing of the rocks in these great movements
form channels of circulation for the mineralizing solutions,
and afford opportunities for them to come into contact with
other solutions, vapors and solids by which their mineral
content is precipitated and forms ore bodies."

After the reign of the reptiles, which period had pre-
ceded the formation of the Rocky Mountains, the birds be-

came a prominent form of animal life; and after their relative decline the mammals became the dominant type. But
these first mammals were rather different from those of today. They were of generalized forms, which have since
differentiated into our modern types. For instance, says
Professor George, "The horse, deer, and rhinoceros families
with their special and distinct features may be traced back
to a peculiar five-toed animal having a full set of rather
simple teeth, and of no greater size than an average dog.
The dog, cat and bear families are traced to an animal similar to the ancestor of the horse, deer and rhinoceros. Evolution was very rapid and bone deposits show remains of
both the modern differentiated forms and the earlier generalized types."

The variations in altitude in Colorado have brought
about the existence of wonderfully diversified flora and
fauna. In the high mountains are species typical of the far
north; in the arid south and southwest, desert types exist;
while temperate zone species abound as the typical and most
numerous varieties. Many species here are peculiar to Colorado. Scores of these have but recently been discovered and
described, while no doubt there are numerous undiscovered
ones awaiting the search of the careful scientist. These
altitude variations are exemplified most strikingly in the
belts of different trees encountered as one ascends or descends the mountains. The Life Zones are as follows (data
furnished by Prof. T. D. A. Cockerell):

(1) The Arctic-Alpine, the region above timberline.
It is characterized by the absence of trees, and the presence
of numerous small plants and brilliant flowers. Among the
fauna are the mountain sheep (which descend to the valleys
during the colder part of the year), the pika, or cony (a
little animal allied to the rabbit, but with short ears and no

tail), the snowshoe rabbit, and the ptarmigan (related to the grouse, and white in winter and mottled in summer).

(2) Hudsonian, so called because it is typical of the Hudson Bay region. This is the zone of "black timber," including the Engelmann spruce, bristle-cone pine, and balsam fir. Chipmunks, Fremont squirrels, weasels, bears (in summer), elk, deer and mountain lions live in this region. The most conspicuous bird is the white-headed jay, or camp robber.

(3) Canadian, with mixed, more open vegetation. The aspen and lodgepole pine thrive here, and this is the natural habitat of the columbine, the state flower. Mammals, birds and especially insects are abundant. This zone roughly includes altitudes from 8,000 to 10,000 feet above sea level.

(4) The Transition, or Coloradian Area, extending along the foothills and into the mountain parks. It is relatively dry and the vegetation is mostly sparse. The Yellow pine, Douglas fir, and mountain maple are common. Sagebrush, especially on the western slope, is widespread.

(5) Upper Austral, including the lower altitudes and the region of the plains. The western cottonwood, along the water courses, and the piñon pine are typical trees. Varieties of yucca and cactus are common. The antelope, buffalo, prairie dog, coyote, and jack rabbit are or were representative animals.

The different life zones are not marked by hard and fast lines but tend to merge into each other; varying of course with conditions of slope and with the latitude. Certain hardy plants and animals can live in more than one -zone.

The coming of white men altered the habitat and life of various animals. For example, elk, deer, bears, and coyotes, once primarily animals of the plains, are now confined

BLUE COLUMBINE, STATE FLOWER OF COLORADO

Upper: "THE COKE OVENS," COLORADO NATIONAL MONUMENT
Lower: ALEXANDER LAKE, GRAND MESA

chiefly to the mountains; while the buffalo and antelope, most common game animals of the plains, have become almost extinct. The coyote has learned to thrive on man's domestic flocks of chickens and sheep, and the jack rabbit has increased in numbers by feeding on the cultivated crops of the farm.

The thousands of species of plants and animals native to Colorado cannot, of course, be listed or described here. But a few of those that have most directly affected the early history of the territory are here mentioned. The short, curly, nutritious buffalo grass that covered the plains of eastern Colorado made possible the vast herds of buffalo in that region. The buffalo in turn furnished food, clothing and shelter for the plains Indians; and for white emigrants and explorers provided not only food but fuel on the treeless plains in the form of buffalo chips. With the passing of the buffalo, the grasses of the plains pastured the long-horned cattle and led to the development on a grand scale of the open range livestock industry of Colorado.

The precious beaver, hiding in secluded mountain streams, lured trappers to untrod regions and brought about a thorough exploration of the state long before the gold rush brought the settlers. When the world market for beaver skins declined and a demand arose for buffalo hides, then it was that the wholesale slaughter of the buffalo cleared the plains for the livestock boom.

The location and the importance of some of the native plants and animals of Colorado are evinced in the names of such creeks as the following: Cherry, Plum, Grape, Lodgepole, Pine, Cedar, Bear, Turkey, Snake, Deer, Elk, and Trout. Wild berries and fruits determined the sites of Indian summer campgrounds, as groves of cottonwoods fixed the winter retreats. The bark and twigs of the sweet cottonwood nourished Indian ponies and pioneers' horses during severe winters; and cottonwood logs were made into pioneer cabins. Pine and spruce provided logs and lumber for the first houses, timbers for mines, and poles for the Indian lodges and *travois*, and for white man's fences and bridges. Sod and adobe became building materials for pioneers on the treeless plains. Native fish and game provided food for pioneers and sport for late comers.

Rivaling the flora and fauna in affecting and directing the course of history in Colorado are the metals and minerals buried in the earth. It was rumor of gold that brought the first white men—the Spaniards—to Colorado, and gold discoveries inaugurated the first permanent settlement. Large bodies of silver ore brought boom days to the "Silver State." Vast deposits of coal affected industry. Over two hundred metals and minerals useful to man are found in the state.

Taken in the large, the topography, climate, resources, and general physical conditions in Colorado are such as have made possible great development in this area. At first neglected for regions thought to offer superior resources, Colorado was comparatively late in attracting the permanent settler. But once occupied and tested she has proved to be a land of great promise, rich and favored.

✦ ✦ ✦

SELECTED REFERENCES FOR FURTHER READING

Baker and Hafen (Eds.), History of Colorado (1927), 35-200
J. C. Smiley, History of Denver (1903), 17-41
O. J. Hollister, The Mines of Colorado (1867), 13-16, 22-59
J. L. J. Hart, Fourteen Thousand Feet (1931)
R. D. George, Geology and Natural Resources of Colorado (1927)
Francis Ramaley, Colorado Plant Life (1927)
T. D. A. Cockerell, Zoology of Colorado (1927)
P. A. Rydberg, Flora of Colorado (1906)
Arthur Lakes, Geology of Colorado and Western Ore Deposits (1893)
E. R. Warren, The Mammals of Colorado (1910)
Colorado Magazine: "The Conifers or Evergreens of Colorado" (Jan., 1925); "Colorado Mountain Passes" (Nov., 1929)

CHAPTER II

IN THE DAYS OF THE CLIFFDWELLERS

The Story of the People Who Vanished

FOUR hundred nineteen years before Columbus set foot on American soil there was being built, of sandstone rocks and sturdy logs, one of the most notable structures in North America. The site chosen for this building, which was a big apartment house, was picturesque as well as utilitarian. A monster cave in a precipitous canyon had appealed to the brown-skinned architects as a likely site and the masons had set to work. Stone hammers squared the building blocks, while stone axes felled trees on the mesa above the cave for the building logs and joists. When finally completed this great communal house contained over one hundred living rooms, besides twenty-three ceremonial rooms (kivas) intended for social and religious purposes.

The builders of this house could neither read nor write. They had no horses, cattle or sheep, no wheeled vehicles, no firearms, no metals of any kind. And yet they were good farmers, excellent stone workers, skillful potters and weavers, and had a high degree of intelligence. Their building stands today, after more than eight and one-half centuries, in excellent repair. Any visitor to Mesa Verde National Park in southwestern Colorado may inspect this great structure. It is known today as the "Cliff Palace."

But how did we come to know of these people, who had already deserted their homes and vanished before our forefathers came to the "New World"? Let us see what we have been able to learn of this interesting people even though they left us no written records.

The first white men to penetrate southwestern Colorado came upon remarkable stone house ruins scattered about the mesas and nestled in caves and cliffs in the canyons. Father Escalante and his party, while traversing this area in 1776, noted such remains and found them long since deserted. Subsequent traders, hunters and prospectors came upon quantities of potsherds and ruins of stone houses. But the most remarkable of these prehistoric remains, such as the Cliff Palace of the Mesa Verde, were not discovered by white men until late in the 1880s.

The Wetherill brothers, Richard and Al, while wintering their cattle in the canyons of the Mesa Verde in 1887-8, discovered many of the larger ruins of the area. With C. C. Mason they made further explorations and were amazed at the size and extent of the cliff houses they found. Soon "pot hunters" went into the region and dug about in the ruins to secure the relics buried there. As more people became interested in the historic significance of these finds, public opinion was aroused at the prospect of these amazing remains being pilfered and destroyed. To safeguard these priceless relics of the past, a movement was inaugurated which resulted in the creation of Mesa Verde National Park in 1906.

Under the direction of Dr. J. Walter Fewkes, the national government began excavation and restoration work at Mesa Verde in 1908 and during the same year the State Historical Society of Colorado and other interested organizations began work at McElmo Canyon. Archaeologists—the historians of vanished peoples—continued their researches and study in the region and by careful observation learned much regarding the people who built these houses. The

MORTUARY POTTERY FROM BURIAL-REFUSE MOUNDS IN
SOUTHWESTERN COLORADO

CLIFF PALACE, MESA VERDE NATIONAL PARK

structure and location of the buildings; the skeletons and
clothing unearthed; the basketware and pottery; the stone
and the bone tools; the remains of food—all have helped
modern scholars to reconstruct the life of these primitive
Coloradans. The degree of skill attained in the manufacture and decoration of their pottery, the successive designs
and colors employed, and the character of other handiwork
of these people reveal their culture and the successive stages
of its evolution.

An accurate dating of ruins is a recent accomplishment.
Dr. A. E. Douglass, an astronomer of the University of
Arizona, in his study of sun spots and their relation to climate on the earth, took up the study of tree rings as a record of climatic changes. He found that dry years or wet
left their indelible record in the thickness of the ring of
growth on a living tree. By taking cross sections of logs
from prehistoric ruins, studying these and comparing them
with log records of known dates, he was, after years of research, finally able in 1929 to perfect a tree ring record and
chart that goes back over 1200 years. Then by taking a
log from a particular ruin and matching its rings in his
chart he was able to date the log. It was in this way that
Cliff Palace was given the date of 1073 A.D.

But from many ruins no logs are procurable, and dependence must be on other indications. Stratigraphy, or the
sequence of strata, has revealed valuable data. For example,
where the remains of one culture are found directly upon
those of another in an undisturbed condition it is conclusive
proof that the lower is the older. Several sites have revealed
such testimony and have thus aided in unraveling the story
of successive developments.

After careful and prolonged study the archaeologists
have developed a fairly accurate general account of the evo-

lution of pre-historic culture in the Southwest. They have divided the known development into two general periods— the *Basketmaker* and the *Pueblo* (including the Cliffdweller), each with a number of subdivisions. Preceding the Basket-maker, or earlier culture, it is assumed that nomadic people, resembling the modern Digger Indians of the Nevada re-gion, lived in the Southwest. They probably had brush wickiups, lived upon such small game as rabbits, prairie dogs and doves and on insects, berries, roots and grass seeds. They were no doubt ignorant of agriculture and of pottery making.

A decided advance came when these primitive people learned of corn and how to grow it. Corn appears to have been developed in the highlands of Mexico or Central Amer-ica or in Peru and from thence spread northward. It was destined to be one of the most important factors in the de-velopment of the prehistoric peoples of the Southwest. This introduction of agriculture marks the beginning of the Bas-ketmaker Period proper. The culture and period take their name from the extensive manufacture and use of baskets, which are found with burials of these people.

The farming of the earliest Basketmakers was very crude and haphazard, but as they gained in skill and their efforts were rewarded with fuller harvests, it became possible for them to expend less time in obtaining food and to de-vote more time to other things. They were thus enabled to develop fine basketry and fur cloth, and to improve their woven sandals. They made caches to hold and preserve their corn, some of which were made by digging holes in the floor of caves and lining these cists, or bins, with flat stones. Most of the Basketmaker remains thus far discovered have been found in dry caves. In some of these, the mummified bodies of Basketmakers have been found, accompanied by

/

offerings of food, baskets, weapons, tools, ornaments and other things, intended as equipment for the future life. A close study of such remains gives a good picture of the life and arts of these people.

The skeletons indicate a people of medium size. They were long-headed, not having the deformed or flattened skull so common with the later Pueblo-cliffdwellers. The corn found is of a single variety and this of a very primitive type. These people also raised squashes, but apparently had no beans or cotton. Their cloth and blankets were woven of yucca fibre and rabbit fur. They made human-hair cords, and wove fibre bags and sandals. The typical sandal was of the square-toed variety with a buckskin or fiber fringe at the end. Their most typical work, however, was their basketry, which is found in the form of trays, bowls, jars, and large panniers. Apparently they had not learned of the bow and arrow, but instead used in their hunting, wooden darts, or spears, and the atl-atl, or spear thrower, a device which added length and therefore greater force to the arm. Their meat was roasted over the coals or on spits before the fire, and stews were made in water-proof basket-pots, hot stones being thrown into the stew to make it boil.

In the course of time the Basketmakers learned, either by their own invention or from neighbors to the south, that vessels made of clay, dried in the sun and finally baked in the fire were not only easier to make than were the woven baskets, but they served better as water jugs and cooking pots. "At about the same period," says Dr. A. V. Kidder, one of the principal authorities on the Basketmakers, "they began to enlarge their storage cists into dwellings, to wall them higher with slabs, and to provide them with pole-and-brush roofs." These two great advances—pottery and improved houses—are the chief features of the late Basketmaker period. The early crude pottery, much of it basket-marked, was mostly gray, with some undecorated red piece: and a primitive form of black-on-white ware.

Products of this period have been found in the Step House ruin at Mesa Verde underneath the regular Cliff-dweller remains. The archaeological expeditions of the State Historical Society in the Pagosa-Piedra area (conducted by J. A. Jeancon) and in the region northwest of Mesa Verde (by P. S. Martin) revealed late Basketmaker remains. In fact some of the ruins excavated show that Pueblo struc-tures were built on the very sites and upon the ruins of late Basketmakers' homes. No hard and fast line can be drawn between the two and the change no doubt covered many years, but there were certain new and distinct fea-tures introduced which characterize the Pueblo (including the Cliffdweller) Period.

The skeletal remains show a decided change in the physique, a taller stature and a different skull shape, which have led archaeologists to believe that a new people of a different racial strain came into the region at this time. Whereas the Basketmakers were long headed, the Pueblos were broad headed. It is possible that this broadening of the skull, so typical of the Pueblo-Cliffdwellers, was just a flattening of the posterior portion, caused by the use of hard cradleboards for the babies, but there is evidence that a new racial element was introduced at the beginning of the Pueblo Period. The invading Pueblo Indians, if such they were, may have driven out the Basketmakers or may have assimilated them.

The bow and arrow, cotton, beans, domesticated tur-keys, better pottery with improved designs, are some of the new features that first appear with the Pueblo Period. There seems to have been a gradual evolution in the building of the primitive Pueblo people's houses. The earlier type has been called the "pit house," because it is partly under ground. The portion of the walls above ground was made of upright poles plastered with mud or was built of cobblestones. The next stage was the building of single rooms entirely above ground, the walls being constructed of cobblestones or flat rocks. Then follows a grouping of five or six rooms into a unit, and finally the construction of large communal houses, or pueblos, often containing more than a hundred rooms. Some of these large pueblos were built in caves or cliffs, such as the famous ones in Mesa Verde.

Archaeologists have divided the Pueblo Period into a number of successive culture divisions, each distinguished by certain pottery designs, features of house construction and such, but these we shall not detail here. Suffice it to say that there was a gradual development and improvement during the period, which culminated in the culture exemplified by the large communal houses in Mesa Verde.

These imposing structures were built, according to the tree-ring record, during the two centuries 1050 to 1250 A.D. This was the Great Period, or Golden Age, of prehistoric culture in Colorado and the Southwest. In Europe these same two centuries saw the Norman Conquest of England (1066), the development of Feudalism, and the famous Crusades to rescue Jerusalem from the Turks (1096-1212). This was over two centuries before the invention of printing; the world was still thought to be flat; and over four-fifths of the earth's surface was as yet unknown to Europeans. All in all, our ancestors also were rather backward in the days of the Cliffdwellers.

The concentration of people into the large communal houses, which was a distinct feature of the Great Period of the Pueblos, was probably brought about by invasion and attacks of nomadic people, forefathers of our modern Utes and Apaches, or through war or rivalry between different clans or inhabitants of separate pueblos. In any case, the building of pueblos in inaccessible cliffs, the construction of watch towers and such other defensive features, clearly indicate that security from attack was a controlling motive in the lives of these people. It would seem that there was just enough danger to cause the highest social and community effort. Life was not so easy that it produced indolence or stagnation, yet not so hard that it stifled progress. This nice balance between necessity and opportunity probably accounts for the Golden Age of the Pueblos.

The architecture of this period was notable. The large communal houses which the Pueblos built on the mesas and in the caves were imposing structures of hewn stone. The masonry work was excellent, with straight walls and even courses of stone. Some of these buildings were, in places, three or four stories high; the general plan of the structure being similar to the present Pueblo buildings in New Mexico.

The floors of upper stories were supported by log beams. Across these were placed small poles which were then covered with cedar bark or twigs and finally coated with a layer of adobe. The regular living and storage rooms were rectangular and small. The doors also were small and were of two types, rectangular and T shaped.

The most interesting rooms were the kivas, which were used for religious and ceremonial purposes and also as club rooms for the men and boys. Apparently each clan or fraternity had its own kiva. In the big communal houses there was usually one kiva to every five to fifteen ordinary rooms. The kiva was unique in character. It was built underground, or largely so, and was usually round, with a diameter ranging from ten to sixty feet. In the center of the flat roof was a small opening by which the men entered the room and through which the smoke from the kiva fire escaped. Near the center of the floor was the fire pit, and a banquette or sort of bench extended around the wall. In the floor near the fire pit was the opening of a ventilator shaft or tunnel which ran underneath the floor and then extended upward to the surface beyond the kiva. In some recently excavated ruins north of Cortez, Colorado, Dr. Martin found these tunnels extending into towers some little distance from the kivas. Our knowledge of the purposes and uses of the kivas are derived from their structure and from a comparison with the kivas of modern Indians. There are certain questions however, in regard to these interesting rooms and the life they fostered which may never be answered. Of the people also, who built these houses and lived their lives in them we would gladly know more than we do. But from rather extensive remains we can reconstruct fairly well their character and manner of life.

These people were primarily farmers, their crops being grown on the mesas or in the narrow valleys. Irrigation they understood, as is evidenced by the remains of small ditches and dams at various places in the region. Corn was their principal crop, but squashes, beans, gourds, and melons also were grown. They had cotton, but whether it was raised by themselves or obtained from neighbors to the south or west is not known. They hunted for deer and other wild game, using the bow and arrow and the spear as weapons. They domesticated the turkey, used its feathers in weaving, and probably used its flesh for food. Wild berries, fruits, and seeds no doubt added variety to their diet.

The community appears to have been emphasized more than the individual family among the Pueblo-Cliffdwellers. The small size of the rooms would indicate that these were

used more as retreats from severe weather than as homes
in our modern sense of the word. There were no chairs,
tables, bedsteads, or such furniture in their houses. Mats,
baskets, and pottery were the chief furnishings. No doubt
the Pueblos spent most of their time in the open. The grinding bins, where the women ground their corn, were usually
outside the houses, as were the fires over which they cooked
their meals.

The Pueblos were industrious and peaceable. Supplies
of food, water and wood had to be carried, often for considerable distances, to their communal houses; and where
their homes were in the inaccessible cliffs, the bringing in
of supplies was no little task. When home from the fields
or the hunt the men mended their weapons and tools,
chipped new arrowheads and spear heads, and engaged in
the ceremonies of their religious and social life.

Various arts and industries absorbed the time of the
women about the pueblo. The grinding of their corn, the
making and decorating of their pottery, their weaving and
basketry, not only produced the necessities and conveniences
of life, but afforded opportunities for the social intercourse
they loved. The brown-skinned children played about the
courts and walls of the big houses, ran among the piñon
and cedar trees on the mesa tops and clambered up and
down the canyon trails. The girls had wooden dolls to dress
and tend while the boys played at building houses of pebbles
and practiced shooting with their bows and arrows.

The social and ceremonial life of the Pueblos must have
been rather full and elaborate. The large number of kivas
with their unique and peculiar features, were the sacred
chambers for much of this activity. Solemn councils with
time-honored ritual were held in the privacy of the kivas
and on special occasions colorful dances and impressive cere-

DESIGNS FROM MESA VERDE BLACK-ON-WHITE WARE

FAR VIEW HOUSE, MESA VERDE NATIONAL PARK

monies or parades entertained the entire community. The
sun, the springtime, the life-giving corn, the harvest, the
rain, their ancestors, the spirits of another world—all no
doubt received due homage in their various festivals and
ceremonies.

These prehistoric people had no metals and therefore
had to make their tools and implements out of stone, wood
and bone. From hard rock they fashioned axes, hammers,
arrow and spear heads, knives, and metates, or grinding
stones; bones they converted into awls, needles, and scrap-
ers; and from wood they made planting sticks, needles,
cradle boards, sandal lasts, toys, and ceremonial sticks of
various kinds.

There is great variety in their woven and textile work.
Yucca fibre, cotton, cedar bark, grass, willows, fur and
feathers, were the principal materials used. The tough fibre
from the yucca leaf was their chief dependence. This was
used in making cords, ropes, feather cloth, sandals, bands,
and bags. The finest cloth for bands and blankets they wove
from cotton; cedar bark and grass were the materials for
making rings for pot rests; while willow withes were used
in making baskets and mats. Some of their baskets exhibit
remarkable workmanship and rare beauty, being made into
winnowing trays, plaques, panniers, and bowls of various
shapes.

One of the characteristic and most highly developed
products of the art and industry of the Pueblos was their
pottery. Although they did not have the potter's wheel or
any such mechanical device, they produced pottery of a high
order. The primitive potter would roll out a long fillet, or
rope, of clay and coil it into a disc, pressing and pinching
each layer firmly onto the preceding one. As the disc grew
he would build it outward and upward into the shape de-

sired. The earliest pottery was rough and undecorated, but as skill and artistic sense developed, improvements came. The surface was smoothed and polished with a glossy stone, and a colored slip, or sort of kalsomine, was applied. Then they began to decorate the vessels with black lines and gradually evolved beautiful designs of geometric type and conventionalized animal forms in great variety. It is these unique decorations that make Mesa Verde pottery not only famous but easily recognizable. This pottery is preserved in many forms. Bowls, mugs, ollas, and ladles are the most common pieces, but there are many jars, pitchers and canteens as well as a number of other more unusual shapes and types.

Such, briefly, are some of the features of the prehistoric Pueblo people of southwestern Colorado, a people who had already forsaken their picturesque homes before the white man came into the Southwest (Coronado came in 1540). What became of them? This question has been rather puzzling to the casual observer. Some have thought that there must have been a wholesale destruction of these people by famine, disease or some cataclysm of nature, but there is no evidence to substantiate these views. There have been similar desertions of pueblos in New Mexico during historic times, some of the pueblos occupied in Coronado's day having been deserted since. Attacks by hostile tribes, failure of a spring, droughts, strife between various clans, some unusual event superstitiously interpreted as an ill omen, are causes which have led to the abandonment of pueblos within historic times.

In all probability similar causes led the prehistoric Pueblos of Colorado to forsake their picturesque homes in the cliffs and on the mesas. The inroads of nomad tribes, such as the Utes and Apaches, no doubt figured prominently in the result. It is likely that the desertion of the cliffdwellings came gradually, that seceding or ousted clans and the inhabitants of certain pueblos moved away to the south or west to be absorbed by other people already living in those sections. Some of the present day Pueblo Indians of New Mexico have definite traditions that certain of their ancestors came from cliff houses in the region of present Colorado. Zuni and Hopi Indian traditions also tell of forefathers who lived in the cliffs to the north. In addition, there is the similarity of house structure, of customs and manner of life that indicates a relationship between these living Indians and those prehistoric inhabitants.

All things considered, it seems indisputable that blood of our prehistoric Pueblo-Cliffdwellers runs in the veins of some of the modern Pueblo Indians of New Mexico and Arizona.

✦ ✦ ✦

SELECTED REFERENCES FOR FURTHER READING

A. V. Kidder, An Introduction to the Study of Southwestern Archaeology (1924)

E. L. Hewett, Ancient Life in the American Southwest (1930)

Baker and Hafen, History of Colorado, 201-256

W. H. Jackson, Ancient Ruins of Southwestern Colorado (Ann. Rep., U. S. G. S. for 1874)

G. E. A. Nordenskiold, Cliff Dwellers of the Mesa Verde (1893)

J. W. Fewkes, Antiquities of the Mesa Verde National Park: Spruce-Tree House, Cliff Palace, and Prehistoric Villages, Castles and Towers of Southwestern Colorado (Bur. of Am. Eth. Bulletins 41, 51, and 70)

Archaeological Exploration Reports of the State Historical Society of Colorado, in Colorado Magazine, Vols. I-X

A. E. Douglass, "The Secret of the Southwest Solved by Talkative Tree Rings" (National Geographic Magazine, Dec., 1929)

CHAPTER III

THE INDIANS OF COLORADO

The Nomad Lords of Mountain and Plain

FOR many years before the white man came—no one can tell how long — roving Indians wandered about the mountains and plains of present Colorado. The Utes, or "Blue Sky People," occupied the mountain area, while "Buffalo Indians" ranged the great level plains to the east.

When Coronado came seeking the fabled riches of Quivira in 1541, he met the early Indians of the plains and described them in a letter to the king of Spain:

"After nine day's march [from the Rio Grande in New Mexico] I reached some plains, so vast that I did not find their limit anywhere that I went, although I traveled over them for more than 300 leagues [a Spanish league is 2.63 miles]. And I found such a quantity of cows [buffalo] in these, of the kind that I wrote Your Majesty about, which they have in this country, that it is impossible to number them . . . And after seventeen day's march I came to a settlement of Indians who are called Querechos [herdsmen], who travel around with these cows, who do not plant, and who eat the raw flesh and drink the blood of the cows they kill, and they tan the skins of the cows, with which all the people of this country dress themselves here. They have little field tents [lodges] made of the hides of the cows, tanned and greased, very well made, in which they live while they travel around near the cows, moving with these. They have dogs which they load, which carry their tents and poles and belongings."

Early Spanish records tell of *Yutahs* (Utes) and other
wild tribes venturing into the New Mexican settlements to
barter. Alluring articles the white men spread before their
amazed visitors. There were magic weapons and tools—
thunder-sticks that killed with lightning swiftness; arrow
tips that did not break or chip; long, smooth-edged knives
that quickly flayed a carcass; and axes so sharp and sure
they felled a lodge pole with a single stroke. Gorgeous articles of adornment the white men offered: soft, pliant robes
dyed with colors from the sunset; brilliant beads gathered
from the rainbow; shining trinkets and tinkling bells that
danced and sang as one walked along. And most wonderful of all, was a kind of prancing, hornless elk that
seemed designed for man to ride upon. For these attractive
objects the Indian gave his buckskins, buffalo robes, jerked
meat, and enemy captives.

In time there developed an annual fair at Taos, New
Mexico, and at other frontier Spanish settlements, to which
the Indians came to barter for white man products. Spanish traders frequently made return visits to the Indian country with goods for trade.

The Indians, long accustomed to raiding enemies to
supply their wants, early learned that surprise attacks upon
the Spanish settlements were a most fruitful method of securing horses. Such horse-stealing raids grew more frequent and although punitive expeditions were sent against
the marauders, the residents of New Mexico were unable
to stop the intrusions. As the years passed, horses multiplied so rapidly in the Southwest that in time they over-
ran the plains, whereupon Indians increased their pony herds
from the wild bands.

By the time the first Americans began to enter Colorado territory, in the early 19th century, the Indian had re-

formed his system of life. Two hundred years of contact with Spaniards in the Southwest had had their effect. The Indian had become an expert horseman. Mounted, he procured his game more easily, extended the range of his raids and wanderings. He was acquainted with firearms, and had adopted metal tools and utensils to replace the crude knives, axes, and arrowpoints made of stone. His ancient garb of skins was ornamented with beads and gewgaws and modified with touches of bright-colored cloth from white man stores.

It is these Indians as we find them in the 19th century that concern us most in Colorado history, for it is with them that our American explorers, traders, and pioneer settlers had their dealings.

When the American pioneers came to Colorado the territory was occupied by three principal Indian tribes—Utes, Arapahoes, and Cheyennes. Of the three, the Utes, a branch of the great Shoshonean Family, were the oldest residents. They claimed the whole mountain area and the western slope, having occupied this region for several centuries. They were a short, stocky tribe, so dark-skinned that other tribes referred to them as the "black Indians."

The Arapahoes came next. They are classed in the Algonquian Family and are supposed at a remote period to have lived near the Great Lakes and to have engaged in agriculture. But they forsook the sedentary life, took to the plains and adopted a nomad existence. The region about the headwaters of the Arkansas and the Platte they looked upon as home. They were taller than the Utes, and lighter skinned. One of their peculiar customs gave the tribe its name, Arapaho, meaning "Tatooed on the Breast."

The Cheyennes, another branch of the Algonquian Family, were late comers to Colorado. They were living in

settled towns and were growing crops on the Cheyenne
River of South Dakota long after the first Spaniards visited
Colorado. Before 1800 a portion of the Cheyenne nation
moved southwestward onto the plains, took to the horse
and the roving life. Well received by the Arapahoes, a
warm friendship developed between the two tribes, even
though the two languages were so different that the sign
language had to be employed for communication. The Arap-
aho-Cheyenne friendship and union have persisted to this
day.

Quite different was the relation between the Arapahoes and the Cheyennes on the one hand, and the Utes on
the other. A bitter enmity existed between the Indians of
the mountains (the Utes) and those of the plains. Sallies
into enemy territory were frequent; skirmishes often resulted. Even after the white settlers came to Colorado the
conflict continued between the Indians of the mountains
and those of the plains. War parties occasionally held their
scalp dances in pioneer Denver for the edification of the
whites.

Other Indian tribes that frequented Colorado territory
were the Sioux, Kiowas, Pawnees, Comanches, Apaches, and
Shoshones. But in as much as their visits were temporary
they can scarcely be spoken of as Colorado Indians.

These various western tribes, while having much in
common, had each its own characteristic physique, customs,
and beliefs. The spoken language of one tribe was almost
never understood by another, but there had developed a sign
language which was universal among the inhabitants of the
western plains and mountains. By this medium of signs and
motions, communication between different tribes and with
white men who learned the sign language, took place with
little difficulty.

The Indian manner of life contrasted strikingly with ours of today. No settled towns with permanent houses; no farming. The culture and very life of the plains Indians were builded upon the buffalo. This migrant animal sup-plied their basic wants and provided them with food, shel-ter and clothing. It is therefore little wonder that the In-dians held the buffalo in high esteem and in some of their ceremonies rendered him a form of worship.

The roving life on the treeless plains necessitated the use of a portable shelter. Buffalo skin tepees, or lodges, de-vised by the plains Indians, were made of skins sewed to-gether and shaped to fit over a framework of lodge poles to form a cone-shaped tent. These skin houses were light, easy to erect, dismantle, and transport; strong to resist the wind; and impervious to rain or snow. The tepee varied in size, the dimensions of the enclosed circular room ranging from ten to twenty feet in diameter. The lodge covering was made of from eleven to twenty-one buffalo skins expertly sewed together with sinew thread. There was a flap door in the side of the lodge, a fire place in the center and a smoke vent in the top. The beds were ranged around the walls. The better lodges were equipped with an inner lining made of buffalo skin which could be hung to the lodgepoles as an added protection against inclement weather.

The procuring of sustenance was the constant concern of the Indian. Meat was his chief food, but wild berries, fruits and roots, gathered in season, were dried and stored for future use. Often the dried fruits were pounded fine, mixed with buffalo fat and dried meat and thus made into what was called pemmican. This rich and nutritious food, after being heated, was poured into skin bags or containers. In this form it could be preserved for months at a time.

The vast buffalo herds furnished the principal meat

Upper: UTE TEPEES NEAR DENVER
Lower: UTE ENCAMPMENT AT LOS PINOS AGENCY, COLORADO
(Photographs by W. H. Jackson, 1874)

LITTLE RAVEN, ARAPAHO CHIEF

supply for the Arapahoes and Cheyennes, and contributed greatly to Ute sustenance; but antelope, deer, elk, rabbits, and other game also were hunted. These secondary game animals were depended upon more by the Utes than by the natives of the plains. Dog meat also was a common food, especially for the Cheyennes and Arapahoes, and white dog was relished as the choice delicacy at feasts.

The Indians were more provident than they are usually credited with being. While it is true that they feasted lavishly on the hunt, they did not "feast one day and starve the next." Following a big buffalo kill the chief labor in camp for days was the drying and curing of the meat for future use. The meat was cut into long slices which were hung on lines or on especially prepared racks. Sometimes a fire was built beneath to facilitate the drying and to enable the smoke to aid in the curing process.

In the days preceding the introduction of those wonderful hunting aids—the horse, metal knives, and firearms —the industry and ingenuity of the Indians must have been taxed to the utmost in their struggle for existence. In those primitive times the Colorado natives possessed only weapons of stone, wood and bone. The bow and arrow (the date of invention of which is unknown) was their best weapon. This was supplemented by clubs, spears and by axes, hammers, and knives of stone.

An early method of getting the buffalo was to build a V-shaped chute with diverging arms extending far out on the prairie, the point or angle of the chute leading to the edge of a cliff or cut bank over which the buffalo were expected to fall. If the cliff was high the fall would kill or cripple the buffalo, but if low it was necessary to build an enclosure at the foot of the bank to hold the animals after their plunge. With all preparations completed, the Indian hunters made a long tour around a small buffalo herd and gradually led or drove it toward their trap. After a suc' cessful drive the red men killed the trapped and crippled buffalo with stone axes or with arrows and spears. Antelope were often led and driven through similar chutes to pens and pits on the prairie, the well known curiosity of these animals being taken alvantage of to lead them to their doom. Game was often trapped in a somewhat similar way in narrow mountain valleys or in pens made in the timbered areas.

After the Indians were equipped with horses, the buf' falo hunt took on a different form, for with fleet mounts they could overtake the animals, ride among them, and shoot them as they ran. The hunt was planned and executed as a concerted tribal measure, no individual buffalo hunting being permitted. Runners from the tribe having located a buffalo herd and the ceremonies necessary to insure a successful hunt having been performed, the mounted and equipped hunters ride off with their swiftest horses at break of day in a body toward their game. They ride without saddles, and a rawhide rope tied to the horse's lower jaw serves as bridle. Each hunter, stripped to breechclout and moccasins, carries his bow and arrows or gun in his hands.

When the buffalo herd is reached the charge begins. The men with fleet mounts soon approach the dark, humped cattle, and passing the old bulls in the rear of the herd press on to the cows and young animals in the lead. The herd splits in many places and horses and buffalo race side by side. "Over the rough billowing backs of the buffalo," writes G. B. Grinnell, "the naked shoulders of the men show brown and glistening and his long black hair flies out far behind each rider, rising and falling with his horse's stride. The lithe bodies swing and bend, and the arms move as the riders draw the arrows to the head and drive them to the feather into the flying beasts. It is hard to see how those who are riding in the thick of the herd can escape injury from the tossing horns of the buffalo, now mad with fear, but the ponies are watchful, nimble, and sure-footed, and avoid the charges of the cows, leap the gullies, and dodge the badger holes. In a few moments the herd is turned, and all are once more racing back over the flat from which they started; but all along where they have passed, the yellow prairie is dotted here and there with brown car-casses . . ." (G. B. Grinnell, *Story of the Indian,* 77.)

Presently the women and children with their horses and travois come up to skin the buffalo, cut up the meat, and haul it back to camp.

Let us take a glimpse at a typical village of Arapahoes or Cheyennes temporarily located in a choice section of the bottomlands of the Platte or Arkansas.[1] Cone-shaped lodges, arranged roughly in a circle, stand near the river bank. Some are new and white, while others are patched and weather-stained and smoke-browned at their tops. On some are painted in gay colors symbolic designs or figures of men and animals depicting the brave deeds of the owner of the tepee. From slender-pole tripods beside the lodges of the principal men are suspended the medicine bundles of priests and the arms and equipment of the warriors, the decorations of feathers, fringes, and scalps waving in the breeze.

With the break of day, plumes of blue smoke rise from the tops of the lodges and spangles of bright sparks fly from the smoke vent. Women come out of the various lodges and hurry down to the stream for water. Young men loosen

---

1. This description is gathered and adapted largely from the writings of G. B. Grinnell, authority on the Cheyenne Indians.

those most valuable horses that have been tied near the lodges during the night and the freed animals trot out into the prairie to feed. The noise and bustle about the camp increases—there is the chattering of the women, the darting about of tousle-headed children, the yelps of dogs kicked from the lodges, the whinnying of little colts and answering neighs from their mothers.

From the lodges come the men, wrapped in their robes; beside them trot the boys—all moving down toward the stream. At the river bank they drop their robes and dive in. A splashing, ducking, racing and shouting follows as they plunge in the chilly water. The invigorating swim over, they return to the lodges to be greeted by the teasing odor from pots steaming with meat for the morning meal. Eagerly the men comb their long hair, put on their leggings and moccasins, and belt their robes or blankets about them.

Breakfast is now served. A sharpened stick or a big spoon fashioned from a buffalo horn or from the horn of a mountain sheep, is used to dish out the food onto a wood platter or onto plates. Fingers take the place of knives and forks to serve the eager appetites. There is a sudden pause in the noisy eating. The voice of the old crier is heard as he moves through the camp shouting commands from the chief or publishing the latest news.

The meal over, everybody turns to the routine duties or pleasures of the day. Some of the men set out to hunt antelope, deer and elk; others form in little groups to plan a war raid or a sacred ceremony; while others remain about their lodges to smoke and gossip or to make or repair hunting and war equipment. Two or three white-haired old men sit close together and recount the days of their great exploits, while little boys crowd close to hear the marvelous tales. Some young braves sit in the sun braiding their black hair, plucking their eyebrows and whiskers, and painting their faces; while a number of half-grown boys ride off to tend the horse herd.

To the women falls what we would consider the principal work about camp. With fleshers in hand, some of them are scraping and tanning hides, stooping for hours at this back-breaking work. Some are drying meat; others, equipped with stone hammers and stone anvils are pounding up dried fruit—pits and all—for the making of pemmican. Here a group is patching lodge covers or sewing hides to make new ones; there a number are making moccasins, leggings and shirts and skilfully decorating them with porcupine quills or gay-colored glass beads. One party leaves to gather berries and choke cherries; another, equipped with sharpened sticks, sets out to dig edible roots; while a third goes off in search of wood.

Though hard at work, the women are not without their enjoyment. The little groups laboring together keep up a lively chatter. Gossip, jokes and stories enliven their duties and make light the day's work. And at times some of them drop their tasks to indulge in games of chance or skill on which they excitedly wager various articles of value.

The children are left to their play, except the tiny ones, who are tied in their stiff little baby boards with only their heads left free. Those old enough to be released from their cradle straight-jackets, crawl about the ground and soon have hands and faces plastered with dirt. The children old enough to toddle about, delight to follow the dogs and annoy them with sticks. The girls are dressed in little smocks that reach to the knees, but the boys go unclothed except perhaps for a string of beads or a charm hung around the neck and a buckskin thong about the waist.

The play of the children is all in imitation of their

elders. The little girls have dolls or puppies for babies, and clothe and care for them with much concern. They wash these babies in the stream and sing them to sleep with plain- tive lullabies. They play at moving camp, using a dog for horse and harnessing him to a small travois to carry their bundles.

The boys' play is largely based on the hunt and war. All boys have their bows and arrows. The small ones shoot at rocks, sticks, and prairie dogs. The older ones hunt squir- rels, blackbirds, and rabbits and proudly bring to camp the trophies of their skill. Sham battles are of frequent occur- rence; the opposing forces armed with limber switches throw mud balls at the enemy. Yells of defiance, cries of terror, promote the semblance of a battle. Sometimes they tie pieces of buffalo hair to sticks and hold a scalp dance. They go on pretended buffalo hunts, riding stick horses and lashing them into a fast gallop with their quirts. Swimming in the river, playing in the sand, and making images from mud on the river banks, are favorite amusements.

As the afternoon wears on, the aspect of the camp begins to change. The women put aside their work and turn to recreation. They enjoy their gambling games and gather in groups to gossip, chatter and laugh.

With the near-setting of the sun, they re-kindle their fires. Some turn to prepare the evening meal while others fetch water from the river. Berry-pickers come straggling in with stained bags bulging with fruit. Squaws with stag- gering burdens of wood on their bent backs, wearily deposit their loads. The men ride in from the hunt; their horses laden with meat. Soon the camp is bristling with activity. Feasts are arranged in various lodges and as the savory roasted meat is served, jollity and good will warm the hos- pitable groups.

"As darkness settles down over the camp, the noise increases. The shrill laughter of the women is heard from every side, partly drowned now and then by the ever-recurring feast shout. From different quarters comes the sound of drumming and singing, here from a lodge where some musicians are beating on a parfleche and singing for a dance, there where a doctor is singing and drumming over a sick child. Boys and young men are racing about among the lodges, chasing each other, wrestling, and yelling. In front of some lodge in the full light of the fire which streams from the open doorway, stand two forms wrapped in a single robe—two lovers, whispering to each other their affection and their hopes. Dogs bark, horses whinny, people call to each other from different parts of the camp. The fires shine through lodge skins and showers of sparks float through the smokeholes. As the night wears on the noises become less. One by one the fires go out and the lodges grow dark."

The needs and industries of the Colorado Indians of a century ago were comparatively few and simple. Their clothing was made from the dressed skins of buffalo cows, deer, antelope, elk, and mountain sheep. Such skins were tanned and smoked so that the garments made from them would not shrink and could be softened after being wet. The sewing was neatly done with sinew thread.

The women usually wore loose, leather gowns which reached to below the knees and were belted at the waist; also moccasins and leggings. The dresses of the older women were often worn, patched, and black with grease and dirt; but those of the younger ones and of the wives of chiefs were clean, white, and handsome.

The men wore shirts or robes, leggings, breechclouts and moccasins. In early times they used no hats or caps; but imposing war bonnets and elaborate, feathered head-dresses were worn in their dances and ceremonies. As contact with the whites increased, the primitive Indian clothing gave way in favor of white man attire.

The Indians were very fond of ornament, as their clothing testifies. Fringes of buckskin or of hair trimmed seams of shirts and leggings. Strings of elk's teeth, or of bear or eagle claws were coveted decorations. Everyone delighted in paint, which was lavishly used on faces and bodies. Designs worked with colored porcupine quills and glass beads brightened the better moccasins, leggings and dresses. After the traders came, cheap spangles of all kinds, looking glasses, bracelets and a variety of tinsel and trinkets were worn.

The women made the clothing, provided the lodge and household utensils at marriage, cooked the food, tended the children, helped in securing and preserving the food, and did much of the labor involved in moving camp. The men engaged in the hunt and war, conducted most of the ceremonies, fashioned male weapons and utensils, and carved many of the sacred artifacts.

The bow and arrow was the most important Indian weapon. The bow, from three to five feet long, was generally made of juniper or hickory wood or of straight pieces of horn, spliced, glued together, and wrapped with sinews. The bow-string was of twisted sinew. The fashioning of good arrows required great skill and once made they were carefully conserved. Shoots of cherry, current bushes, or tough willows were peeled, straightened, scraped and dried. Turkey or buzzard feathers were fastened to these shafts with glue and sinew string, the feathers having first been split and carefully trimmed. The arrow's flight depended largely on its feathers. In early times arrow tips were made of flint or bone, but after the coming of white men, metal

points came into general use. Barrel hoops were then in
great demand for making of arrow heads, these sheet-iron
arrow-points being filed and whetted to a sharp edge.

The bow and arrow was an excellent weapon; the missile, silent and deadly. At its most effective range—from
forty to seventy yards—an Indian could shoot with bow and
arrow more rapidly and more effectively than could the average white man with a revolver.

The lance was useful in war and in the buffalo chase.
It consisted of a shaft six or seven feet long, tipped with a
sharp point of flint, iron or steel securely bound with sinew
or with rawhide thongs. In battle, warriors frequently carried circular shields made of dried, tough bullhide. Many
shields, peculiarly painted and ornamented, were thought to
exert a spiritual as well as a physical protection. The early
ax and the maul had a head of stone, with a groove for handle
attachment. War clubs, similarly constructed, used smaller
stones.

Articles of horse equipment were many and important.
Ropes were made of twisted hair of the horse or buffalo,
or of rawhide. The bridle usually consisted merely of a piece
of rope tied about the horse's lower jaw and extending with
a single strand back to the rider's hand. A common type of
Indian saddle was high peaked both front and back, the
pommel and cantle being made from elkhorn prongs or of
forked sticks covered with rawhide. The stirrups were short
and were of wood covered with green, or fresh, hide. The
saddles of recent times were often elaborately ornamented
with leather fringes, brass tacks and with bead and quill
work. One variety of saddle, or riding pad, consisted of
a flat buffalo-skin bag filled with grass or buffalo hair. This
mattress-like bag served as both blanket and saddle. In war
or on the buffalo hunt the men rode without saddles.

The Indians developed no wheeled vehicles, but in their place employed the *travois*. This consisted of two long poles about the size of lodge poles, placed on either side of the horse, the small ends of the poles crossing above the horse's shoulders and the large ends dragging the ground behind. Two braces at the rear of the horse, held the poles apart. Attached to the poles and the braces was a rawhide network which was strong enough to carry a weight of several hundred pounds. On this travois, or "prairie buggy," might be carried rolls of buffalo robes, lodge covers, or pieces of camp equipment. Travois were often used for the carrying of small children or of old or sick adults. Such conveyances sometimes were equipped with a cage which had a skin covering to shelter the occupant from sun and rain.

The early camp equipment was primitive. Vessels and containers were often made from the paunch or intestines of the buffalo. Bowls and platters were of wood; spoons were fashioned from horn. Sometimes pottery was obtained from the Pueblo Indians of New Mexico. After contact with the whites, the utensils of wood, horn, turtle shell, bone, and skins were gradually replaced by brass buckets, iron pots, and tin cups. In a similar way metal axes, hammers, knives, and needles came to replace cruder articles of stone and bone.

The parfleche, a sort of rawhide trunk or carryall, was an article of general use. Buckskin bags and sacks of various sizes were employed in the carrying and safe keeping of miscellaneous articles. Willow shoots strung on sinew, padded with layers of grass formed mattresses for the beds. Buffalo robes and blankets constituted the bedding. Pipe bowls were usually fashioned from red, black or green pipestone. Their long wooden stems, frequently carved, were often decorated with hair and feathers.

Of musical instruments the drum was most important. Its deep reverberations announced the religious ceremony or the occasion of festivity. Drums varied in size from a few inches to several feet in diameter. They were made of horse or buffalo hide stretched over a willow framework. Rattles to be shaken in accompaniment to dancing and for use in "making medicine" were usually of rawhide shaped into a sphere, enclosing a number of pebbles. Gourds were some' times used as rattles, as were turtle shells with bear claws attached. Notched sticks were rasped together to accentu' ate rhythm and a sort of fiddle frequently was made with a notched stick and a sounding board. The beat of the drum, the shake of the rattle, and the rasping of the sticks or fiddle were always accompanied by the accented chant of the musicians.

War whistles were usually cut from bird bones, those of the eagle and the sandhill crane being most highly es' teemed. The flute, about eighteen inches in length, was fashioned of wood, the finger holes being burned out with a hot iron. Some flutes were designed simply for making music; others were fashioned by men supposed to possess peculiar ability to imbue instruments with power to charm a girl into loving the serenader. Frequently on summer eve' nings as the plaintive call of the flute sounded through the camp the pulse of some girl quickened as she recognized a certain music message. She hastened to finish her work in the lodge, then stole out into the night to meet her lover.

But the music of these people is chiefly vocal. They are unwearied singers. Love, war, religion, sorrow, joy— alike are themes for their songs. Their singing is generally in unison, the women using a high, reedy, falsetto tone an oc' tave above the male singers. Their singing is not for objec' tive effect, but to express the fervor of an emotion.

Contrary to certain popular conceptions, the Indians are fond of social life, are great talkers, and have a keen sense of humor. They like to visit each other's lodges; relish story-telling and conversation; and delight in feasts, dances and ceremonies. They enjoy horse racing, and various games of skill and of chance.

The Sun Dance, or ceremony of the Medicine Lodge, was the greatest ceremony of the Indians of Colorado, being observed, though with variations of detail, by the Cheyennes, Arapahoes, and Utes. With certain modifications it has persisted to the present day. Both social and religious features are prominent. It has become an occasion of glad reunion of relatives and friends.

As formerly practiced there was a division of the performance into the secret rites and the public exhibition. The secret rites occupied from one to four days, were held in a special tepee and consisted of smoking, feasting, praying, and the cleansing of participants. The public performance took place in the sun dance lodge. This lodge was erected according to prescribed rules. It was circular in form, with a diameter of from sixty to one hundred feet. The altar and the tall center pole with its "thunder bird nest" were the most important features. Within this lodge those participating remained from one to four days without food, dancing and resting at alternate periods. The dancing which was toward the center pole, representing the sun or "Man Above," was performed to the accompaniment of songs of the musicians who were seated about a big drum to the south of the lodge entrance.

The sun dance was primarily a form of sacrifice to ward off evil and win the good will of the spirits. The fasting and the continued dancing are the present-day forms of sacrifice, but in earlier years various forms of torture were

THE SUN DANCE OR MEDICINE LODGE CEREMONY
AS PRACTICED BY THE PLAINS INDIANS

CHIEF OURAY AND OTTO MEARS (1870)

practiced. The most common forms were: (1) to drag around one or more buffalo skulls by a riata attached to a skewer inserted under the skin in the man's back; or (2) to insert in the skin of the breast two skewers which were attached to a rope fastened to the tall center pole of the lodge, the dancer striving to free himself by jerking back- ward until the skewers tore through the skin. On the last day of the dance members of the tribe other than the danc- ers placed articles of clothing in the medicine lodge as a form of personal sacrifice.

Different ceremonial and social dances, such as the Bear Dance, the Buffalo Dance, and others were practiced by the Colorado Indians. In some of these women as well as men participated. Space forbids a further description here.

The Indian was deeply religious in his primitive way. Strongly aware of superhuman powers about him, he strove continually through word, prayer and deed to propitiate those unseen spirits that controlled the welfare of him and his tribe. He was inclined to look upon the sun, the moon, animals, trees, mountains and rivers as persons possessing power and intelligence. There were forces in nature he could not understand—thunder, lightning, earthquakes, disease.

Much was mysterious and much beyond his power to control. Hence in humility he prayed often and earnestly to the gods, the spirits and the ghosts who peopled his uni- verse, asking them to protect him from evil and give him success on the hunt and in war.

Certain men—priests or medicine men—seemed to un- derstand more of the mysteries than did the common man, and on these persons devolved the performance of special rites and ceremonies. These medicine men were often power- ful individuals, "making medicine" for recovery of the sick; reading the signs which controlled the movement of hunting and war parties; and directing the general conduct of the camp.

The chief god of the Cheyennes was the Wise One Above. Another god lived under the ground and four powerful spirits dwelt at the four points of the compass. In ceremonial smoking, the pipe was pointed in these six directions out of respect for these powers. The Arapahoes and the Utes had similar beliefs and practices. Animals were believed to exert over man certain influences—some good, some evil. The coyote and the spider were looked upon as being very wise; the buffalo, as typifying force or power as well as the quality of dashing blindly onward. Too, the buffalo was reverenced because he was considered a favorite secret helper who could intercede with the great powers, in behalf of man. Other animals, such as the beaver, bear, eagle, owl, etc., were thought to possess peculiar powers.

Since sickness might arise from either natural or supernatural causes, treatment for disease showed a mingling of natural and spiritual methods. Roots and herbs were commonly administered with healing effects. A vapor bath in a sweat lodge, followed by a plunge in the river was frequently prescribed—a remedy that sometimes proved fatal to the patient. The medicine man employed various devices to drive out the evil spirits which caused disease. He might sing, shake his rattle, or go through various contortions to frighten away the evil power. Amulets and charms were often worn as protection from malignant, unseen influences.

When a man died, close relatives exhibited their grief by wailing or by cutting off their hair or gashing their bodies with knives. There was diversity in burial customs. The Cheyennes dressed the dead man in his finest clothes, wrapped the body in blankets or robes, wound it tightly with rope and usually placed it upon a pole scaffold or up in a tree. The Arapahoes commonly buried their dead in the ground, while the Utes placed theirs in caves in the cliffs. A man's war equipment and some personal effects were placed beside him. One or more of his horses were killed. When Chief Ouray of the Utes died, five horses were killed to accompany him.

Government among the Colorado Indians was demo-cratic. The will of the tribe was the controlling force, and chiefs paid careful attention to public opinion. There was no formal set of laws, but established customs and rules were carefully observed. There were several bands of Utes, each with a chief or head man. The Cheyennes and Arapahoes were similarly divided into bands or subdivisions of the main tribe. While there was occasional federation of bands or of tribes it was rather uncommon for such concerted action to persist for long. The Indian was too fond of his free-dom and too individualistic to relish subordination to others. It is his failure to unite with his fellows which accounts for the comparative ease with which the Indians were dispos-sessed of the West. Had there been effective cooperation among the tribes the story of white conquest would have been a different tale.

Tribal bands usually had a chief, who had won his position by marked ability. The extent of power attained by him depended largely upon his force of character. Some chiefs were absolute rulers; others were almost powerless, their commands being ignored with impunity. In general the chief must have wisdom as well as valor, must be kind to the weak and liberal with the unfortunate. Among the Cheyennes the chief was elected for a period of ten years, with right to re-election. Among the Utes and Arapahoes he commonly retained his position throughout life and some-times chose his successor.

A council of chiefs or of the leading men usually considered important matters affecting the tribe and decided
questions of general policy. In council each man was given
an opportunity to speak and was accorded respectful attention. No interruptions or wrangling occurred. Soldier
bands and fraternal societies often exerted great influence.
Women frequently assumed leadership and important control in the tribe.

Since time immemorial, intertribal conflicts have occurred. But the coming of the horse increased the fre-
quency of pillaging raids among Indian tribes until war became common, almost the usual, state of affairs. War came
to be regarded, especially by the Cheyennes, as the noblest
of pursuits. A craving for glory, desire for more horses,
eagerness for revenge, and the very love of the fighting were
motives that urged on the warrior in his career. Death in
battle was esteemed glorious. It was almost impossible for
a young man to marry, sit in council, take part in a feast,
or enter a dance until he had shown his courage by touch-
ing or killing an enemy in battle. Says Stanley Vestal, "Enemies were as necessary to their culture as markets are to
ours."

Before going on the warpath, the tribe must consult
the medicine man to learn if signs and omens be favorable.
Then certain ceremonies must be observed and prayers offered to propitiate the spirits. Upon setting forth to war
each man carried his personal belongings—arms, food, and
clothing. When the enemy country was reached, scouts
were sent in advance to locate the enemy and safeguard the
advancing party. Stealing of horses was usually accomplished silently and stealthily at night; attack upon a camp
came usually at dawn.

An Indian war party took careful precautions for its

own safety, preferring to fight from cover rather than in the open. A common strategy, especially when fighting white soldiers, was to send a small party on swift horses to charge the enemy and then to flee, endeavoring thus to lead the pursuers into an ambuscade. In war the Indians were cau-tious, usually refraining from attack until they had a dis-tinct advantage over their foe.

In battle the chief honor went to the brave who was first to "count coup" on an enemy, that is, to touch or strike him. Scalps were taken as trophies to dance over. The cap-turing of horses from the enemy tribe was considered a worthy achievement, to be rewarded with honor.

The return of a victorious war party was the occasion for great rejoicing in the home camp. Honors were heaped upon the warriors; wild singing, dancing and feasting stirred the village. The scalp dance often lasted not only through the first night but continued through several successive nights of wild celebration.

The Indian had strong primitive emotions. He was cruel; delighted in revenge, enjoyed the torture of an enemy. In war he neither gave nor asked quarter. He was vain, su-perstitious, sensitive to ridicule, childlike.

On the other hand, as regards certain emotions and indeed the social graces, the Indian had much to commend him. Freehanded hospitality was part of the daily life of the camp, not being denied even to an enemy. Food was always placed before a visitor or stranger. And in contrast to our own social conditions, there was never feasting in one lodge and starving in another. In the family circle there was kindness and affection. Children were almost never given physical punishment, lest their spirit be broken. The Indian was a loyal friend and his promised word was sacred. To him the wilful breaking of treaties by the white

men was as shocking as the Indian barbaric cruelties were
to the civilized mind. In fortitude he was supreme. He
endured hunger, privation and misfortune with stoic forbearance. He underwent torture bravely. Murder and sui-
cide were rare. Drunkenness became common only after the
white man's introduction of liquor.

Today most of the Indians have gone from Colorado.
The government has removed them to widely separated reservations. On the Wind River of central Wyoming the last
remnant of the Northern Arapahoes are tilling the soil. In
southern Montana the Northern Cheyennes are building
their herds. In the oil lands of Oklahoma the Southern
Arapahoes and the Southern Cheyennes see unexpected
wealth. In northwestern Utah the Uncompahgre Utes are
enjoying the quiet of their mountain valleys. Within the
borders of Colorado now only the Southern Utes remain
(numbering 813 in 1930). In the southwest corner of the
state on their two reservations they are being schooled to
stock-raising, herding, and farming.

Although the Indian's heyday has passed, he has not
gone without leaving his impress upon the state. Indian
nomenclature is evident almost everywhere. The Yampa,
Uncompahgre, Saguache, Arikaree, Apishapa, are but some
of the Colorado streams which retain their Indian names.
Seven of Colorado's counties, a number of her towns, and
miscellaneous geographic features have names of Indian origin.

Many of the foods on the American table today are
gifts of the Indian. Potatoes, corn, squash, and turkey are
but the principal of these.

Valuable lessons in hunting, in frontier crafts and industries and even in agriculture have been taught the white
man by the American Indian.

But it is in the realm of art, music and literature that the Indian has left his most valued heritage. Unique designs and color combinations characterize his art. Expertly fashioned handicraft in the form of arrowheads, baskets, and quill and bead work on buckskin are works of intrinsic beauty.

The plaintive native music has a charm all its own. It has been given in solos, is rendered effectively in orchestration, and has been charmingly produced in opera. The Indian rhythm appeared not only in music but in the dance. A native grace and primitive uniqueness characterized the expression of his emotions through this medium.

Weird Indian legends, creation myths, and adventure tales enrich our literature. Fundamentally the Indian was poetic. He thought in terms of nature and his language was rich in pictures and metaphors. His poetry was verbal, like that of the earliest bards of our own ancestors. Poetry, which is "the wedding of thought with word," cannot be adequately translated, but a few words and expressions from Indian tongues give an inkling of their intrinsic beauty: "The Never Summer Range"; "Talking Leaves" (the Indian term for book or a letter); "May the Giver of all Good make ever Sunrise in your Heart"; the cowslip "that opens the swamps by blossoming in the spring." Certain Indian names exhibit the essence of poetry—Alights-on-the-Clouds, Face-to-the-Storm (incorrectly rendered "Rain in the Face"), Laughing Water, Fall Leaf, Blue Cloud People (the Arapahoes), Dwellers of the Turquoise Sky (the Utes). In oratory the Indian excelled. He was eloquent, sincere. His symbolism and figures of speech, even in translation, are strikingly effective.

The Indian has been a persistent theme in our own literature and art. Although often unfaithfully and sometimes

grotesquely portrayed in "Western" motion pictures and
magazines, he is none the less a figure of great literary and
artistic possibilities. In painting, in sculpture, on the printed
page, he has an abiding place. The Indian's true story is
inherently rich in romance, drama and tragedy and will ever
command our attention.

"Greek art and culture," says Chauncey Thomas, "did
not affect the Roman more than the Indian has affected the
American, and in due time History will so record the fact."

✦ ✦ ✦

SELECTED REFERENCES FOR FURTHER READING

Clark Wissler, The American Indian (1922)
G. B. Grinnell, The Story of the Indian (1898)
G. B. Grinnell, The Cheyenne Indians (1923)
F. W. Hodge, Handbook of American Indians (1907)
A. J. Fynn, The American Indian as a Product of Environment (1907)
R. I. Dodge, Our Wild Indians (1882)
Irving Howbert, The Indians of the Pike's Peak Region (1914)
G. W. Manypenny, Our Indian Wards (1880)
H. L. Scott, "The Early History and the Names of the Arapaho" (American
    Anthropologist, July-Sept., 1907)
U. S. Commissioner of Indian Affairs, Annual Reports of Indian Agents of
    the Colorado Region (1847-1881)
Colorado Magazine: "With the Indians in Colorado" (Mar., 1930); "Condi-
    tions and Customs of Present-day Utes in Colorado" (May, 1929);
    "Major Thompson, Chief Ouray and the Utes" (May, 1930); "Rela-
    tions with the Cheyennes and Arapahoes in Colorado" (Aug., 1927);
    "The Death of Ouray, Chief of the Utes" (Sept., 1930); "Indian Petro-
    glyphs of Southeastern Colorado" (Jan., 1931); "Pictographs of Colo-
    rado" (Jan., 1925); "General Mano Mocha of the Utes and Spanish
    Indian Policy in Indian Relations" (July, 1932)

CHAPTER IV

WHITE MEN DISCOVER COLORADO

Spanish, French and American Explorers

WITHIN fifty years after Columbus discovered the New World, Coronado was leading his armored knights of Spain far into the interior of North America—to the very border of present Colorado. Strange as it may seem, what we now know as the Far West was really visited by white men before the eastern part of the United States was explored. It came about in this way: Spain, the first European nation to colonize in the New World, made her first settlements in the West Indies and in Mexico. From these bases her explorers rapidly pushed northward to the Pueblo Indian villages of New Mexico and beheld the Grand Canyon of the Colorado eighty years before the Pilgrim Fathers landed at Plymouth. Thus the earliest history of Colorado deals with the pioneer work of the Spaniards.

Gold was the lure that brought these early adventurers across the sea, and gold in quantity the earliest Spaniards found. In Peru, in Mexico the conquerors avidly gathered in the precious metal. Exquisite jewelry, dishes and ornaments fashioned in gold (tribute paid by the natives) were melted into slugs and carried across the Atlantic to enrich the king and nobles of Spain. It was the hope of finding another Mexico or another Peru which produced the famous Coronado expedition of 1540. Stories told by Cabeza de Vaca whetted the Spanish appetite. This adventurer had been shipwrecked on the Texas coast in 1528 and for six years had wandered among the Indian tribes before finding his way to Mexico. To the Spaniards he repeated stories told by Texas Indians of wealthy cities to the northward. Conquered natives in Northern Mexico told similar tales and the Spaniards listened eagerly. "The 'Seven Cities of Cibola' lie to the northward and in them the doors to the houses are studded with jewels and whole streets are lined with the shops of goldsmiths."

Such great cities and vast wealth must be conquered. To accomplish this a great expedition was planned by the Viceroy of New Spain and placed under the direction of Francisco Coronado. This was one of the most elaborate and splendidly equipped expeditions ever to set out in the New World. Cavaliers were equipped with dazzling metal armor. Their spirited mounts were draped with gay-colored blankets, leathern armor and silver-mounted trappings. In the rear of the horsemen marched foot soldiers armed with swords, crossbows and arquebuses. A third division was composed of several hundred Indian allies, their naked bodies splashed with black and vermilion. There were one thousand horses, pack mules loaded with elaborate equipment, droves of cattle, sheep, goats and pigs to be used for food on the way and to stock the new country. At the head of all flashed the splendid figure of Coronado encased in golden armor.

But the glamour of the search and the splendor of appearance wore away as the cavalcade marched day after day over parched uplands, farther from home and friends and deeper into the heart of an unknown land. We cannot here recount the events of the long tramp to New Mexico but must record that the towering cities they had visioned proved to be only prosaic adobe pueblos. The semicivilized natives who peered at them from the tops of their flat-roofed houses were poor farmers who worked hard to raise the corn and squashes they ate, who labored patiently against the handicaps of an arid climate. No gold was here to gladden the sight of weary Spaniards and though the pueblos were easily subdued there was no wealth to reward the conquerors.

Presently stories were told that wealth could be found at "Quivira" to the eastward. Indians gladly led the way hoping to lose the intruders on the wide-spreading prairies. On the journey across the open plains the Spaniards first saw the "hump-backed cow" and gave us our first description of the American buffalo. But at Quivira, in modern Kansas, they found no gold, only disappointment and misfortune. Disheartened, they turned their bronzed faces homeward, and tramped a weary retreat to Mexico. On the return journey they may have crossed the southeastern corner of Colorado. If so, they were the first white men to tread the soil of the state.

The apparent failure of the Coronado expedition gave a decided check to further northern exploration. It was only gradually that the frontier of settlement, based on mining and stock raising, pushed northward from Mexico City. At the end of the sixteenth century, nearly sixty years after Coronado's journey, an advance in settlement again brought the Spaniards to the borders of Colorado. This important step was the conquest and colonization of New Mexico under Onate in 1598. Families came and settlements were founded. Farming and stock raising were developed and missionary activity was rewarded with many Indian converts to Christianity. This province remained for many years the northern outpost of Spanish civilization.

With Spanish towns within a hundred miles of the present southern boundary of Colorado it is evident that

the pioneers of New Mexico soon spanned the short distance and wandered over Colorado soil. As there were no
boundaries and the Spanish claim to territory extended in-
definitely northward, we cannot know whom to honor as
the first explorer of Colorado. It was probably some humble
Spaniard following a flock of sheep, a trader journeying
northward to barter with the Utes, or an adventurous prospector lured by visions of gold in the Sangre de Cristo
Mountains. During the century that followed the founding
of New Mexico by Onate, the development of the province
was very slow. The Indians put under tutelage began early
to smart under the discipline, and occasionally bands of discontented natives ran away. Several of the earliest recorded
expeditions into Colorado territory were conducted by Spaniards in pursuit of such fugitives. One of the most prominent of these expeditions was led by Juan de Uribarri in
1706. With forty Spaniards and one hundred Indian allies
he journeyed northeastward from the frontier town of Taos
to the Arkansas River in the vicinity of present Pueblo,
and continued eastward for five days to a region known as
El Quartelejo. Here Uribarri took formal possession of the
territory. With great ceremony he claimed the land for his
king, Philip V of Spain, and called it *Santo Domingo,* a
name soon forgotten. This is the first record of the naming or claiming of Colorado soil. Just 155 years afterward
the territory was rechristened with another Spanish name
—*Colorado.* This name, Spanish for "red," was first applied to the great river which rises on the western slope
of the Rocky Mountains. Subsequently it was given to
present Colorado, when this Territory was created by the
Congress of the United States in 1861.

Until the beginning of the eighteenth century Spain's
control of western North America was practically undis-

puted. Then came threatening from the eastward the ex-
panding power of France. With a foothold on the St. Lawrence and the Great Lakes, France further extended her
claim when the famous LaSalle floated down the "Father
of Waters" to its mouth in 1682, claimed the Mississippi
Valley and named it *Louisiana*. French traders and explorers began soon to ascend the rivers which enter the Mississippi from the west.

But the Spaniards guarded jealously their empire. As
they heard of Frenchmen among the plains Indians they
grew more alarmed and in 1720 sent an expedition of over
one hundred men under Pedro de Villasur through eastern
Colorado to make a reconnaissance of the French activity.
Villasur followed the South Platte (which he called the
Rio Jesus Maria) out of Colorado and into Nebraska,
where he was attacked by Indians, led probably by Frenchmen. At dawn, flights of arrows and showers of musket
balls began the slaughter. The Spaniards were caught in an
indefensible position and were doomed. Only a half dozen
escaped to tell the gruesome tale in Santa Fe. The disaster
so weakened the Spanish forces of New Mexico that no
further attempt was made to occupy the territory of eastern
Colorado.

And the Frenchmen came ever nearer. They had heard
of Spain's empire in the Southwest and were anxious to
visit this region where gold and silver were rumored to be
abundant. As early as 1724 a Frenchman named Bourg-
mont traveled westward from the Illinois country to the
eastern border of present Colorado. This is the first recorded visit of French explorers to our soil. Fifteen years
later the Mallet brothers led an expedition to Santa Fe, taking a path which brought them through eastern Colorado.
During the next two decades a number of other French

traders traveled through our state on their way to New Mexico. But the French advances were not welcomed by the Spaniards, who desired no foreign trade and feared the loss of the country they now ruled.

The international rivalry between France and Spain for the region of Colorado and the prairie country to the east came to a sudden close in 1763, when the treaty of peace closing the French and Indian War ceded to Spain all of France's territory and claims west of the Mississippi. Colorado was now undisputed Spanish soil and so remained until the Louisiana Territory (secretly re-ceded to Napoleon) was purchased by the United States in 1803.

During those forty intervening years (1763-1803) there was little permanent development in the Colorado region. An outstanding expedition of the period, however, deserves attention. It came about as a result of important developments outside Colorado. The French threat to Spanish possessions had hardly been removed when a danger from Russia and England arose in the far northwest. It was the creeping of the Russians down the Pacific Coast from Alaska which spurred the Spaniards to found their famous missions and settlements in California. With these Pacific Coast outposts established, an overland route was needed between New Mexico and California, and it was to open such a pathway that the Dominguez-Escalante expedition set forth.

In the very month and year when the Declaration of Independence was being signed in Philadelphia, these Spanish pioneers set out from Santa Fe to explore an unknown land. Twelve companions accompanied the two Spanish padres, Atanacio Dominguez and Silvestre Escalante, as they set forth in this eventful July. A northwestward course brought them into Colorado near the present site of Pagosa

Junction. In journeying westward they crossed the beautiful streams which rush down from the snow-capped San
Juan Mountains. These rivers were known to the New
Mexicans and had already received their musical Spanish
names—*Piedra, Los Pinos, Florida, Las Animas, La Plata*
and *Rio Mancos*. Turning northward the party reached the
Rio Dolores (River of Sorrow), but after following it some
distance they found the country rough and broken, and
turned eastward to seek an Indian guide.

Upon crossing the Uncompahgre plateau, Escalante
records: "We entered the pleasant valley of the river of San
Francisco, called by the Yutas the Ancapagari [Uncom-
pahgre], which the interpreter tells us means Colorado
Lake, from the fact that near its source there is a spring
of reddish water, hot and disagreeable to the taste." Down
the broad valley they tramped to a point a little below present Montrose, when a northeastward course brought them
to the Gunnison River. Following the North Gunnison
(called by them *San Javier* and by the Indians "Tomichi")
they found Ute Indians and induced an Indian guide
to accompany them. After crossing the Grand Mesa and
then the Colorado River near present DeBeque they turned
northward over the Roan Plateau and descending Douglas
Canyon reached the White River (called by them *San Cle-
mente*). From this point, on the 10th of September, they
turned to the northwest and made their exit from Colorado
territory. The further journey does not so much concern
us. They traveled westward to Utah Lake and thence into
southern Utah. Here, as winter threatened, they decided
to return. Accordingly they made their way eastward, ford-
ing the Colorado River at the "Crossing of the Fathers" (so
named for them and located about forty miles above the
new Colorado River bridge) and returned to New Mexico.

Although the Escalante expedition failed to open the route
sought to California, it nevertheless ranks as the first and
most important exploration of much of western Colorado.
Raids made by wild Indians of present Colorado upon
the frontier settlements of New Mexico caused a punitive
expedition to be directed against these marauders in 1779.
It was led by Governor Anza of New Mexico, the man
who three years before had been the founder of San Francisco, California. With a force of about 600 men the Governor set forth to find and punish the raiders. Traversing
the San Luis Valley and continuing northward to South
Park, he traveled to the east of Pikes Peak and turning
southward returned to New Mexico. On the campaign he
twice met and defeated the hostiles, in the second engagement killing the Comanche chief, *Cuerno Verde* (Greenhorn). This second fight took place on Greenhorn Creek,
near the eastern base of Greenhorn Mountain, and it is from
this defeat of *Cuerno Verde* that the mountain and stream
took their name.

Several years thereafter the Comanches signed a peace
treaty at Santa Fe and indicated a willingness to give up the
nomad life and settle down in fixed villages. This plan the
Spaniards were eager to promote. A site for a settlement
was selected on the *Rio Napestle* (Arkansas River) probably near the mouth of the *San Carlos* (St. Charles), near
present Pueblo. The Governor sent laborers and materials
to help in building houses, supplied seed for planting, and
provided sheep and cattle, expending 691 *pesos* (dollars)
in the project. The settlement, begun in 1787, was the first
such enterprise to be attempted in Colorado so far as our
records show.

But the *San Carlos* village, so hopefully begun, was
doomed to early failure. In the following January a person

of prominence in the tribe died at the new pueblo and this, according to Comanche beliefs, was a divine sign of disap' proval of the project. The Indians accordingly deserted the *San Carlos* village site in a body and hurried away to more favored ground. This was a great disappointment to the Spaniards who had inaugurated the plan and had helped in founding the settlement, but they were unable to over' come the Indian superstition and induce them to return. After the Indian desertion it was proposed to occupy the deserted site with Spanish families, but the project appears not to have been carried out. More than half a century was to elapse before a permanent settlement was to be founded on Colorado soil.

With the closing years of the eighteenth century, the days of Spanish dominion in North America were nearing their end. A young and vigorous nation was being born on the Atlantic seaboard through the successful revolt of the English colonies from their mother country. One of the most important events in the early history of this young nation was the purchase of the Louisiana Territory in 1803. At one stroke the area of the United States was doubled and a vast and fertile region acquired for American expansion. It was through this fortunate event that most of the eastern half of present Colorado came under the Stars and Stripes.

To the Americans the vast country beyond the Missis' sippi was largely unknown land. But the aggressive pioneers of the United States were not to remain long in ignorance. Lewis and Clark set out in 1804 to explore the far North' west and two years later a similar expedition began its journey to the far Southwest. This second expedition was led by a gallant young Captain from the United States army whose name is indelibly linked with Colorado—Zebulon Montgomery Pike.

In July, 1806, Captain Pike and his little party of twenty-two men set out from St. Louis on their journey of discovery. Proceeding up the Missouri River they visited the Indians of the Kansas region and procured horses for the overland journey. The Pawnee Indians on the Republican River attempted to dissuade them from continuing farther westward, for the Indians had been recently visited by a large and imposing Spanish expedition from New Mexico that had traveled far out onto the plains to turn back American explorers. This party, which had been led by Don Facundo Malgares, consisted of six hundred mounted troops with over two thousand horses and mules. Don Malgares had given presents to the Pawnees, had instructed them to permit no Americans to go westward beyond the Pawnee villages. Judging by the size and equipment of the two expeditions the Indians must have thought that the Spaniards were much more powerful than the nation Pike represented. Accordingly, they tried to turn back the Americans, but Pike replied that he "had been sent out by our *great father* to explore the western country . . . " and that "the young warriors of his *great American father were not women* to be turned back by words." In the face of Pike's determination the Indians gave way.

Pike continued to the Big Bend of the Arkansas and followed that stream into present Colorado. On November 15th he caught his first glimpse of the Rocky Mountains, viewing the peak that was destined to bear his name. "At two o'clock in the afternoon," writes Pike, "I thought I could distinguish a mountain to our right, which appeared like a small blue cloud; . . . When our small party arrived on the hill they with one accord gave three *cheers* to the *Mexican mountains*." On the 23rd Pike reached the site of present Pueblo. Near the mouth of Fountain Creek he built a

breastwork of logs for defense against the Indians. It was
the first structure erected by Americans in Colorado.

A high peak loomed up to the northward. Pike decided to try to reach its summit in order to survey the surrounding country. Though it was late November and snow
covered the ground, he heroically set forth. Two and one-
half days of marching and climbing brought him only to a
point near the summit of Mount Miller, at the head of
Turkey Creek. He records:

"27th November, Thursday.—Arose hungry, dry, and
extremely sore, from the inequality of the rocks, on which
we had lain all night, but were amply compensated for toil
by the sublimity of the prospects below. The unbounded
prairie was overhung with clouds, which appeared like the
ocean in a storm; wave piled on wave and foaming, whilst
the sky was perfectly clear where we were . . . The summit
of the Grand Peak [Pikes Peak] which was entirely bare of
vegetation and covered with snow, now appeared at the distance of fifteen or sixteen miles from us, and as high again as
what we had ascended, and would have taken a whole day's
march to have arrived at its base, when I believe no human
being could have ascended to its pinical [pinnacle]. This
with the condition of my soldiers, who had only light overalls on, and no stockings, and every way ill provided to
endure the inclemency of the region; the bad prospect
of killing anything to subsist on, with the further detention
of two or three days, which it must occasion, determined us
to return."

Though he did not reach the summit of the high peak
he was the first American to describe it. He did not name
it for himself, but modestly called it "Highest Peak." The
trappers who followed him, however, insisted on calling it
"Pikes Peak," and so it is known today.

Returning to the camp on the Arkansas, Pike with his party turned westward. December was ushered in with a foot of snow. The men, dressed in cotton overalls, were poorly equipped for winter travel, but some buffalo bulls, opportunely killed, provided hides for making moccasins. On December 4th Pike camped near the present site of Florence and the next night reached the mouth of the Royal Gorge. A detour was now made to the north, and South Park and the upper Arkansas were explored.

For the two days before Christmas the men were practically without food, but in the vicinity of present Salida buffalo were encountered and eight were killed. Christmas was now celebrated with glad hearts, for though they had no food except meat, and that without salt, there were buffalo steaks in plenty. Sleds were constructed, drawn down the river over the ice, and on Pike's birthday (January 5th) the previous camp at the site of Canon City was reached.

As the horses were unable to travel and supplies were meager, Pike decided to build here a blockhouse for deposit. Leaving two men in charge he set out with the remainder to the southward seeking the Red River. After encountering great hardships they crossed the Sangre de Cristo Range and beheld the broad San Luis Valley with the shining thread of the Rio Grande winding across its level floor. Towards this stream they turned and passing near the site of Alamosa reached the Conejos River and encamped five miles above its mouth. Here they built a fort of cottonwood logs. It was thirty-six feet square and twelve feet high, with sharpened pickets projecting over the walls. From the top proudly floated the Stars and Stripes.

Pike thought that he was now on the Red River, while he was in fact on a branch of the Rio Grande and therefore on Spanish soil. He was made aware of this in Febru-

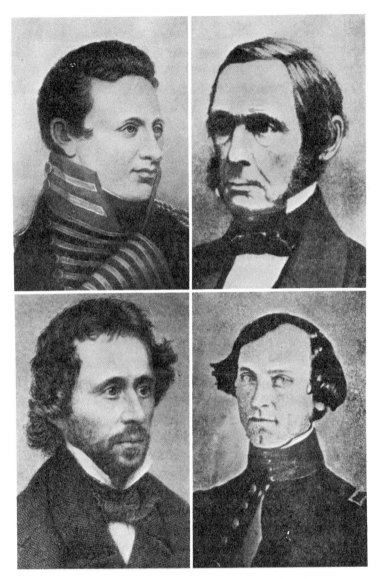

EARLY AMERICAN EXPLORERS OF COLORADO
Upper: Zebulon M. Pike and Stephen H. Long
Lower: John C. Fremont and John W. Gunnison

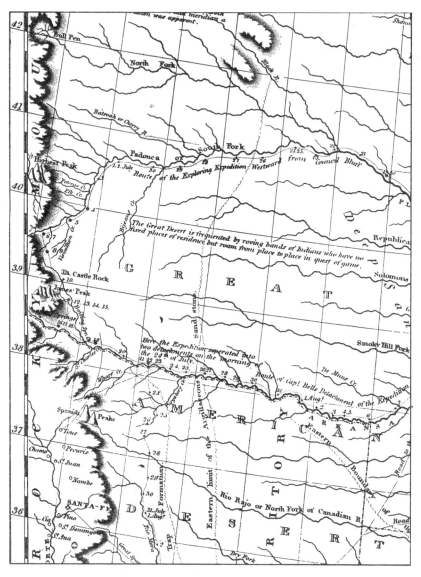

THE "GREAT AMERICAN DESERT"
Map accompanying report of Maj. Long's Expedition, 1820

ary (1807) when one hundred Spanish troops came on the scene. They politely invited him to come to Santa Fe, and being convinced that the troops came with orders to fetch him he decided it would be foolhardy to resist. Hence Captain Pike now left the territory of present Colorado and was escorted through New Mexico and to Chihuahua. The Americans were looked upon as intruders, were tried before the Spanish officials and finally released on the Louisiana border some months later.

Pike gathered much valuable information on the geography and resources of the Southwest. When his report was published (1810) it was eagerly read not only in the United States but was published in England and quickly translated into German, French and Dutch editions. Captain Pike not only aided the development of the great Southwest but was the first American explorer of Colorado. Later, as a General in the United States army during the War of 1812, he led the successful attack on York (now Toronto), Canada, and was killed in the charge.

As yet the boundary line had not been drawn between American and Spanish possessions, but in 1819, when Florida was purchased from Spain the boundaries were defined. Through present Colorado the boundary followed the Arkansas River to its source and thence due north to the 42d parallel of latitude. This line continued as the international boundary until the War with Mexico gave the United States the remaining portions of Colorado.

It was more than a decade after Pike's expedition that the second official explorer touched Colorado soil. Major Stephen H. Long now entered this territory leading his expedition up the Platte River in the summer of 1820. The party of nineteen men traveled on horseback, using pack animals for the transportation of supplies. The season was favorable and the marches of twenty-five miles per day were made regularly with little difficulty.

On June 27th they reached the eastern boundary of present Colorado. Large herds of buffalo were here encountered, their dusky bodies blackening the whole surface of the prairie. Bands of wild horses also were seen. It is interesting to note that although Americans were just entering Colorado the Spaniards had been in the Southwest for three centuries and the horse, transplanted to the New World, had so thrived that he was now running wild upon the plains.

On the 30th the Rocky Mountains were seen, the explorers viewing first the famous peak that now bears the name of Major Long. Without turning westward to attempt an ascent of Longs Peak the party continued up the South Platte past the sites of Greeley, Denver, and the other cities that today dot the banks of the stream. Following Plum Creek the explorers crossed the Divide and followed Monument Creek to present Colorado Springs.

Here Dr. James, historian of the expedition, decided to attempt to reach the summit of the high mountain to the west. With two companions he set out in the early morning, each man carrying a small blanket, several pounds of buffalo meat and a pound of parched corn meal. After a hard day's climb they encamped on the side of the mountain and with the break of day again resumed their climb. They reached and passed timberline and in the treeless region beyond made frequent halts to gather specimens of the rare flowers which here were seen. In the afternoon the goal was reached and for the first time a white man's shadow was cast on the summit of "America's most famous mountain."

Major Long labeled the mountain "James Peak" in honor of this ascent, but the public continued to call it

Pikes Peak, and James' name was later transferred northward to the mountain now pierced by the Moffat Tunnel.
Long's party continued southward to the Arkansas and
after examining the valley to the Royal Gorge turned east-
ward and journeyed back to civilization. In his report Major Long gave a disheartening picture
of the country. On his map he labeled the plains region
east of the Rocky Mountains "The Great American Desert,"
and asserted that the whole region was "uninhabitable by a
people depending upon agriculture for their subsistence."
This opinion persisted in the public mind and appeared in
the school books for more than a generation and was a factor
in retarding the development of the West. Although we
may now criticize Long's report, who could have foreseen
what wonders the railroad, the irrigation ditch and scientific dry-farming would do in blotting forever from the map
the "Great American Desert"?

✦ ✦ ✦

SELECTED REFERENCES FOR FURTHER READING

Baker and Hafen, History of Colorado, 257-298
J. C. Smiley, History of Colorado (1913), 1-114
Bolton and Marshall, The Colonization of North America (1920)
H. E. Bolton, Spanish Borderlands (1921)
Edwin James, Account of an Expedition from Pittsburgh to the Rocky Moun-
    tains [Long's Expedition] (1823)
Hart and Hulbert, Zebulon Pike's Arkansaw Journal (1932)
Colorado Magazine: "Spanish Expeditions into Colorado" (Nov., 1924);
    "Origin of the Name of the Purgatoire River" (Feb., 1928); "San
    Carlos; A Comanche Pueblo on the Arkansas River, 1787" (May, 1929);
    "Zebulon Montgomery Pike" (July, 1931)

Chapter V

DAYS OF THE FUR TRADE

*The Trail Blazers—Seekers of Beaver Skins
and Buffalo Robes*

HUNTERS and trappers were the real pioneers of the West, the original trail blazers and pathfinders of Colorado. To be sure Indians and wild animals had previously beaten trails to watering places, river crossings, and over mountain passes. But it was the persistent search for beaver that familiarized the white man with the western wilds, and eased the way for official explorers and settlers.

Even before the Louisiana Territory was purchased by the United States in 1803, adventurous Americans were pushing their way westward beyond the Mississippi. Daniel Boone, famous backwoodsman of Kentucky, had been for seven years on the Missouri frontier before he was visited by the Lewis and Clark expedition bound for the Oregon country. When Captain Pike reached Santa Fe in 1807 he found residing there an American who two years before had traded with the Indians and hunted in South Park of present Colorado—James Purcell, the first American in the state of whom we have record.

Frenchmen had for years engaged in the fur trade, trapping the Great Lakes region, following the streams in their canoes. From them the Americans learned the art of fur-gathering, and in the earlier years employed keelboats and pirogues, using the streams as highways. Before the year 1800 and for many years thereafter parties of trappers and traders (for they traded with the Indians for furs as well as trapped) went regularly far up the Missouri River. Then as wandering bands worked southward to the region of the central Rockies they found the streams too shallow for regular navigation. Hence they were forced to change their methods—the horse replaced the boat. Creeks and small streams were rich with beaver, and the Indians of the mountains and plains were possessed of much peltry; so the white men came in increasing numbers.

With beaver skins selling at $6 and $8 apiece, with markets in St. Louis, New York, and London demanding prime beaver for the manufacture of the fashionable tall hat, with virgin streams dotted with the houses of these industrious denizens of the wilds, where better for thrifty and fearless Americans to trap for beaver than in these Colorado streams?

Riding horses, trailed by pack animals carrying beaver traps and a few meager supplies, these trapper bands broke trails into the central West. 'And when they reached the mountains, the stream or upland park never before visited was the one most likely to yield the greatest return in skins. There was thus a money reward for trail blazing. The very nature of their work made these hardy men the real pathfinders of Colorado. It is to them we are indebted for the first thorough exploration of our territory. The training they here received equipped such men as Kit Carson, Jim Bridger and Thomas Fitzpatrick to become the scouts and guides to official explorers such as Fremont and Gunnison and to the emigrant parties that later trekked into the far West.

These western trail blazers were young men, strong, hardy, adventure-loving. Most of them were from the frontier settlements where book learning was rare, where physical strength and courage were the qualities prized. As they journeyed into the West they little realized that they were performing important explorations which later generations would be anxious to learn about. But most of them could not have written a record of their discoveries even had they thought it worthwhile. Fortunately, some few were able to, and did,-keep records of their travels. From letters published in eastern newspapers, from diaries, from records in fur company account books and other stray sources, present historians gather the bits of information which tell all too briefly the fascinating story of the life and work of these pioneers. Though the record is broken and the data far from complete, much more is known than we can present here. Our brief space will permit mention of only a few events and characters.

Ezekiel Williams of Missouri, with a party of nineteen men, entered Colorado in 1811 to trap on the upper Arkansas. The following spring he sought beaver in the South Park country. From there half of his men crossed to the streams of the western slope and are lost from the record. After returning to the Arkansas, four of his remaining men went to Santa Fe, while the others remained with him another year hunting and trapping in Colorado. Three of these later were killed by hostile Indians, and Williams and his two surviving companions spent a wretched winter (1812-3) as captives of the Arapaho Indians. In the spring Williams managed to escape, cache his furs and make his way back to Missouri.

The following year he joined a party of twenty-one westbound trappers under Joseph Philibert, hoping to recover his furs and rescue his two companions. Upon arriving at the Arapaho village on the Arkansas he learned that his two men had been killed by the Indians. Williams uncached his furs and with the help of two of Philibert's men transported them back to the States. Williams' party had suffered greatly in the venture but this did not deter others from setting forth hoping for better success. In fact, the Indian difficulties encountered by Williams' men were unusual, for during the fur trade days in Colorado the trappers and Indians of this region usually maintained friendly relations with each other. Many of the trappers and traders including such prominent characters as Carson, Fitzpatrick, Bridger, Lupton and Bent married Indian women, while certain squawmen lived with the tribes and adopted generally the Indian mode of life.

On his second trapping expedition to Colorado in 1815, Philibert was accompanied by A. P. Chouteau and Julius DeMunn. These latter, on the outward journey, purchased Philibert's outfit and the services of the men he had left to trap in the mountains.

During the two succeeding years Chouteau and DeMunn conducted a successful trapping business in Colorado, maintaining about fifty trappers in the field. Not only did they gather furs by trapping, but through trade with the Cheyennes, Arapahoes and Kiowas obtained peltries. One large trading council with these Indians was held on the Platte River a few miles south of present Denver. Twice DeMunn went to Santa Fe to seek permission to trap south and west of the Arkansas, in territory which was considered as belonging to Spain; but each time permission was delayed or refused. On a third attempt in the spring of 1817 he was escorted back to the Arkansas River by 200 Spanish troops. The Americans now decided to turn northwestward toward the Columbia River, but on encountering deep snow in the Colorado Rockies they turned back.

The prosperous trading venture of Chouteau and DeMunn came to a sudden termination in the summer of 1817.

Already the bundles of furs were assembled at the mouth of the Huerfano River in readiness for transportation east-ward, when Spanish troops came upon the trappers and took them and their furs to Santa Fe. After forty-eight days' imprisonment the men were tried, sentenced to leave Span-ish territory and to forfeit all their property except one horse apiece. It was poor reward for the months of work and the dangers they had faced. An account of the outrage was carried to the United States government but not until more than thirty years afterward was the damage claim of these Americans paid.

News of the confiscation of property by the Spanish officials was carried to the Missouri frontier and had the effect of deterring others from seeking furs on the borders of New Mexico. But with the achievement of Mexican in-dependence from Spain in 1821 matters changed. The ex-clusive and monopolistic system of old Spain was replaced with one more friendly to the United States. In New Mex-ico especially were conditions improved, for American vis-its and Yankee trade were now welcomed.

Perhaps the first Americans to trap in the portion of Colorado that then belonged to Mexico (that region south and west of the Arkansas, as defined by the treaty of 1819) were the Glenn-Fowler men who traveled up the Ar-kansas River in the fall of 1821. Jacob Fowler, one of the leaders of this party of twenty men, kept a journal which though rated low in English grammar and spelling ranks high in history. It is a valuable diary of the entire journey and gives some important data on early Colorado.

Fowler reached the present boundary of Colorado on November 5th and in the latter part of the month reached an Indian camp near the present town of Fowler. Here the weather turned cold, a foot of snow fell, and the river froze over. Fowler quaintly writes: "the Indean Children that is able to walk and up to tall boys are out on the Ice by day light and all as naked as the Came to the World . . . We Have Seen more than one thousand of these Children on the Ice at one time and Some that Ware too young to Walk Ware taken by the larger ones and Soot on a pece of skin on the Ice and In this Setuation kick its [legs] Round and Hollow and laff at those Round it at play—I have no doupt but that to take one of our White Children and Put it In Such Cold Weather in that Setuation it Cold not live Half an Hour."

There were 900 lodges of Indians here and the na-tive hunters furnished the white men with meat, not per-mitting the whites to hunt the buffalo lest they should drive the "Indians' cattle" away.

In January, 1822, Fowler built a three room house of cottonwood logs at the present site of Pueblo and did some trapping in the vicinity. Later in the month emissaries pre-viously sent to Santa Fe returned to the Arkansas with a welcome to the party. The trail by Greenhorn Creek, along the upper Huerfano, across Sangre de Cristo Pass and through the San Luis valley they now followed to Taos— the first Americans known to have traversed this "Taos Trail" through southern Colorado.

In February, 1822, Fowler conducted a trapping ex-pedition into the San Luis Valley, reaching the South Fork of the Rio Grande above Del Norte. On the last of April he left the valley and after returning to Taos took his furs and journeyed back to the American frontier on the Mis-souri.

In the 'twenties, Taos became a base for trapping oper-ations in southern and western Colorado. The San Luis Valley, the San Juan, the Gunnison and the Colorado River regions were all visited by trappers, and a harvest of furs was gathered.

James Ohio Pattie in his *Personal Narrative* has left us an account of the adventures of the parties he accompanied. We cannot follow his numerous wanderings in western Colorado, but shall quote his description of his crossing of the continental divide in the winter of 1826-7: "The passage occupied six days, during which we had to pass along compact drifts of snow higher than a man on horseback. The narrow path through these drifts is made by the frequent passing of the buffaloes, of which we found many dead bodies in the way. We had to pack cottonwood bark on the horses for their own eating, and the wood necessary to make fires for our cooking."

In 1824 William Becknell, "Father of the Santa Fe Trail," and William Huddart had trapping parties on the Western Slope, where they fell in with another fur trader, Antoine Robidoux, and his trapping band. Robidoux conducted a fur business for many years in western Colorado and built Fort Robidoux near the mouth of the Uncompahgre River. The itineraries of most of these expeditions were never written and never can be, but we know that all of Colorado was overrun by the adventurous fur gatherers in the '20s and '30s. For many of these, the trails beckoned on and on, and the journey ended only when some grizzly caught the hunter unprepared or some Indian sent a deadly missile from ambush.

While trapping parties were working into Colorado from the southeast, others were coming in from the north and northeast. One of the most prominent of these fur gathering organizations was the Rocky Mountain Fur Company, begun by General William Ashley of Missouri. With Ashley there came into the West a group of young men many of whom became famous as western explorers. Jim Bridger, Jim Beckwourth, Thomas Fitzpatrick, Louis Vasquez and Jede- diah Smith were numbered among these.

After operating in the Montana and Wyoming coun- try Ashley's men pushed southward into Colorado territory. In the winter of 1824-5 Ashley led an expedition up the South Platte, the Cache la Poudre and after turning north and west crossed to the valley of the Green River. Here he bu·lt two "bull boats," made of buffalo skins sewed together and stretched over a wooden framework, and in these rude crafts set out to explore the lower Green River and search for rich beaver regions. In the meantime the majority of his men, after being divided into small bands, set out in various directions to trap in the mountain streams. A suit- able place on Green River he designated as the place of rendezvous, or general meeting, for the first of the following July.

With great difficulty Ashley made his way through Flaming Gorge Canyon, over Ashley Fall, and around the various cataracts which imperiled his way in the Green River canyons, and was the first white man to reach the Brown's Hole country of northwestern Colorado. After threading further canyons and portaging around Disaster Falls and other dangerous rapids he forsook his boats in eastern Utah. Adventure and hardship he had found aplenty, but beaver were scarce. He now returned by land to the place of appointed rendezvous near the northwest corner of Colorado. This general meeting was one of the earliest of the trapper gatherings, but for more than ten years thereafter such rendezvous were a regular feature of the fur trade system.

The mid-summer rendezvous became one of the most typical and interesting institutions of the fur trade days.

The owner of the company or some business manager brought in a train of supplies and trade goods from the East to dispense to his men or barter to the independent trappers and the Indians. Trappers who for months had lost themselves in the mountains gathered in to this fair of the wilderness. The brief holiday invited jollification and dissipation. Races and contests of skill were arranged, and gambling and the drinking of bad whisky were indulged in. Flour, sugar, and coffee were procurable and the continuous meat diet of months was now varied by the introduction of these luxuries from the States. Beaver skins were money and with these hairy banknotes the trapper could satisfy every primitive need. Indians came in, set up their lodges and participated in the fiesta. White trappers with Indian wives bestowed upon their spouses the trinkets and gay draperies that appealed to the feminine heart. Most of the trappers were of the open-handed sort who in the day or two of prodigal living squandered their year's earnings. Around the campfire the adventures of the past year grew ever greater with the telling, and a shake of the head or a word of praise was the last boon of the trapper who no longer cast a lengthened shadow out into the night.

From 1824 to 1827 Ashley prospered greatly in the fur trade, and was able in the latter year to retire a rich man. Some of his former employes took over the business and each year trapping expeditions were conducted by them into northern and western Colorado.

In 1831 Captains Gant and Blackwell launched a fur trade venture in Colorado with seventy men, but it met with ill success. Trappers were coming in such great numbers that the fur areas were being depleted. Streams once alive with beaver were stripped of fur animals, and competition between the various companies became keen and ruthless.

And not only were the fur resources being exhausted, but the demand was falling off. A change of style in London and New York was recording its effect in the Rocky Mountains. The silk hat had been invented and the beaver hat was being supplanted. The bottom fell out of the fur market, beaver skins dropped to $1 apiece, and the industry was ruined.

Although companies failed and many trappers changed occupation, the fur trade days were not ended. From beaver skins the fur men turned to buffalo robes and these latter became the chief article of commerce in Colorado during the late '30s and early '40s.

The coming of wagons made possible this development. Trappers on horseback had blazed the early western trails, but very quickly. wagon wheels followed the horse paths. On the earliest and most famous western pathways—the Santa Fe and the Oregon trails—wagons were employed in 1822 and 1830 respectively. Thereafter the annual caravans of prairie schooners grew longer with each year. At first Colorado territory had been barely touched at its northeast and southeast corners by these historic highways, but soon wagons continued along the Arkansas and the South Platte to the mountains. Now buffalo robes, which had been too bulky and cheap for carriage on pack animals could be handled profitably by wagon transportation.

With the development of the buffalo robe business notable changes were made in the methods of the fur trade. The rendezvous gave way to the permanent trading post. Whereas beaver skins had been garnered largely by white trappers, buffalo robes were obtained by trade with the Indians, and although some bartering took place at the Indian villages much came now to be conducted at the white man's fort, where his trade goods were safely housed.

In Colorado were located several of the leading trading posts of the West. Ranking first in importance and among the earliest to be established was Fort Bent, on the Arkansas. This famous establishment was built in 1828-32 and was located on the north bank of the Arkansas about midway between the sites of the present cities of La Junta and Las Animas. It was built by the Bent brothers and Ceran St. Vrain, who organized the first big and successful business organization in Colorado. Their fort was so situated that it could command the robe trade of the plains, the fur trade of the mountains, and participate in the overland caravan traffic to Santa Fe. Since it became the model for subsequent posts, we shall describe some of its chief features.

The fort was built of large gray adobes and was in rectangular form, about 180 by 135 feet. The walls were from two to four feet thick and fifteen feet high. Round bastions projecting from the southeast and northwest corners of the enclosure rose above the wall and were provided with loopholes for musketry and cannon. Midway in the eastern wall was a large gateway fitted with two great, heavy plank doors plated with sheet iron. Over the gateway rose a square watchtower, capped with a belfry and flagstaff. Within the fort were rows of low rooms backed against the outer wall and having doors opening into the central court. These were like the common Mexican houses with dirt floors and with clay and gravel roofs which were supported by pole beams. The rooms comprised the warehouses, living rooms, kitchen, and the quarters for the post attaches. Sheds provided shelter for the yokes, harness, and other caravan equipment. At the back of the fort was the corral, enclosed with an adobe wall. On the river bank, 200 yards south of the fort, was an adobe ice house. This was filled with ice in winter, and in summer a supply of fresh meat was here preserved.

COLORADO FUR TRADERS OF THE 1830s
Upper: Kit Carson and William Bent
Lower: Jim Baker and Jim Bridger

A PORTION OF THE WALL OF FORT LUPTON (1913)

REPLICA OF BENT'S FORT IN STATE MUSEUM, DENVER

Life about the fort was picturesque. Bronze-faced hunters and bearded trappers in their fringed buckskin suits
made this their headquarters. Their Indian women in
beaded and quill-decorated deerskin dresses glided about
with moccasined feet, through the rooms, across the grav-
elled courtyard, and perhaps mounted the flat roofs to peer
over the protecting outside wall. Naked children playing in
the shadow of the great wall revealed but slight traces of
white blood through the darker hue of their mothers' race.
Clerks and traders had feverish days of merchandising followed by languid weeks of lounging and smoking and the
telling of tales. Mexican mestizos and French Canadians
furnished additional features for the scene, and when the
trading parties of Arapahoes and Cheyennes came in, the
drab fortress was transformed into a colorful, semi-oriental
mart.

For two decades this fort stood as the commercial center of a vast area. But it was not alone, nor did it monopo-
lize the field. Farther up the Arkansas, six miles below present Pueblo, Gant's Post was built by traders Gant and Blackwell in 1832; but it was short lived. Maurice LeDoux is
said to have had a trading post farther up the stream in
the vicinity of present Florence in the '30s. Fort Pueblo
was built by independent traders as early as 1842 and became a famous post which was occupied most of the time
until 1854, when its inhabitants were massacred by the Indians on Christmas day. Other temporary posts no doubt
were maintained for brief periods at different places on the
Arkansas.

On the South Platte River between present Denver and
Greeley a little string of four adobe forts, or trading posts,
was established in the late thirties. Fort Lupton, one mile
north of the present town of this name, was built by Lan-

caster P. Lupton in 1836. Lupton, as a lieutenant of the
First Dragoons accompanying Colonel Dodge to the Rocky
Mountains in 1835, saw the possibilities of the fur trade,
resigned from the army, established his fort, and spent the
next decade in Colorado as a trader. About six miles north
of this fort Henry Fraeb and Peter A. Sarpy built Fort
Jackson the following year. It was maintained but a short
time, being sold to the Bent and St. Vrain Company in the
fall of 1838. One mile south of Platteville are the ruins
of Fort Vasquez, built by Louis Vasquez and Andrew Sub-
lette in 1837. Perhaps at no other place are the evidences
of the old and the new in Colorado history more strikingly
contrasted. What once stood as a proud outpost of civilization—the walled fort with commanding bastion—has become in less than a century a crumbling relic of an almost forgotten day. The winding, dusty, trappers' trail to the fort
and beyond is now a thin, long line of glaring concrete, while
the walls which sheltered the initial commerce of Colorado,
now in crumbling ruin, vibrate to the throbbing of modern
transportation. The fourth of the South Platte trading posts
was Fort St. Vrain, first known as Fort Lookout. It was
built by the Bent & St. Vrain Company on the east bank of
the Platte, about one mile north of the mouth of St. Vrain
Creek.

At least two fur trade posts were established in west-
tern Colorado. One of these was built on the Gunnison
near the site of Delta. The founder, Antoine Robidoux was
in the region as early as 1824, but just when he built his
log fort is unknown. It was already in ruins when Captain
Gunnison passed the site in 1853. The other post, Fort
Davy Crockett, named for the Texan hero of the Alamo,
was located in Brown's Hole on the Green River in the extreme northwestern corner of Colorado. We do not know

the founder, or date of founding, but in 1839 it was in possession of three Americans—Thompson, Craig and St. Clair.
The two forts in western Colorado were used largely as headquarters for beaver trappers, whereas those on the South
Platte and the Arkansas catered primarily to the Indian
trade in buffalo robes. Fortunately, we have preserved by
the State Historical Society of Colorado an inventory of
the goods at Fort Jackson in 1838. This gives a good idea
of the articles used in the Indian trade. Among the items
listed are: looking glasses, finger rings, wrist bands, ear bobs,
glass beads of all colors, bells, powder horns, battle axes,
scalping knives, brass kettles, blankets, vermillion, bright-
colored cloth, powder, lead and alcohol.

With competition keen among the white men for the
Indian patronage, they all resorted to trade in whisky.
This would draw robes from the Indians when nothing else
was effective. The Fort Jackson accounts show whisky selling at $4 per pint and buffalo robes being received at $3 and
$4 apiece. Much trade was on the basis of one pint of whisky
for one buffalo robe. The better element among the traders
tried to abolish the liquor traffic, but the Indians were so
eager for the "firewater" that it was almost impossible to
enforce in this far region the prohibition laws of the government, which forbade the sale of liquor to the Indians. The
Arapahoes, in an interview with Colonel Dodge in 1835,
thus listed the desirable things of this world: first, whisky;
second, tobacco; third, horses; fourth, guns; fifth, women.

During the fur trade days (roughly from 1810 to
1850) Colorado was not only overrun by the trappers and
traders but was visited by official explorers and travelers who
left us interesting accounts of what was seen and done in
this virgin land before plows turned the sod or miners bur-
rowed holes in the mountains.

We have already told of the expeditions of Captain
Pike and Major Long. The next government expedition to
this region was led by Col. Henry Dodge, who with his 120
men of the First Dragoons, in 1835 followed the general
route of Major Long to and from the mountains. Then in
1842 John C. Fremont came to Colorado on the first of his
five famous expeditions into the West. On all of these notable journeys he crossed Colorado territory. In 1845
the First Dragoons, now led by Col. Stephen W. Kearny,
made another tour through Colorado, holding councils with
the Indians and endeavoring to impress them with the power
of the United States Government. Captain John W. Gunnison in 1853 conducted the first official survey through
Colorado, seeking a railroad route to the Pacific Coast. He
came up the Arkansas and Huerfano, crossed the Sangre
de Cristo and Cochetopa passes, and descended the western
slope river that was thereafter to bear his name. Continuing westward, he reached central Utah where he was massacred by hostile Indians. Colonels Dodge, Fremont and
Kearny and Captain Gunnison on their various western expeditions, all had with them as guides and scouts such early
trappers as John Gant, Kit Carson, Thomas Fitzpatrick and
Bill Williams to lead the way and safeguard the march of
the less experienced soldiers, explorers, and engineers.

During the fur trade period several travelers visited Colorado territory, seeking adventure and a knowledge
of the country. A number of these wrote interesting books
which give much first-hand information on this region.
Thomas Farnham, bound for Oregon, and Dr. Wislizenus,
seeking western experience, both crossed Colorado in 1839
and recorded their experiences in books. It is intersting to
note that Dr. Wislizenus' book, the first to report a crossing of Colorado territory, was published in German and

entitled *Ein Ausflug nach den Felsen-gebirgen im jahre 1839*
(A Journey to the Rocky Mountains in the Year 1839).
Rufus Sage in his volume entitled *Rocky Mountain Life,*
gives valuable information gathered in his two years of wandering about Colorado territory (1842-4). Lewis Garrard
penned an excellent picture of life about Fort Bent, on the
Santa Fe trail, and in New Mexico, in the years 1846-7 in
his *Wah-To-Yah and the Taos Trail.* George F. Ruxton
was an adventurous Englishman who in his *Wild Life in the
Rocky Mountains* interestingly recounts his journey from
Mexico into Colorado and his experiences in hunting and
traveling in our territory in 1847. The historian, Francis
Parkman, got much of the color for his valuable historical
writings on a journey to the West in 1846. His *Oregon
Trail,* which tells of the journey, is not only an English
classic, but an original source for Colorado history.

These men mingled with the trappers and traders, sat
by their campfires, thrilled to their stories of adventure.
They learned from the mountain men the arts of hunting,
trapping and reading Indian signs on the trail. Most of these
writers were fascinated by the life and characters of the
region and felt the pull which the Wild West exerted upon
its visitors.

The trappers and traders of the fur trade days were
an interesting lot. French Canadians, Mexicans and Americans mingled together. Their tanned faces and long hair
made it difficult to distinguish one from another, or all from
a band of Indians. In a beaver cap and a fringed buckskin
suit gayly decorated with Indian designs, or in a slouch
hat, calico shirt and cotton overalls the trapper was equally
at ease. With his powder horn, shot pouch and muzzle-
loading rifle he was self-supporting and independent. For
money he had little need; by primitive barter his simple

wants could be supplied. A lodge made of buffalo skins furnished him winter shelter while for summer nights a bed of buffalo robes was spread beneath the stars. A horse to ride, one to carry his trappings, others for his squaw and children (had he married a native woman) and he could journey wherever the trails led.

Most of these Mountain Men were illiterate, but books gave no instructions for trapping beaver or shooting grizzlies. The men were educated for the life they led. They could read the tracks of moccasins, the sign of beaver and the trace of travois; they could mould their bullets from bars of lead and strike a fire with flint and steel. Some were bad characters, fugitives from the law and civilization, while others were specimens of the best in rugged manhood. With them a man was rated by his strength and skill, his courage, and his integrity. The open country, the freedom from restraint, the thrill of adventure tied them to the wilds. A number of these pioneer fur men have become famous, others perhaps equally deserving of honor are little known. Kit Carson is the best known of these early frontiersmen, brave, modest, truehearted; his name has come to be synonomous with the valor of the West. Equally skilled in frontier arts were Thomas Fitzpatrick, Jim Bridger, and William Bent. There were many others who were prominent as trappers, fur traders, and scouts. Among the most active and well known in the Colorado region should be mentioned the following: Jim Baker, Louis Vasquez, John Hatcher, Tom Tobin, Jim Beckwourth, John Albert, Henry Fraeb, Lancaster P. Lupton—and the list could be extended to great length.

Some writers have characterized the fur trade period in Colorado as of no consequence in our history. From one view-point this seems justified. Practically all the trappers and fur men had left this territory before the discovery of gold inaugurated the permanent and rapid settlement of the region. The trading posts were in ruins and grass was growing in the enclosures when the '59ers crossed the Plains.

But are not first explorers making history though they do not open mines, take up homesteads or found cities? Are not the men who make the paths that become our highways, who trace out the passable canyons and reveal the habitable valleys performing a service for those that follow? Shall not those whose hardihood laughed at exposure, whose courage cowed not at danger be remembered with honor? The trappers and fur men were the trail blazers of Colorado and as such we may give them a favored place among our pioneers.

✦ ✦ ✦

SELECTED REFERENCES FOR FURTHER READING

H. M. Chittenden, The American Fur Trade of the Far West (1902)
Baker and Hafen, History of Colorado, 298-350
J. C. Smiley, History of Colorado, 114-193
Elliott Coues (Ed.), The Journal of Jacob Fowler (1898)
H. C. Dale, The Ashley-Smith Explorations (1918)
W. F. Wagner (Ed.), Zenas Leonard's Narrative (1904)
Hafen and Ghent, Broken Hand, the Life of Thomas Fitzpatrick (1931)
Edwin Sabin, Kit Carson Days (1914)
Rufus Sage, Rocky Mountain Life
G. B. Grinnell, Bent's Old Fort and Its Builders
Lewis Garrard, Wah-to-Yah and the Taos Trail
Francis Parkman, The Oregon Trail
Colorado Magazine: "Fort Jackson and the Early Fur Trade on the South Platte" (Feb., 1928); "Old Fort Lupton and Its Founder" (Nov., 1929); "The W. M. Boggs Manuscript About Bent's Fort" (Mar., 1930); "Fraeb's Last Fight" (May, 1930); "Antoine Robidoux, Kingpin in the Colorado River Fur Trade" (July, 1930); "Mountain Men—Louis Vasquez" (Jan., 1933); "Furs and Forts of the Rocky Mountain West" (Nov., 1931, Mar., 1932)

CHAPTER VI

FIRST SETTLEMENTS AND INDIAN PROBLEMS

*Founding the First Towns and Forts on the
Indian's Land*

THE fur trade posts mentioned in the preceding chapter could hardly be called settlements, even though at some of them the trading operations were supplemented by a little agriculture and stock raising. Corn and vegetables were raised at Fort Bent and Fort Lupton and probably at other posts soon after they were established. Then, as the fur trade waned, trappers decided to forsake the roving life for one of farming, and several little settlements were begun. One of the first of these was known as *El Puebla*, located five miles above Fort Bent, near present La Junta. Farnham, on his way to Oregon, visited it in July, 1839, and described it as composed of "American and Mexican trappers who, wearied with the service, have retired to this spot to spend the remainder of their days in raising grain, vegetables, horses, mules, etc., for the various trading establishments in these regions." But this settlement so promisingly begun was soon abandoned.

A *Pueblo* (Spanish word meaning town, village, or inhabited place), at the site of present Pueblo was started in 1842, if not before. Fremont visited it the next year and said that here "a number of mountaineers who had married Spanish women in the valley of Taos, had collected together, and occupied themselves in farming, carrying on at the same time a desultory Indian trade. They were principally Americans . . ."

Contemporary with this Pueblo at the mouth of Fountain Creek was a settlement of some fifteen or twenty families near the mouth of Hardscrabble Creek, about thirty
miles above Pueblo on the Arkansas River, which Rufus
Sage writes of in 1843 and Fremont in 1844. Various other
villages and ranches were started on the Arkansas and its
branches in the forties—the Bent-Hatcher farm on the Pur-
gatoire, twenty miles below Trinidad, in 1846-7; the settlement on the Greenhorn, a little below the present town of
Rye at least as early as 1846; and the temporary Mormon
settlement near Pueblo in 1846-7. This Mormon colony,
comprising some 275 persons, was made up largely of soldiers of the "Mormon Battalion" who had enlisted in the
United States army in our War with Mexico. They were
the sick and disabled sent to the upper Arkansas to recup-
erate during the winter. Here they built a temporary settlement of log cabins and a log church on the south side of
the Arkansas River near present Pueblo, but in the spring
of 1847, they journeyed northward to the Oregon trail and
continued westward to Salt Lake valley. "Uncle Dick"
Wootton, J. B. Doyle, Charlie Autobees and others took
up ranches on the Huerfano and San Carlos rivers in the
early '50s.

But all of these settlements and ranches appear to have
been deserted prior to the gold discoveries and consequent
migration of 1858-9. In most cases the abandonment was
caused by Indian hostility. Of the various Indian attacks
the most tragic was the massacre at Pueblo on Christmas
Day, 1854, of which we shall hear more hereafter.

The international boundary line between the territory
of Spain and that of the United States was agreed upon by
treaty in 1819. Through the region of present Colorado
this boundary followed the Arkansas River to its source

and thence ran due north to the 42d parallel of latitude. That part of Colorado lying south of the Arkansas and west of the headwaters of this stream was thus recognized as Spanish territory. In 1821 Mexico won her independence from Spain and inherited as her northern boundary the treaty line run in 1819.

When Texas won her independence from Mexico in 1836 she wrung from the defeated Mexican general, Santa Anna, the promise of the Rio Grande as a boundary. Had this been acknowledged it would have given to Texas not only Santa Fe and the other towns east of the Rio Grande in New Mexico, but also that portion of present Colorado lying between the upper waters of the Arkansas and the Rio Grande. Texas, during her nine years of independent exist-ence as the "Lone Star State," continued to claim the land east of the Rio Grande and sent out two military expedi-tions to New Mexico to make good her claim, but these failed and Mexico continued to control that portion of New Mexico and Colorado located east of the Rio Grande.

It was perhaps the threat of Texan conquest which prompted the Governor of New Mexico to give grants of land in an effort to stimulate colonization in this disputed area. In any event, some large and important tracts in pres-ent Colorado were thus given as grants in the early forties. Today the title to thousands of acres of land in southern Colorado is traced back to these grants.

In December, 1843, the Sangre de Cristo Grant (over a million acres), comprising present Costilla County, was granted to Stephen Luis Lee and Narciso Beaubien; the Nolan Grant, immediately south of Pueblo, to Gervacio Nolan; and the Vigil and St. Vrain Grant to Cornelio Vigil and Ceran St. Vrain. Previously, the Maxwell Grant and the Tierra Amarilla Grant, the northern portions of which

FORT MASSACHUSETTS
First United States Military Post on Colorado Territory

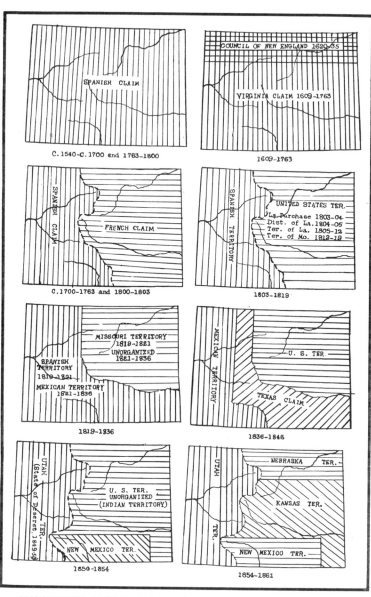

SUCCESSIVE CLAIMS AND JURISDICTIONS OVER COLORADO
TERRITORY

extend from New Mexico into Colorado, were given to private parties by Mexico. The Conejos Grant was also given, but its terms were not complied with and it was not ratified.

Before any permanent settlements were made on these grants the whole region of the Southwest changed hands. This transfer came as a result of the War with Mexico, one of the major features of which was the campaign of General Stephen W. Kearny and his "Army of the West." In June, 1846, over 1,600 volunteers were assembled at Fort Leaven-worth on the Missouri River to accompany General Kearny into the Southwest. The army was in detached sections, and along the dusty Santa Fe trail the infantry and dragoons marched in the blistering sun, while a great caravan of 1,500 wagons, with about 15,000 oxen and 4,000 mules, carried the supplies, ammunition and field pieces.

Taking the mountain division of the Santa Fe Trail they reached a rendezvous about nine miles below Fort Bent, where plans were perfected for the conquest of New Mexico. Fort Bent, temporarily converted into a military storehouse and hospital, rendered distinct service to the army.

Governor Armijo, the crafty *commandante* at Santa Fe, made a show of resistance, but his forces dissolved be-fore the American advance, and Santa Fe was taken without bloodshed on August 18, 1846. Charles Bent, one of the owners of Fort Bent, was appointed the American governor, and Spanish and Mexican rule was forever ban-ished from the region. We cannot follow here the further campaigns of the war, but when it was over, the treaty of peace (1848) transferred the great Mexican Cession to the United States. The major portion of Colorado ter-ritory thus came for the first time under the Stars and Stripes.

Affecting the Mexican Land Grants was the provision of the treaty that all private property rights should be respected. It thus fell to the United States to determine the genuineness and the extent of these grants. Congress ratified the full areas of the Sangre de Cristo, Maxwell, and Tierra Amarilla grants, but reduced the size of the Nolan and the Vigil and St. Vrain grants. The case of the Conejos Grant dragged on for years and was finally outlawed by the court.

An effort had been made at settlement on the Conejos Grant, near the junction of the Antonio and Conejos rivers, in 1843, but the Ute Indians quickly drove out the colonists. In 1849 a settlement was begun on the Costilla River, on the Sangre de Cristo Grant, just south of the present boundary between Colorado and New Mexico. It was reenforced by more settlers the following year. Then in 1851 the town of San Luis on the Culebra River was begun, and in 1852 and 1853 San Pedro and San Acacio were established. These little villages in present Costilla County were the first permanent settlements in present Colorado.

In 1854 the first permanent settlement west of the Rio Grande in the San Luis Valley was made on the Conejos River and named Guadalupe. Conejos and other towns were founded shortly thereafter. Each of these depended on irrigation and thus the dates of the irrigation ditches of the region give a good index to the growth of settlement. It is worthy of note that more than forty ditches in the San Luis Valley antedate those of any other part of the state.

These pioneer settlements of Colorado were begun by humble farmers who dug ditches to irrigate their land, plowed the soil with crude wooden plows, and raised crops of wheat, corn and beans to feed their families. Cattle and horses were fed on the grass of the valley, and sheep and goats grazed on the hillsides. The homes of these pioneers were low adobe houses with clay and gravel roofs, dirt floors, and whitewashed walls. The houses were usually grouped about a central plaza or square in the typical Spanish style. Furniture was necessarily limited and what they had was mostly crude, homemade. A table of boards and some stools sufficed in many cases. A tick filled with straw or corn shucks often was used for a bed, and in the daytime the blankets and quilts were rolled into a bundle against the wall to serve as a seat.

The opportunities for social life were limited, but occasional fandangoes were arranged, when the music of the violin and the Spanish guitar brought hours of gayety and recreation. The visit of the priest or Father and the performance of the rites of the Catholic Church were welcome occasions. Then at Conejos in 1858, they established their first church in Colorado and named it "Our Lady of Guadalupe."

These pioneers had not only to build homes and make a livelihood in a new land, but in the earlier years were faced constantly with the peril of Indian attack. It was to safeguard settlers, to hold in check hostile Indians, that Fort Massachusetts was established to the north of the settlements in 1852. This post, built on Ute Creek, near the base of Mount Blanca, was the first United States military fort in Colorado. Six years later it was replaced by Fort Garland, six miles southward, which post was garrisoned so long as Indians threatened the region. Several of the old adobe buildings of this fort are still standing.

The Indians had been a problem in the New Mexico region from the time the white men first came there, and when control of the land passed from Mexico to the United States the Indian problem was inherited also. Within a month after the conquest of New Mexico by General Kearny in 1846, the United States army was dealing with the Utes of Colorado. Major William Gilpin, fifteen years later to become the first governor of Colorado Territory, was sent north from Santa Fe to hold the Indians in check. On September 20, 1846, he returned to Santa Fe with some Indians, who held a council with General Kearny and received presents from him. Later in the month Gilpin went with a command of eighty-five men into the San Luis Valley and induced sixty of the principal Utes to accompany him to Santa Fe, where they met Colonel Doniphan on October 13th and agreed to remain peaceful. Late in the following month Major Gilpin conducted a campaign against the Navajoes, which took him into the San Juan River valley of southwestern Colorado and northwestern New Mexico. These Indians also were induced to make peace.

In 1849 the first formal treaty of peace, ratified by the United States Senate, was made with the Utes. By it they agreed to make peace and to begin settlements and devote themselves to agriculture. That the Utes really knew what they were promising in this treaty is doubtful, for we know that they were strongly opposed to settling down to till the soil. Their instincts and desires led them to the free life of the hunter. But they were glad enough to receive the $5,000 worth of presents which the government sent them each year.

When game was scarce they looked with envy on the flocks and herds of the white pioneers and could not always resist the temptation to kill the lone herder and help themselves to his flock. Such acts led to punitive measures and peace was often broken. A number of United States Indian agents were in turn appointed to the Utes of southern Colorado, the most successful of whom was Kit Carson. But even this experienced frontiersman was unable to maintain peace by presents and "big talks."

In 1854 and 1855 difficulties had reached such a point that important military campaigns were directed against the Utes and the Jicarilla Apaches of southern Colorado, who were menacing the white settlers. In 1854 several minor conflicts occurred between the soldiers and these Indians. Then on Christmas Day, 1854, at Pueblo on the Arkansas, a brawl occurred in which the fifteen men at the fort were killed and the one woman and two boys were carried away captives. Raids were made on several ranches in the Arkansas Valley, some men were killed, and the ranchers were driven out.

News of these occurrences was quickly carried to Fort Union and Santa Fe, New Mexico. General Garland, commander of this military district, decided upon a vigorous campaign. Six companies of mounted volunteers were called for and obtained and these were added to the regular troops. They set out for Taos and Fort Massachusetts, Colonel Thomas T. Fauntleroy and Lieutenant Colonel Ceran St. Vrain, with Kit Carson as chief scout, leading the campaign. In the meantime the Indians also realized that actual war was on, so they turned to the San Luis Valley for an attack upon the little settlements there. Some men were killed and cattle and sheep were driven off. Even the garrison at Fort Massachusetts was endangered. The commander took precautions. All the trees and brush about the fort were cut away, the haystacks were moved nearer the fort, breastworks were thrown up about the blockhouse, and sentinels kept a tireless watch. The Utes decided not to attack the fort.

After the regulars and volunteers from New Mexico joined the force at Fort Massachusetts an aggressive campaign began. In the Saguache Valley, on March 19, 1855, the first war party was encountered, Chief Tierra Blanca in his red woolen shirt, in command. The Indians found themselves outnumbered, took to their heels, and in the running fight towards Cochetopa Pass most of them managed to escape. For several days the troops pursued, but as the Utes scattered and hid themselves in the mountains the troops were unable to find them.

The soldiers now returned to Fort Massachusetts. After three weeks rest, again they set out, St. Vrain leading his men to the east of the Sangre de Cristo Mountains, while Colonel Fauntleroy moved northward over Poncha Pass. Some distance above present Salida, on April 29th, Fauntleroy made a surprise attack on a band of Utes, killed forty, captured others, and recovered some horses, sheep and supplies. Other minor fights took place during May and June. The Indians received such punishment that finally they asked for peace. A meeting was arranged and on September 10-12th some prisoners were exchanged and a treaty was agreed upon. Although this treaty of 1855 was never ratified by the United States Senate, peaceful relations were generally maintained thereafter with the Utes. Kit Carson and Diego Archuleta were their agents for some years, and distributed regularly to them the government annuities.

The United States government opened dealings with the plains Indians of the Colorado region as early as 1846. In this year Thomas Fitzpatrick, already famous as a trapper and guide, was appointed the first Agent to the Indians of the upper Platte and Arkansas. Upon coming out to his agency in the spring of 1847 he found the Comanches and Kiowas of the southern plains attacking emigrant parties and even United States soldiers on the Santa Fe trail. But upon reaching Fort Bent he met the Cheyennes and Arapahoes and found them friendly. With them he held several councils, was able to keep them peaceful and prevent their joining the marauding Comanches. For plundering Indians Fitzpatrick had no love. He advised the government to use vigorous measures against them, writing thus in one of his reports: "I am well aware that the intentions of the government tow^rds the Indians are conciliatory and humane. But those of this country who know not our strength, and attribute our forbearance to dread of their great prowess, must be dealt with in precisely the opposite manner."

In line with a more vigorous policy, Major Gilpin, now back from the Mexican War, was sent out on the plains in the fall of 1847 with 850 men to punish the marauders. He conducted a winter campaign in present southeastern Colorado and southern Kansas and drove the hostile Indians from the Santa Fe trail. Indian attacks now became less frequent in this region.

In 1848 and subsequently Agent Fitzpatrick worked for a great peace council and treaty with all the Indians. This was finally authorized by the government and arranged for the first of September, 1851. The Cheyennes and Arapahoes, who claimed all of eastern Colorado north of the Arkansas, accompanied en masse their agent to the great council.

This was the largest Peace Council ever held in the far West. To the treaty grounds below Fort Laramie, present Wyoming, over 10,000 Indians gathered. Besides the Cheyennes and Arapahoes, came Sioux, Snakes, Crows, and delegations from the Assiniboine, Minnetaree, and Arikara Indians. When all were convened and rigged out in their colorful regalia and costumes the assemblage appeared more like a country fair and a grand exhibition than a peace council. There were military maneuvers and horsemanship exhibitions. There were dances and dog feasts given by one tribe in honor of another. Upon the firing of the cannon and raising of the flag at the willow bowery which the squaws had built for the ceremonies, the chiefs and head men of the various tribes solemnly assembled. Here the pipe of peace was passed around and white men and red made speeches explaining their rights and needs. Space will permit but one quotation here. Cut Nose, of the Arapahoes spoke thus:

"Grand Father, I thank the Great Spirit, the Sun and the Moon for putting me on this earth. It is a good earth, and I hope there will be no more fighting on it—that the grass will grow and the water fall, and plenty of buffalo. You, Grand Father, are doing well for your children in coming so far and taking so much trouble about them. I think you will do us all much good; I will go home satisfied. I will sleep sound and not have to watch my horses in the night, or be afraid for my squaws and children."

For fifteen days the Council convened. At its close twenty-seven ox-wagon loads of presents were distributed. Father De Smet, the famous missionary among the Indians, was present and thus writes: "The great chiefs were for the first time in their lives, pantalooned; each was arrayed in a general's uniform, a gilt sword hanging at his side. Their long, coarse hair floated above the military costume, and the whole was crowned by the burlesque solemnity of their painted faces." To the lesser braves and the women were given other presents—cloth, beads, trinkets of all kinds, coffee and sugar.

A small delegation of Indians was taken by Agent Fitzpatrick to the East to be impressed with the vast numbers of white men and their great cities. They inspected United States forts and the navy yard; were received by President

and Mrs. Fillmore at the White House, where the delegation in full regalia squatted on the carpet of one of the par-
lors while speeches were made and medals were presented
to the chiefs. It was assumed that if the Indians saw how
numerous and powerful the whites were they would be
cowed into submission and remain peaceful.

The Fort Laramie treaty of 1851 pledged the Indians
to peace, fixed the boundaries of the territory of the various
tribes, and granted the whites the right to travel through
the Indian country and to establish forts on the overland
trails. For this privilege and in payment for destruction of
wild game and for damage done to the Indians' hunting
grounds the whites agreed to bring out and distribute to the
Indians $50,000 worth of goods each year for fifteen years.
Under this treaty that part of Colorado north of the Arkansas and east of the mountains was definitely assigned as
Cheyenne and Arapaho territory, and it remained thus until
the rush of miners into the region created a new situation
which led to another treaty with these Indians in 1861.

Two years after the Fort Laramie treaty was made,
Fitzpatrick formed a similar treaty with the wild tribes of
Comanches, Kiowas and Apaches who roamed over southeastern Colorado. Annuities to the amount of $18,000 per
year were to be given them. In return they agreed to keep
the peace. The Indians of the plains of eastern Colorado during the next decade were generally peaceful. When the
pioneer gold seekers came to the Rocky Mountain region
and settled on the land vouchsafed to the Arapahoes and
Cheyennes by the treaty of 1851, these Indians did not
resist the intrusion.

We thus see that from the early '40s to 1858 development of the present Colorado territory was slow and
halting. The fur trade days were nearly over; the few

pioneers who attempted to found homes and make a living from the soil were insecure. No mines had been opened, and since farming land was plentiful nearer the centers of population in the East, there was little inducement for pioneers to migrate to the territory.

But all this was changed suddenly in 1858 when gold was discovered on the South Platte River. This was the magic touch needed to transform the dormant region into a glittering Eldorado, to place on everyone's tongue the enchanting words, "the Pike's Peak Gold Region." A new day for Colorado was ushered in, a day of great achievements and rapid progress. It is to the story of these events we shall next turn our attention.

✦ ✦ ✦

SELECTED REFERENCES FOR FURTHER READING

H. L. Conard, "Uncle Dick" Wootton (1890)
John T. Hughes, Doniphan's Expedition (1847)
G. H. Heap, Central Route to the Pacific (1854)
Lewis Garrard, Wah-to-Yah and the Taos Trail
Steinel and Working, History of Agriculture in Colorado (1926)
Justin H. Smith, The War with Mexico (1919)
Commissioner of Indian Affairs Annual Reports of 1849-1859
Colorado Magazine: "The Fort Pueblo Massacre and the Punitive Expedition Against the Utes" (Mar., 1927); "Status of the San Luis Valley, 1850-1861" (May, 1926); "Mexican Land Grants in Colorado" (May, 1927); "Relations of the Cheyennes and Arapahoes in Colorado to 1861" (Aug., 1927); "Early Settlements of Southern Colorado" (Feb., 1928); "The Hatcher Ditch" (June, 1928); "Early History of Costilla County" (Aug., 1928); "Thomas Fitzpatrick and the First Indian Agency in Colorado" (Mar., 1929); "The Explorations of Gunnison and Beckwith in Colorado and Utah, 1853" (Sept., 1929); "The Mormon Settlement at Pueblo During the Mexican War" (July, 1932)

CHAPTER VII

"PIKE'S PEAK OR BUST"

The Discovery of Gold and the Rush of the Argonauts

RUMORS that gold existed in the Colorado Rockies had been floating about for more than two centuries before the prospecting parties of 1858 found the precious metal in the sands of Colorado streams. Visions of gold had lured Coronado northward on his ill-starred expedition, and after the settlement of New Mexico the Sangre de Cristo and the San Juan mountains beckoned to gold-hungry Spaniards who saw and christened these majestic ranges. Empty prospect holes found by the first American miners in Colorado attest the searches of Spanish gold seekers, but the names of those first lone prospectors may never be known.

Perhaps the earliest recorded prospecting expedition into Colorado was led by Juan Maria de Rivera in 1765. His party of New Mexicans explored the southern base of the San Juan Mountains and crossed to the valleys of the Dolores and the Gunnison. Ore was found on the La Plata River and this it was, no doubt, which gave the name to the river and to the La Plata Mountains (Plata is Spanish for "silver"). Some little mining was also attempted in the Sangre de Cristo Mountains. But during the days of Spanish and Mexican possession of the Colorado region no gold or silver was mined in paying quantities.

The first American to report a discovery of gold in Colorado was James Purcell. To Captain Pike at Santa Fe

in 1807 he told of finding gold on the headwaters of the
Platte River, probably in South Park. But no one seemed
to be much concerned about the story and it was not until
more than fifty years afterward, when gold was panned from
the South Platte headwaters, that men recalled the story of
Purcell. Other trappers and fur traders at various times
told of finding gold in the region. Rufus Sage repeated the
story that in one of their battles the Arapahoes, when out
of lead, had used gold for bullets. But neither the Indians
nor early traders had the prospecting instinct to urge them
on, to make them seek and keep on seeking the elusive metals.

It was the famous gold discoveries in California in
1848 and 1849 which whetted the American appetite for
gold and stimulated interest in prospecting and mining. Although most of the '49ers who so eagerly rushed across the
continent refused to stop long enough to prospect in the
Colorado region, there were some curious few who halted
to pan the gravel in Colorado streams. Among these were
some intelligent Cherokee Indians, formerly of Georgia, who
found "color" on Cherry and Ralston creeks near present
Denver. The showing was too meager to hold them when
there were stories of pans of gold in California, but after
they and others of the '49ers had sought in vain for fortunes in the Pacific state and had returned home, they remembered with greater favor the promising color in Colorado streams.

Since placer mining in California began to wane in
the late fifties, prospectors turned naturally to other regions
in the hope of revealing another Eldorado. In far off Georgia
W. Green Russell and his brothers Oliver and Levi, learned
from the Cherokees of the signs of gold discovered in the
Pike's Peak country and by correspondence it was agreed to
make a joint prospecting trip to the Rocky Mountains to

make a thorough search for gold. This plan materialized and resulted in most important consequences for Colorado. Other prospecting bands came to the mountains in 1858 but this one, known as the Russell Party, was the first, the most successful and consequently the most famous.

In February of that year the Russell brothers with a party of relatives and friends set out from Georgia, and on the Arkansas River, according to prearrangement, combined with the Cherokee party from the Indian reservation. As their oxen plodded up the Santa Fe trail toward the mountains the gold seekers were joined by a few other westbound travelers until the party eventually numbered over sixty persons with fourteen wagons. From Bent's New Fort they turned northwestward to the head of Squirrel Creek, and crossing the divide descended Cherry Creek, halting occasionally to prospect the bed of this stream for signs of gold. Nothing very promising was revealed here nor on Ralston Creek during the succeeding two or three days. Whereupon the Cherokees and some of the whites became discouraged, decided to give up the search, and return home.

Russell and some of the more steadfast of his companions tried to dissuade them, saying they had not yet given the region a thorough search and that the "color" they had found surely indicated richer deposits that persistent seeking would reveal. But the discouraged members had had enough, and forthwith set out on their return, leaving but thirteen determined men to continue the search. This "baker's dozen" wielded pick and pan with indifferent success at various points on the South Platte near present Denver and then during the first days of July, 1858, found "good diggings" at the mouth of Dry Creek, which runs through Englewood, a Denver suburb. Several hundred dollars worth of dust

panned here rewarded their persistence. This was the first
"pay dirt" panned by Americans in Colorado and even
though the diggings proved to be but a pocket which soon
"played out," it was the news of this discovery when carried eastward which caused the great rush to the Pike's Peak
region during the succeeding months.

We must now leave the Russell party at their diggings
while we tell of another and entirely independent party of
prospectors that also came to the Colorado region in the
spring of 1858. This was known as the "Lawrence party,"
from the fact that it set out from Lawrence, Kansas. Although vague rumors of gold in the Rocky Mountains had
floated about the Mississippi Valley for some years it was
the actual sight of some of the yellow metal carried to
eastern Kansas by two Delaware Indians which gave rise
to the Lawrence party. These Indians, Fall Leaf and Little
Beaver, had been out to the Rocky Mountains in the previous summer with the military expedition of Colonel Sum-
ner and Major Sedgwick, and they told of getting their dust
and nuggets from the region of Pike's Peak. A party of
about forty men was quickly organized but Fall Leaf, being hurt by an accident, was unable to accompany them.
Only one of the company had had any experience in mining, but all were confident of being able to pick up the precious metal.

Leaving Lawrence in May with a train of eleven wagons
they journeyed to and up the Arkansas River, being but ten
days behind the pioneer Russell party. Turning northward
to the site of Colorado Springs they made camp, but seemed
more interested in scenery than in prospecting for gold.
After a short stay in this region, during which time a number of the party climbed the summit of Pikes Peak (including Mrs. J. H. Holmes, the first woman to achieve this

from Lawrence
considered that there were enough mining prospects on and
about Dry Creek to warrant the laying out of a town and
accordingly they organized a company on September 7th
and laid out "Montana City," located on the east bank
of the Platte about five miles south of the present State
Capitol. But this first "city" was shortlived; within a month
its promoters had given it up. On September 24th a group
of the Lawrence party organized the St. Charles Town Company and laid claim to a town site on the east side of Cherry
Creek near its mouth. Then all but one of their number
returned to Kansas, leaving this single representative to maintain their claim.

The Russell party returning to Dry Creek diggings in
middle September from their prospecting tour to the Cache
la Poudre made plans for the winter. Part were to return
to the States for supplies and new recruits while the majority
were to set up winter quarters on the South Platte.

In the meantime, news of the Russell gold discoveries
of July had been carried in every direction. In August accounts began to appear in Kansas and Missouri papers and
on September 2d the *Lawrence Republican* told of the arrival of John Cantrell with three ounces of gold "which he
dug with a hatchet in Cherry Creek and washed out with
a frying pan." Cantrell said he could make $17 to $20 per
day with pick and pan. Others reported that from $5 to

$25 per day could be washed from the golden sands. Stor-
ies were told and retold, published and republished, gaining in size and exaggeration with the telling. Excitement
ran high. "It must be a second California, a new Eldorado."
Those first to arrive would gather the richest harvest, and
hence men began the organization of companies to hurry to
the gold mines. Some would not await the coming of spring
lest by that time the richest ground be claimed by others.

Thus, in the fall of 1858, several parties of gold seekers
journeyed across the plains to the new gold fields. The first
of these arrived on October 24th and found the remnants
of the Russell and the Lawrence parties building cabins on
the west side of Cherry Creek near its mouth. Although
some of the Russell party and nearly all of the Lawrence
group had returned to the states for the winter, the newcomers soon made up the loss in numbers. Some of these
would-be miners were greatly disappointed at the meager
gold returns thus far obtained and at the shallow future
prospects, but most of them were hopeful. All were convinced that at least there would be a heavy migration in
the spring and if gold was then found town real estate would
be valuable. At a mass meeting held on October 30th
it was decided to organize a company and found a town
in the angle formed by Cherry Creek and the South Platte
(site of present West Denver). The new town was called
"Auraria," from the name of the Russell brothers' home
town. Auraria, Georgia, had been founded in 1833, at the
time of the gold rush to Lumpkin County. The name was
from the Latin, meaning "gold." The town had been christ-
enend by the famous South Carolinian, John C. Calhoun,
who had mining interests in North Georgia. New Auraria,
founded twenty-five years later on the banks of Cherry
Creek, was the real beginning of present Denver.

On November 16th there arrived at Auraria a company of pioneers from Leavenworth and Lecompton, Kansas, led by William Larimer, an experienced town promoter.
He immediately selected the land east of the mouth of Cherry
Creek as his town site and with some associates organized
the Denver City Town Company. In a sense they were
jumping the St. Charles Company site, but they induced the
sole representative of that company to join the new organization. The town now started was named in honor of James
W. Denver, who was governor of Kansas when the Leavenworth party set forth, but who no longer held the office
when the infant metropolis was named. Auraria and Denver, facing each other across the sandy bed of Cherry Creek,
were to be rivals until 1860, when they were consolidated
under the name of Denver.

But the twin cities at the mouth of Cherry Creek were
not the only ones launched in the Pike's Peak region in
1858. One party of Argonauts coming up the South Platte
in October, turned from the trail near the ruins of Fort St.
Vrain, and, led by Captain Thomas Aikens of Missouri,
reached the mountains at the mouth of Boulder Canyon. On
this promising site they laid the foundations of present
Boulder. At about the same time Antoine Janise, an early
fur trader, and some companions built cabins on the Cache
la Poudre above present Fort Collins and started the town
of Colona, later known as Laporte.

On the east side of the mouth of Fountain Creek (site
of present Pueblo) the town of Fountain City was begun
in November, 1858, by J. F. Smith and associates. Some
cabins they built of logs, while others were constructed of
adobes from the ruins of the old Pueblo fort. The site of
present Colorado Springs was chosen by certain '58ers as
the location of their dream city. This they called "El Paso

Among the pioneer towns of Colorado born in 1858, those at the mouth of Cherry Creek attracted most of the immigrants who came in the fall of that year. It is true that only a few hundred dollars worth of gold had been secured from the whole Pike's Peak region during the year 1858, but most of this had come from diggings near Auraria-Denver. Thus there congregated here two or three hundred hopeful goldseekers who were to spend the winter months prospecting for gold, building cabins, hunting game and planning for the future. These pioneers, being typical Westerners, were buoyant with hope, confident of success. They expected a large migration in the spring and visioned the creation of a great mountain state in the region of the central Rockies.

While these meager beginnings were being made in the Colorado region, exaggerated news of happenings here continued to be spread as by a giant station broadcasting from the Rockies. The public was tuned for keen reception of news of gold, as the panic of 1857 had brought disaster to many, casting to ruin business ventures and private fortunes. Many a man, crushed in the avalanche of misfortune, faced the world with empty hands to begin anew. To such as these the stories of Pike's Peak gold made a strong appeal. With everything to gain and nothing to lose they could afford to take a chance. From the hard times in the East they would fly to alluring wealth in the golden West.

ult..

The gold ca...

stores, newspaper offices and outh...

as tangible evidence of the truth of the roseate stories being told. The frontier newspapers gladly printed all favorable accounts, for a large migration meant prosperity for
themselves and for the outfitting merchants in the river
towns.

During the winter, preparations were made for the
spring migration. Merchants in the Missouri River towns
laid in their supplies—sacks of flour, sugar, beans and coffee; stacks of bacon sides and hams; cases of canned goods;
bales of overalls and shirts; large boxes of boots and shoes;
shovels, picks and pans. Ox yokes and chains, harnesses
and saddles, wagons and carts, wagon bows and covers and
extra axle trees were crowded in sheds and heaped into
piles in the yards of outfitters.

Newspapers were full of sage advice upon the proper
tools for mining, outfits for travel, and routes to be taken.
Guidebooks were published with maps of routes and travel
information, some of these being put out for the purpose
of directing the travel to certain cities and routes. There
developed keen competition among Leavenworth, Atchison,
Westport and other Missouri River towns, each claiming to
be the best outfitting point, the natural gateway to the
mines, and the eastern terminus of the best highway to the
gold fields. There were three principal routes across the
plains: one up the Platte, one up the Arkansas, and a third
up the Smoky Hill River. Each was to draw its adherents,
but the South Platte route was to be in greatest favor.

...equipment and supplies and eagerly set out. There were all kinds of conveyances, from the ponderous covered wagons to the two-wheeled handcart. Some went on horseback, some tramped on foot with packs on their backs, a few set out pushing their belongings in wheelbarrows. Many set forth with little conception of the distance to be traveled (about 600 miles) or of the supplies needed, and great suffering resulted from their indiscretion. Others went well provisioned and equipped, determined to give the reported gold fields a fair trial. "Pike's Peak or Bust," painted on the covers of their "prairie schooners" voiced the determination of resolute pioneers. Men outstanding in character and training formed a large proportion of the throng.

Through April and May the volume of seekers increased. The motley caravan pushed westward, thousands of hopeful Argonauts seeking the golden fleece. By day the string of canvas-covered wagons appeared as a dusty serpent creeping across the plains; and as darkness settled on the level prairie hundreds of camp-fires dotted the trail and formed a line of beacon lights pointing to the West. Many of these wayfarers were to travel but short distances and turn back discouraged; others were to push on in the face of great difficulties, overcome all obstacles, and lay the foundations of a great state. These latter were of the true pioneer type; they qualify as empire builders.

When the vanguard of the great caravans of '59ers reached the mouth of Cherry Creek in March and early

April they found the little log house towns of Auraria and
Denver still waiting for the gold discovery that would justify
their existence. No placers along the Platte or its dry tributaries were paying for one-fourth the labor being expended
on them and but meager discoveries in the mountains had
been reported. New comers pitched their tents beside the
log cabins of the winter sojourners and asked to be directed
to the gold fields. But no finger pointed the way; only expressions of hope could be given.

With the increasing arrivals, matters developed toward
a crisis. Here were scores of people arriving daily who having read exaggerated accounts of the gold fields had made
the long journey in the full expectation that the sands of
Cherry Creek were yellow with gold and that an ample
fortune could be quickly shoveled up in the new Eldorado.
A day or two of hard work panning sand and gravel for a
few cents' worth of gold dust was sufficient to convince
many of the new comers that they had crossed the plains
on a fool's errand. Disappointment turned to disgust and
then to bitterness, and with strong epithets they condemned
the country and its enthusiasts. Some of the '58ers, who
during the winter months had eaten up their supplies and
found little gold, were of like mind. Covered wagons were
faced about and turned back over the prairie trails while em-
bittered gold seekers shook the dust from their feet and sent
forth the cry of a "Pike's Peak Humbug."

But all were not disheartened; the faith of the majority
in the golden future of the country was still unshaken. These
optimists pointed to placers where a little gold was being
found and contended that this dust had surely come from
"lodes" in the mountains that would be discovered when
the snow melted from the mountain gulches and thorough
prospecting was possible. In fact some diggings had been

uncovered on Gold Run and at Deadwood Gulch in the mountains west of Boulder in January and stories of other discoveries were being rumored about.

In the meantime the embryo cities on Cherry Creek were growing, more log cabins were being built, stores, hotels and saloons were opened and town lots were sold and resold. Indeed, so active was this last named business that many new comers were convinced that most of the inhabi-tants of Auraria-Denver were town lot speculators.

In the emigrant throng of 1859 all classes and most occupations were represented. Farmers were in the ma-jority, but there was a generous sprinkling of merchants, doc-tors, lawyers and politicians and numbers of gamblers and ne'er-do-wells. Comparatively few who came had had any experience in mining. Most of these pioneers were young men without close family obligations. Their new experiences were a relief from the humdrum life of the farm and vil-lage back East. They welcomed adventure, enjoyed excite-ment, and were not afraid of hardship.

In the early supply trains were not only stocks of gen-eral merchandise and food, but mining tools, saw mills, and two printing presses. The mining tools went to the placers and the saw mills were soon turning out lumber for finish-ing buildings and replacing rude log cabins. The print-ing presses were quickly put into operation, and on April 23, 1859, the *Rocky Mountain News* and the *Cherry Creek Pioneer* were issued almost simultaneously. The latter died after the first issue, but the former, under its founder and editor, W. N. Byers, persisted, and was to exert a great and wholesome influence upon the territory. Uninterrupted, the *News* publication has continued to the present day.

May came and more gold hunters were losing courage. Converts to the theory of a "Pike's Peak Humbug" swelled the ranks of the "go backs." There were threats of lynching for the enthusiasts who had spread the false reports of gold, and curses and maledictions were directed against the editors and outfitters on the Missouri frontier who had boomed, it was said, this outrageous fraud for their own profit.

"Hang Byers and D. C. Oakes
For starting this damned Pike's Peak hoax,"
was an expression often repeated with much feeling.

The returning emigrants increased in numbers and as they journeyed eastward, spreading the disparaging report, induced all but the most resolute oncomers to turn back with them. The great tide of gold seekers had surged to the foot of the Rocky Mountains, had broken against the mighty wall, and the back flow with strong current was now sweeping eastward. It is estimated that 100,000 goldseekers set out from the Missouri River in the spring of 1859. About 50,000 reached the mountains and about half of these returned home discouraged shortly after reaching Cherry Creek.

It was at this critical juncture that discoveries were made which in reality saved the whole uncertain structure from collapse, and rescued the Pike's Peak region from taunts and derision. On May 6, 1859, John H. Gregory of Georgia discovered the outcropping of a rich lode, or vein, of gold-bearing quartz near the present site of Central City. This was the first lode gold found in the region, the first extensive deposit unearthed in Colorado.

This Gregory, a poor man traveling the Oregon Trail toward the Frazer River mines of British Columbia, had heard at Fort Laramie of gold discoveries on the South Platte. He at once changed plans, turned south, and his persistent prospecting was rewarded by the discovery of the Gregory Lode.

The sudden wealth almost dazed him, and visions of a life unlike he had ever before known were constantly before him. "My wife will be a lady and my children will be educated," he would mutter with a far-away look in his eyes. Editor Byers visited him some days after the discovery and found him almost distracted from nervousness and lack of sleep. The pioneer editor writes: "Reaching out into the brush, where at arm's length lay his frying pan, reversed, he raised it and uncovered two large masses of gold, which had been gathered from the sluice and fused or retorted in the camp fire. This, he said, was the result of the first three days' work after he got his sluices in working order. He said the pieces were worth about $900 each."

Another, but less important discovery by George A. Jackson was said to have been made in January preceding, but it was not until late April that it was made known. Jackson's diggings were placer deposits on Chicago Creek at the present site of Idaho Springs. His was the richest placer yet discovered in the region.

News of the Gregory and Jackson discoveries was hailed with joy; the faith of the hopeful was justified. A stampede into the mountains began which left the towns on Cherry Creek almost deserted. A line of Concord stagecoaches across the plains had been started in the spring, the first coach reaching Denver on May 7th. This pioneer express was just in time to receive the report from Gregory Gulch and to carry it back to the States. The good news sped down the prairie trails to overtake the "go backs" and hearten westbound emigrants. The back flow of the discontented was partially checked and the emigrant tide again rolled westward toward the mountains.

SELECTED REFERENCES FOR FURTHER READING

J. C. Smiley, History of Colorado, 193-260
Frank Hall, History of Colorado, I, 173-186; II, 519-523
O. J. Hollister, The Mines of Colorado
Henry Villard, The Past and Present of the Pike's Peak Gold Regions (New edition edited by L. R. Hafen, 1932)
C. W. Henderson, Mining in Colorado (1926)
Colorado Magazine: "The Pike's Peak Rush, 1859" (Jan., 1927); "Spreading the News of the Early Discoveries of Gold in Colorado" (May, 1929); "The Colorado Gold Rush and California" (Nov., 1930); "To the Pike's Peak Country in 1859 and Cannibalism on the Smoky Hill Route" (Nov., 1931); "The Contract with Specifications for Building Stout's Pioneer Cabin in Denver, 1858" (Sept., 1932)
The Trail (1908-1924)

CHAPTER VIII

LAYING FOUNDATIONS

The Days of "Jefferson Territory"

LIKE ants about their giant hills the goldseekers swarmed and scurried. Already Jackson Diggings and Gregory Gulch were bristling with claim stakes, but round about and beyond, the eager search continued, for who could say when or where the next strike might be? And the search was not in vain. Other rich lodes were discovered near Gregory Gulch. Soon hundreds of dollars in gold was being washed with pan and sluice from the outcroppings of fabulously rich ore bodies. Tents and pine bough shelters sprang up in the narrow, wooded gulches. An active, throbbing life replaced the quiet that for ages had ruled the hills.

It was to these busy camps that the famous Horace Greeley came in June, 1859. Here he addressed the first great mass meeting of miners in the Rocky Mountains, preaching to them temperance and right living, and advocating the creation of a new State in the region. "As yet," he observed in a letter to the *New York Tribune*, "the entire population of the valley sleeps in tents or under booths of pine boughs, cooking and eating in the open air. I doubt that there is as yet a table or chair in these diggings, eating being done around a cloth spread on the ground, while each one sits or reclines on mother earth."

Clusters of cabins became "cities." Black Hawk, Nevadaville, Mountain City, Central City sprang up in the vicinity of the Gregory lode. These soon had their crude business houses and by August a newspaper—*The Rocky*

Mountain Gold Reporter and Mountain City Herald—was being published.

As the incoming rush continued and these first camps became crowded, prospectors scattered into more distant parts. Strikes were made on upper Boulder Creek and its tributaries, and on various branches of Clear Creek. In the former field quartz gold was discovered at Gold Hill, the Horsfal Lode proving a rich deposit. Groups of prospectors going southward entered South Park, where they made dis, coveries of great importance. While panning sand on an upper branch of the South Platte one of these prospecting parties found gold. "It is in scales nearly as large as water, melon seeds, smooth and very bright yellow, worth from 25 cents to $1.30 each," wrote one of the miners to the Denver *News*. To the stream was given the name "Tarryall Creek," but disgusted late comers who found the choice locations already staked off, said it should have been called "Grab all." Subsequently, when some of these disappointed prospectors found good diggings in another part of South Park, they gave the stream and camp the name "Fairplay," as an assurance of justice and good intentions.

News of the discoveries traveled in all directions. In its issue of August 13th the *Rocky Mountain News* at Denver said: "Five days ago the rush began for South Park; ever since a continual stream of miners have passed through our streets. Wagons, carts, pack animals and footmen—all heading one way; all bound for the same destination—the head waters of the Platte."

The flood surged into South Park and splashed over the crest of the continent to the headwaters of the Blue River, which courses to the Pacific. Placers were found at French Gulch, Negro Gulch, and Breckenridge. During that spring and summer of 1859 the central chain of the Rocky

Mountains was prospected from the headwaters of the Rio Grande to South Pass on the Oregon Trail.

Most of the diggings were of the placer variety in which free gold as "dust," "scale," "shot," or "nuggets" was found among the sand and gravel of gulches and stream beds. The simplest method of recovering such gold was by "panning." With this method one shoveled some of the gold-bearing gravel into a pan, added water, shook the pan to permit the heavy particles of gold to settle to the bottom, poured off the water, scraped off the sand and gravel and gathered the yellow gleanings from the bottom of the vessel. This same general principle of recovery was employed in the rocker and sluice, water being used to carry off the sand and gravel.

The sluice, a favorite device, was a long wooden trough with strips of wood nailed across the bottom. Through this sluice, inclined at an angle, a stream of water was directed, and into it was shoveled the gold-bearing gravel. The swift current carried off the sand and lighter rocks, while the heavy gold settled to the bottom of the sluice and was caught in front of the wooden crosspieces. The water necessary for operating sluices was often diverted from streams into ditches and carried for miles to the rich gulches. For the building of such ditches were formed some of the earliest cooperative associations in Colorado. The water thus obtained was alloted or rented to individual miners and to mining companies.

The surface ores on the gold lodes had been so disintegrated by the action of air and water through the centuries that as "dirt" it could be treated by placer methods. But upon following the vein some feet under the surface the ore was found to be hard rock which had to be broken up before the gold could be recovered. This led to the use of

a rude drag-stone mill, the arrastre, an old Spanish device
for grinding ore, and to the employment of crude stamp
mills for crushing the gold-bearing rock. These mills were
sometimes propelled by horse power, often by water power.
After the ore had been reduced by such devices, mercury
was placed in the muddy solution. It united with the gold
particles to form an amalgam from which the gold could
later be separated by heating. In the late summer and fall
of 1859 these methods were being extensively used in the
region of present Gilpin and Clear Creek counties.

The mining activity in the mountain camps created
business for the "valley towns." The ferry across the Platte
at Auraria-Denver drew most of the goldseekers bound for
the mines to this point and these towns grew as they met
the need for a depot of supplies and an outfitting point for
the camps. Golden, founded at the mouth of Clear Creek
Canyon in June, 1859, soon became the leading competitor
of the towns on Cherry Creek. Two miles north of Golden
the town of Golden Gate sprang up on one of the trails into
the mines, while five miles to the south rose Mount Vernon
on another road to the upper Clear Creek diggings.

The discovery of gold in South Park and on the Blue
River brought into existence Canon City and Colorado City,
each located at the foot of the mountains on a trail leading to
the mines. Colorado City (now a part of Colorado Springs)
was located two miles from the deserted El Paso City of
the preceding year. It was so named because it was thought
to be the natural gateway to the mines on the upper branches
of the Colorado River. The name "Colorado" was applied
to this hopeful little town two years before it was given to
the whole territory. Pueblo, or Fountain City, received
some additions in 1859, the village consisting of about thirty
cabins in June of that year.

With the founding of the mining camps and the valley towns the Anglo-Saxon foundations of Colorado were laid. Though the vast majority of gold seekers came not to found new homes but to gather a fortune and return to the old homes to enjoy it, still after sojourning in the new region and seeing its limitless possibilities, many decided to work out their future here.

True, most of the pioneers thought only of mining; but some saw quickly that surer wealth lay in the fertile soil beside the streams. Miners must eat; supplies raised locally would be assured a ready market. Vegetable gardens were planted in the bottom lands along the Platte, and on Clear and Boulder creeks. In June, 1859, radishes, lettuce, onions and peas were on sale in the Denver market. More extensive farming was done on the Arkansas and its branches, especially on the Huerfano and on Fountain Creek during this first year. A number of wagon loads of produce from these farms were brought to Denver and to the mining camps. The *News* of August 13th reports: "Our market is now well supplied with garden vegetables of as fine quality as can be found in the old settlements of the States." During the summer of 1859 much native grass, or wild hay, in the bottom lands was cut, cured and stacked for winter feed for livestock.

According to early treaties, all the land in the Colorado region belonged to the Indians. But the newcomers were confident that their government would soon secure it from the natives. Hence many farmers laid claim to tracts of land and took possession. Groups of farmers then formed "claim clubs" in the accepted frontier style, and elected a secretary to keep a record of the land claimed by each farmer. This arrangement remained in effect until a treaty was made with the Indians by which they gave up the territory wanted by the whites, and until the land was surveyed by the United States, when each farmer could receive regular title to his "squatter's claim."

But the food products raised locally were far from sufficient to supply the demand in the new gold region during the first two or three years. Most goods and supplies were hauled from the Missouri River region by great ox trains, while large quantities were also brought in from New Mexico and from Utah. Major Bradford, a pioneer Denver merchant, shipped from the Missouri River in 1860 eight hundred wagon loads of goods (a "wagon load" meant about three tons, and was usually drawn by three or four yoke of oxen).

From the valley towns, roads were built to the mining camps. There were no public funds for making such improvements so toll road companies were formed which built roads and bridges and reimbursed themselves by the collection of tolls. This remained for many years the accepted method of financing road building. Many of these pioneer roads were extremely narrow and very steep, but even so they were better than pack horse trails, and enabled wagons of supplies to reach all but the most inaccessible camps.

From the East the road along the Platte was the favorite route. Over it came not only the dusty ox trains and supplies, but the fast stagecoaches of the Leavenworth and Pike's Peak Express, traveling night and day and carrying passengers, mail and express from the Missouri River to Denver in seven days. Prior to August, 1860, there was no United States mail service to the gold region, but anxious pioneers were glad to pay the express company twenty-five cents each for letters from home. The autumn of 1859 saw the return of many successful miners to their homes to spend the winter with their families. John Gregory, for example, returned with $30,000 in gold. Others, though less successful, were enthusiastic for the country and trav-eled east with the purpose of coming back the following spring with their families to make a home in the new land.

Approximately 10,000 spent the winter of 1859-60 in the new territory. Most of these were men, but there was already a fair representation of women and children. In fact, during the summer there had been a number of births to families of gold seekers. The first white baby was a daughter born to Mr. and Mrs. Henry Humbell, and was named "Auraria" from the town of her birth. In Colorado City the first child was christened Colorado Johnson, and the first white boy in Denver was named John Denver Stout. Each of these welcome guests was presented with town lots by the appreciative town companies, lots which if held to this day would have made those early comers wealthy.

It was the presence of children of school age which sug-gested the formation of schools as winter approached. The pioneers, absorbed as they were in the development of the material resources of a new country did not lose sight of the educational and cultural development which was necessary for the founding of a great state. On October 3, 1859, the first school in the region was opened at Auraria by O. J. Goldrick, a picturesque Irishman who had arrived at the settlement some days before. He had entered the pioneer town decked out in a silk hat, broadcloth suit and kid gloves, yet driving an ox team with the regular bullwhacker's whip. So arrayed, he naturally had caused considerable amusement, but soon he adjusted himself to the life of the community. Goldrick's school opened in a flat-roofed cabin rented for the purpose. There were 13 students present the first day. It was a private school, the tuition of the pupils providing the teacher's salary. This was the only school in operation

O. J. GOLDRICK
First School Teacher in Colorado

CENTRAL CITY, 1860

in the region in 1859. The following year other private schools in Auraria-Denver were being taught by Miss Indiana Sopris and Miss Lydia Ring. Schools were conducted also at Mount Vernon and at Boulder in this year. The school at Boulder was taught by Abner Brown in a log cabin schoolhouse especially erected for the purpose. This was Colorado's first schoolhouse built for school purposes, for previous schools had been held in rented quarters.

The pioneer gold seekers did not neglect religion. As early as November 21, 1858, services were held at Auraria. Young William Larimer (18 years old) thus describes the first meeting: "It was a morning service. The congregation was small although Mr. Fisher [the preacher] and my father went around and invited everybody to attend. There were no church bells to ring, no finely draped ladies, no choir, no pews to sit in. But seated on buffalo robes spread on the ground, with both the Jones and the Smiths squaws present (there were no other women), Fisher, father, myself and perhaps six or eight others held the first religious service ever held in the country. . . . In the opposite end of the cabin I could hear the money jingle where the gambling was going on at the same time that Mr. Fisher was preaching." (Larimer *Reminiscenses*, p. 117.) During 1859 a number of religious bodies were organized, and during these early years practically all towns and mining camps were provided with religious instruction by various denominations.

The 3d of October, 1859, the day which marked the opening of the first school, saw also the first theatrical performance in the Pike's Peak region. Col. Thorne's Star Company, having crossed the plains from Leavenworth, played *Cross of Gold* at the Apollo Hall, Denver. This announcement appeared at the bottom of their advertisement: "Front seats reserved for the ladies." During the succeeding winter there was no dearth of dramatic offerings in the pioneer metropolis.

But it was rather quiet in the Pike's Peak region during the winter of 1859-60; some of the mining camps were deserted; others were operated on a small scale only; and many of the miners had returned to the States. Improvements, however, were being made in the valley towns, some of the miners having come to these points to spend the winter. In November, 1859, a three story business block, 50 x 60 feet, was completed on the corner of Blake and G (now 16th) streets, Denver. It was the largest building thus far erected in the region. In December building continued, several lumber mills furnishing the material for new and better construction. Plans were being laid for a season of great activity in 1860. The first year's operations on the gold lodes had revealed the urgent need for more effective machinery. Many now planned to bring out stamp mills to crush the obstinate ore.

The spring of 1860 saw another rush to the Pike's Peak region, one better ordered than that of '59. There was less wild excitement and more sober determination. More men now came with their families, planning to build new homes. The emigrants were, on the average, of a higher type than those of the preceding year. The spring migration was of large proportions, the arrivals being estimated at 5,000 a week at the peak of the season. Most of these came by the Platte road and stopped first at Denver, from which center the majority distributed themselves to the various mining districts. Some remained at Denver and set themselves up in business at this rapidly growing place. Early in April, 1860, the rival towns of Auraria and Denver decided to unite as one city, urged on, no doubt, by the threatening competition of Golden. The united towns took the name "Denver." In the moonlight celebration on the Larimer Street Bridge the consolidation was ratified by the assembled citizens on April 5th.

A large portion of the incoming miners of 1860 went into the Gregory Gulch region. Twenty thousand miners were said to be working in the Clear Creek district during this summer, and forty or fifty arrastres and a number of stamp mills were in operation. Some miners went to Boulder and some to the South Park districts, while others organized parties and prospected the Western Slope and other unproved fields. New discoveries were made in South Park and on the Blue River, where the towns of Buckskin Joe (Laurette), Hamilton, Breckenridge, and others sprang up.

But the outstanding revelation of 1860 was the gold find of California Gulch on the upper Arkansas near present Leadville. To this, the richest placer deposit ever found in Colorado, flocked miners by the hundreds. Fully 5,000 people crowded into the gulch and clustered like swarming bees about Oro City, the principal camp.

Gold discoveries by Charles Baker in the San Juan Mountains were reported and to this region a rush began in the fall of 1860. But no profitable mines were found. Instead, many prospectors suffered great hardship and a number perished in the snows of the high San Juan range. Another decade was to pass before the mineral wealth of that region was to be revealed.

The immigration engendered by the discoveries on the upper Arkansas, the Blue, and in South Park gave prominence in 1860 to Colorado City and Canon City, gateways to the region. By May, Colorado City claimed to be second in size of the cities of the Pike's Peak region and was advertising its free road to the South Park mines, its agricultural resources, medicinal springs and the Garden of the

Gods. By June 200 houses were reported completed in the thriving town.

Canon City was also benefiting by the migration to the mines. On September 8, 1860, the first number of the Canon City *Times,* the city's first newspaper, was issued. It told of a shingle mill and steam saw mill in operation, of the discovery of an oil spring eight miles from the city, and of a subscription being taken up for a new church. By November the city was boasting a population of 800 with 40 business houses.

Boulder was a town of about thirty log cabins in 1860. It was the gateway to the mines of Gold Run, Gold Hill, and Utilla and about the town was developing an important agricultural section. At the mouth of Fountain Creek, In- dependence City was launched in 1860 as an addition to halting Fountain City and the Mexican Pueblo. There were a large number of ranches and farms being cultivated in the Arkansas Valley but city development at the Pueblo site had not yet found its stride.

The first United States mail service in the Colorado region was inaugurated in August, 1860. This was weekly service by stagecoach from Julesburg to Denver and from Denver to Central City, to Boulder, to Colorado City, and to Breckenridge. But this regular weekly service was in- capable of carrying the heavy traffic to the mines, and local stage companies supplied the demand. During the sum- mer two and three daily stages were required to carry the passengers and express from Denver to the more active min- ing camps. From the Missouri River to Denver passenger and express stagecoaches ran tri-weekly, the passenger fare being $100.

On April 3, 1860, there was inaugurated the famous Pony Express from St. Joseph, Missouri, to San Francisco,

California, running on a ten day schedule with a charge
of $5.00 per one ounce letter. This was the fastest western
news carrier developed up to this time and it remained the
pride of the West for 18 months, or until the first transcontinental telegraph was completed. Daring, light-weight
riders rode fleet horses in this race with time across the continent. At the stations, ten to fifteen miles apart, the rider
switched his leather bag of precious letters from the lather-
covered steed to a fresh pony and dashed on at break-neck
speed. Over the level prairie and through the mountain
fastnesses the rider must know the path or make it. Hostile Indians might lie in ambush, but he must not hesitate.
Day and night, in sunshine or storm, the precious burden
must go on. In his mail bag went hope and good tidings—
mayhap sorrow—to pioneers, and in his person and wiry
steed rode the romantic spirit of the West. The Pony Express followed the old emigrant road turning to the North
Fork of the Platte from Julesburg and continuing thence to
California. Letters for Colorado pioneers were therefore
dropped at Julesburg and carried the remaining distance
by stagecoach.

During mid-summer of 1860 Denver was a thriving
business center; two daily newspapers were proudly pro-
claiming to the world the rapid growth of the country and
the unmeasured resources here available. In the *News* of
June 6th we read: "Our city—commenced in the winter
of fifty-eight and nine—in the spring of 1859 containing a
motley collection of three hundred log huts, covered with
mud, and on the first of July in that year having but one
room with a plank floor, has in a few months increased
to a city of six thousand people; with its fine hotels, stores,
manufactories, and all the appliances, comforts and many
of the luxuries of civilization . . . Lofty buildings are rising

on the business streets; solid and substantial brick .edifices of which old cities might well be proud . . . Great trains of huge Prairie freighters arrive and depart almost daily, and more than a thousand emigrant wagons arrive every week. "With such a start and such a prospect what will be the future of Denver, the commercial emporium of the Rocky Mountains, the great city of the Plains?"

To facilitate business transactions a unique institution was established at Denver by Clark and Gruber in the summer of 1860. This was a private mint, established for the coinage of gold. Gold dust had heretofore been used as money but miners and business men alike welcomed the new coins as more convenient. The machinery and dies of this pioneer mint are now the property of the State Historical Society of Colorado and are on exhibition in the State Museum, Denver. A number of banks, established in 1860, aided business development. Denver's first Chamber of Commerce also was organized that same year to further business interests of the city.

Farming by irrigation was already becoming an established occupation in 1860. William Kroenig, who had farmed on the Huerfano in 1859 and had marketed his produce in Denver, reported in June, 1860, that over 600 acres were being farmed on the branches of the Arkansas in that year as against 125 acres in 1859. Vegetables, corn, grain and melons were being raised. The lands cultivated were distributed thus: 390 acres on the Huerfano, 150 on the Fountain, 100 on the Greenhorn and 20 on the Arkansas proper. On the South Platte and its tributaries many farms were being opened. Cherry, Bear, Plum, Clear, and Boulder creeks were dotted with farms and the South Platte for several miles above and below Denver was lined with ranches. That this land was becoming highly prized is in-

dicated by the sale of Jack Henderson's ranch on an island
in the Platte about 15 miles north of Denver for $6,000 in
August, 1860. All of this agriculture, developed since the
gold discovery, was a convincing argument to those Easterners who had thought of this region as barren and fruitless.
And in addition to the farming on the branches of the Platte
and Arkansas there continued the agricultural production
in the San Luis Valley, then a part of New Mexico, which
had been gradually expanding during the preceding decade
even though there had been no gold mining in the vicinity
to stimulate it. Thus within two years the foundation of
a great Commonwealth was laid.

One of the most interesting features in pioneer development in Colorado was the rise of civic and political organizations. The Anglo-Saxon race is noted for its inborn
tendency toward self-government and political creation, and
nowhere is the trait better exemplified than in the early history of the Pike's Peak region. A. D. Richardson, upon
his visit to Denver in 1859, writes with both truth and
humor: "Making governments and building towns are the
natural employments of the migratory Yankee. He takes
to them as instinctively as a young duck to water. Congregate a hundred Americans anywhere beyond the settlements
and they immediately lay out a city, frame a State constitution and apply for admission into the Union, while twentyfive of them become candidates for the United States Senate."

From 1854 to 1858 the territory of present Colorado
lay within the boundaries of four existing Territories. All
that portion west of the continental divide was a part
of Utah; that south of the 38th parallel, east of the continental divide and west of the 103° West longitude, belonged to New Mexico; the remaining part was included in

Kansas and Nebraska, with the dividing line on the 40th parallel. Such the divisions remained until Colorado Territory was created in 1861. Thus in 1860 Breckenridge was in Utah, Conejos in New Mexico, Boulder in Nebraska, and Denver in Kansas.

From another standpoint all the region was Indian territory, for prior to 1861 the natives had not made treaties ceding their land to the whites. The newcomers were therefore intruders upon Indian land. But the pioneer Pike's Peakers showed little regard for Indian title and were almost equally uninclined to acknowledge the jurisdiction of existing Territorial governments. From the beginning they visioned the creation of a new mountain state. Any other arrangements were thought of as merely temporary expedients.

The western end of Kansas, in which the gold discoveries of 1858 occurred, had been created Arapahoe County in 1855, but there had been no population and hence no county organization established before 1858. To meet the situation arising from a rush to the gold region, Governor Denver of Kansas, appointed a corps of county officers from among the westbound goldseekers, but before they arrived at the mouth of Cherry Creek earlier arrivals were taking political action.

On November 6, 1858, the handful of pioneers at Auraria elected Hiram J. Graham as their delegate to Washington, and A. J. Smith to represent them in the Kansas legislature. Mr. Graham carried with him across the plains and to the national capital a petition praying the organization of a new Territory in the Pike's Peak region. In January, 1859, two bills were introduced in Congress in conformity with this petition, one proposing the name "Colona Territory," the other "Jefferson Territory." But neither measure attracted the necessary support for passage before Congress adjourned.

As the spring immigration set in, the movement for a spontaneous government rose and spread. The first definite proposal came from Fountain City (present Pueblo) in early April and was soon followed by a like movement in Auraria. At the latter place a convention assembled on April 15, 1859, proposed the creation of the "State of Jefferson," and issued a call for elections in May to select delegates to a constitutional convention to meet in June. The call explained: "Government of some kind we must have, and the question narrows itself down to this point: Shall it be government of the knife and revolver or shall we unite in forming here in our golden country, among the ravines and gulches of the Rocky Mountains, and the fertile valleys of the Arkansas and Plattes, a new and independent State? . . . Let us all unite as one in so great an object . . . It is a glorious cause, and a feeling of pride as well as of duty should lead us to act in it."

But the spring and summer of 1859 were full of uncertainties. When the constitutional convention met in Denver on June 6th the future of the proposed State was rather dubious. In view of this situation the convention decided to appoint committees to draft a constitution, and to adjourn until the first of August to await developments. As the weeks passed and more emigrants returned home the feeling grew that the political fathers had overstepped themselves. Would not a Territorial organization be adequate to the needs of the people and at the same time dispense with the financial burden involved in statehood? After debating this question in its August session the Constitutional Convention decided to submit it to a vote of the people. In the polling on September 5th the State proposition was

defeated; so steps were taken for the formation of a provisional Territory. Another convention met on October
10th. In a three-day session a constitution was drawn up
for Jefferson Territory. Two weeks later it was ratified
by popular vote and a set of officers, with R. W. Steele as
Governor, was elected for the new Territory. All of present Colorado and considerable strips of present Utah and
Wyoming were included within the generous boundaries
of the provisional Territory.

The newly elected General Assembly of Jefferson Territory convened at Denver on November 7, 1859, and proceeded to the making of laws. It created twelve counties
and three judicial districts, incorporated Denver City, and
enacted other needed legislation. But the execution of these
laws was a difficult matter. The spontaneous government
had no legal authority; therefore many refused to acknowledge its jurisdiction or to lend it support. Some considered
themselves under Kansas authority. These elected Richard
Sopris on November 8, 1859, to the Kansas legislature,
where he was duly seated and served his constituents. Approximately one-third of the laws enacted by the Kansas
legislature in 1859-60 were local laws concerning present
Colorado territory.

Financial rocks rendered the sea rough for the newly
launched government of Jefferson Territory. When, in late
December, the Assembly levied a poll tax of one dollar
to defray the expense of government, the opposition crystallized. Six hundred miners from the mountain camps signed
a pledge to resist the collection of the tax and promised the
collectors bullets instead of dollars. The collection was not
made. In fact Jefferson Territory was more imposing on
paper than in reality.

The actual effective governments in the Pike's Peak

region before the creation of Colorado Territory were the local governments of mining districts and towns. These were as extra-legal as Jefferson Territory and equally spontaneous, but their operation in a smaller area made them more effective.

When prospectors revealed rich diggings or lodes and men flocked to the scene it was imperative that some regulations be formed to safeguard rights and protect holdings. By a common impulse these miners assembled in the open air and in that great, democratic institution, the mass meeting, decided all questions that arose. They organized mining districts and established their boundaries, fixed the size of claims and the amount of work necessary to hold them; elected officers of the district and created miners' courts to settle all disputes which might arise.

Not only were matters affecting property rights regulated by these spontaneous local governments, but codes of criminal and civil law were also enacted by majority vote and put into effect. The rules were simple, clear, and therefore all the more effective. A person accused of a crime was given a hearing before a jury and straightway the verdict was executed, without the prolonged delays that so often defeat justice today. Crimes were usually punished by whipping, banishment from camp, or hanging, depending upon the seriousness of the offense. But in all cases an appeal could be made to a meeting of all the citizens of the district, which was the court of last resort.

In the valley towns criminal cases were handled in the same general way as were similar cases in the mining districts. Simple democratic methods, a fair trial and speedy justice were the laudable features of these pioneer processes of law and justice. Among the farmers, "claim clubs" regulated property rights. The record of the miners' courts, the

people's courts, and claim clubs in the Pike's Peak region
is a praiseworthy one; it exemplifies a high sense of justice
and fair dealing.

While the local governments just described were handling civic problems as they arose, and while the Territory of
Jefferson was attempting to care for the more general political needs of the region, efforts were continued to per-
suade Congress to establish a regular legal government for
the territory. As the General Assembly of Jefferson Territory sat in session in November, 1859, B. D. Williams, who
had been elected Delegate from the provisional Territory,
was journeying to Washington to seek recognition for himself and the Territory he represented. Bills were introduced
and debated in Congress but again the session (1859-60)
closed without Congress' having recognized or established
a Territorial government for the Pike's Peakers.

The year 1860 passed with little change in the political
situation, except that Jefferson Territory declined somewhat in prestige. Since experience in the region was proving the local governments stronger than a general one, Denver in the fall of 1860, heeded this lesson and established
an "Independent City Government" with a mayor and
council. This was well supported and operated successfully
until replaced by a government created under Colorado Territory.

For a third time the pioneers of the Pike's Peak region
appealed to Congress, in December, 1860, for a Territorial
government. At last their wish found favor and a majority
vote was in sight for the bill. The matter of a name was now
debated. Among those suggested, "Idaho" appeared to be
first choice. Then someone observed that states may appropriately be named for great rivers within their boundaries
and the name "Colorado" was proposed. Senator Gwin of

California objected: "It is the handsomest name that could be given to any Territory or State," he said, and he wanted it reserved for present Arizona Territory. But his objec-tion was overruled. The bill passed both houses of Congress and became a law when President Buchanan attached his signature on February 28, 1861. The Territory of Colorado was born and christened, and Jefferson Territory graciously bowed her exit.

✦ ✦ ✦

SELECTED REFERENCES FOR FURTHER READING

Baker and Hafen, History of Colorado, 433-440, 475-490
J. C. Smiley, History of Colorado, 260-362
Frank Hall, History of Colorado, I, 186-258
O. J. Hollister, The Mines of Colorado
T. M. Marshall, Early Records of Gilpin County (1920)
Steinel and Working, History of Argiculture in Colorado (1926)
Horace Greeley, An Overland Journey in 1859 (1860)
A. D. Richardson, Beyond the Mississippi (1867)
W. H. H. Larimer, Reminiscences of Gen. William Larimer, etc. (1918)
J. E. Wharton, History of the City of Denver (1866)
Rocky Mountain News (1859-1861)
The Trail (1908-1924)
Colorado Magazine: "Early Mail Service to Colorado, 1858-1860" (Jan.,
    1925); "Steps to Satehood in Colorado" (Aug., 1926); "Western Ex-
    periences and Colorado Mining Camps" (Mar., 1929); "Across the
    Plains and in Denver, 1860" (July, 1929); "The First School in Den-
    ver" (Mar., 1929); "Colorado's First Woman School Teacher" (May,
    1929)

CHAPTER IX

PIONEER LIFE

How the First Settlers Lived

"GO West, young man, go West, and grow up with the country," was the sage counsel of the famous Horace Greeley. Among the thousands who took his advice were the vigorous young founders of Colorado. To portray the life and conditions which these pioneers experienced while laying the foundations of the state is the object of this chapter.

It is the spring of 1860, the brown earth is turning green with tender grass and the odor of growing things is in the air. The valley roads are muddy from spring rains but on the plains the buffalo grass is ready for cropping and there is no need for further delay. The pioneer family has secured its outfit; food, bedding and perhaps a few pieces of household furniture are packed in the wagon, and the journey begins. On the front seat sits the father, dressed in his overalls and calico shirt and beside him the mother in checkered calico dress peers from beneath her starched sunbonnet. Back of the seat in the little house made by the canvas cover stretched tightly over the wagon bows, the quilts are arranged to make a comfortable nest for the children. Perhaps a milk cow or two are led behind the wagon or driven along by the boy on his pony. There may be a rack of chickens tied to the side or rear of the wagon and perhaps a dog and cat accompany the family.

After a few days of travel out from the Missouri River, through the rolling country of eastern Kansas, past the fron-

tier towns and outlying farms, they reach the Platte River
at Fort Kearny and follow the main traveled road along the
south side of this shallow winding river shining in the sunlight. This is the Oregon Trail which for over a decade
has been carrying the heavy emigration to Oregon, California and the valley of the Great Salt Lake.

The novelty of the first days are soon over and travel is
settling down to a routine, which at times grows monoto-
nous. Early rising is the rule, for hobbled horses and wandering oxen that have strayed far from camp through the
night must be gathered in. Only small fires are made, for
there is no wood on the treeless plains and drift wood is
scarce in the river bed. But out on the open prairie buffalo
chips are plentiful and these make a fire sufficient to fry the
salt pork and flapjacks for breakfast.

With the morning meal over, the train is soon in motion, wagon trailing wagon in a long creeping line. A little
before noon a camp is made. The horses and stock are allowed to graze for several hours, while the noon meal of
the emigrants is prepared and eaten during the halt. At
sunset the afternoon drive ends and the night camp is made.
The horses are unharnessed; the cattle are placed in charge
of a herder. Campfires are lighted, and supper is prepared.

As darkness envelops the company the emigrants gather
in groups about the fires to tell the experiences of the day,
plan the morrow's travel, or discuss some bit of news that
has been dropped to them by passing stagecoach or pony
express. Perhaps the strains of the violin and guitar compete with the far off yelp and howl of the lonesome coyote.
On a moonlight night a group clusters about the melodeon,
where the singing of folk and love songs recalls fond memories of the home and friends being left behind. Many a
courageous mother, through a film of memories, has fallen

to sleep on a dampened pillow in her bed in the covered wagon.

Indians, not yet openly hostile, occasionally visit the emigrant train to beg for "beescuit" and "tobac" and do a little petty stealing when they can. The white children shy back or cry and their mothers are far from comfortable when these painted, befeathered "bucks" come nosing about the wagons, but a few gifts and a stern "vamoose" from the men usually suffices to send the visitors away.

Vast herds of shaggy buffalo are met on the plains. The numberless, dusky bodies darken the prairie for miles. On occasion the emigrant train must be halted while the moving mass of lumbering bison pass across the trail. On hot sultry days swarms of gnats and flies annoy the animals and pester the travelers, and at times clouds of dust rise in billows that nearly suffocate both man and beast. Then on other days the scene is changed; heavy clouds pour out their volumes amid the flash of summer lightning and the crack and rumble of resounding thunder.

Twenty miles per day is the average drive. Four to six weeks of travel bring the emigrant caravan across the plains. From Fort Kearny to Denver no white inhabitants occupy the land, save the resident keepers of the stage stations along the line of travel. The sameness of the landscape grows wearisome before the mountains come into view. Mrs. Daniel Witter, a pioneer mother, writes: "I never shall forget those dear old mountains. The first sight we had of them 75 miles out, they looked like silver and gold piled up in the sunlight and I thought, 'Well, we can dig most any place and get the gold,' but oh, how disappointing such thoughts."

The six hundred miles of plains were crossed also by modes of travel other than the emigrant wagon. While the ox-trains with their wagon bosses and bullwhackers were usually two months upon the road, the stagecoaches required only six or seven days. Many pioneers to Colorado chose this speedy passenger carrier for their trips across the plains. The coach traveled day and night, stopping at the stations only long enough for change of teams and for passengers to take their meals. Nine people could be accommodated in the three inside seats of the coach and additional ones might ride on the front and rear seats of the upper deck. One passenger writes: "A through ticket and fifteen inches of seat, with a fat man on one side, a poor widow on the other, a baby on your lap, a bandbox over your head, and three or four more persons immediately in front leaning against your knee, makes the picture, as well as your sleep' ing place for the trip." But all coaches were not so crowded and pioneers often looked upon a stage trip across the plains as a vacation jaunt, much to be preferred to the pro' longed journey by covered wagon.

Four spirited horses pulled the coach and responded quickly to the word of the arrogant driver or the crack of his silver-mounted whip. The body of the coach was swung on heavy leather thorobraces which took the place of springs and permitted the coach to rock slightly to and fro. In the front and rear were the triangular leather "boots" which carried the mail and express. The Concord stagecoach was one of the most elegant passenger carriers of pioneer times and many an emigrant was proud to ride the famed vehicle to the Pike's Peak country.

For the stagecoach passengers or the covered wagon emigrants the immediate destination usually was Denver. From this center they then distributed themselves to the other towns and the mining camps. Though far from being the beautiful city that greets one today, the little pioneer town was none the less welcome to weary emigrants. It marked the end óf the plains journey and symbolized the Colorado which was to be their home. In 1860 most of the buildings were as yet in the Auraria section (West Denver) but the higher ground to the east of Cherry Creek was being dotted with frame buildings. Larimer and Blake streets were crowded with freight wagons and ox teams and the business houses which lined them were doing a thriving trade in provisions and supplies. The town was treeless except for a few huge cottonwoods along the river, the streets were ungraded and billows of dust went swirling through them on dry summer days. There were no lawns or flowers about the houses and the sidewalks were but trails through the sand. There were no street lights, no fire department, no police force. There was no water piped into town nor none as yet in ditches along the sidewalks. Instead, private wells or barrels of water hauled from the river furnished the culinary supply, but a six mile ditch had been surveyed for bringing water from the Platte to the city and was later to supply the growing metropolis.

The year before, in early 1859, the best houses were rude log cabins with dirt floors and canvas or dirt roofs. Of their furnishings A. D. Richardson, a pioneer journalist, writes: "Chairs were glories yet to come. Stools, tables and pole bedsteads were the staple furniture, while rough boxes did duty as bureaus and cupboards. Hearths and fireplaces were of adobe, as in Utah, California and Mexico. Chimneys were of sticks of wood piled up like children's cob houses and plastered with mud. A few roofs were covered with shingles split by hand, but most were of logs spread with prairie grass and covered with earth." The Denver House was the leading hotel in early 1859. Henry Villard, (later president of the Northern Pacific Railroad), who took lodg-

CONCORD STAGECOACH AND COVERED WAGON

DENVER IN THE EARLY SIXTIES

The *Rocky Mountain News* building, shown here, was washed away by the famous
Cherry Creek Flood of May, 1864

ing there in 1859, says that it "was about 60 feet long and 30 wide. Its four sides consisted of roughly-hewn logs. It had a slanting, skeleton roof, covered with canvas. In the interior were neither floors nor ceilings, nor walls, nor solid partitions to divide the space; but canvas nailed on frames served to set it off for different purposes to the height of seven feet. The front part was occupied by a bar for the sale of strong drinks only, and a dozen gambling tables . . . Next to the barroom came another space, enclosed by canvas partitions where the meals were served. Immediately behind it six apartments for sleeping purposes, divided only by the same light material, were set off on each side of a passage. . . . There was no furniture but the gambling and other tables and benches and chairs, made out of rough boards. Bedsteads were provided of the same material, without mattress or pillows, and also tin wash basins, which the guests themselves filled out of barrels of water standing in the passageway, and emptied, after use, on the dirt floor."

But now, in 1860, the log houses of previous years were being boarded up with siding or were giving way to neat frame structures with board floors, glass windows and shingle roofs; and even substantial brick buildings were going up. Painted buildings were becoming common, while artistic signs on the business fronts announced the line of trade being carried on within. There were several two story business blocks housing small shops and providing offices for lawyers, doctors and real estate agents.

Already a great variety of businesses were represented in the city. Supply and provision stores and saloons were the most numerous, but there were hotels, boarding houses, livery stables, blacksmith shops, drug stores, dance halls, theaters, meat markets, barber shops, warehouses, bakeries,

banks, clothing stores, and at least one each of such establishments as a gun shop, jewelry store, bookstore, millinery
store, chair factory, ice house, mint and brewery. And to
supplement the permanent business houses were enterprising
small traders of whom the pioneer newspaper editor writes
in June, 1860:

"Some are in tents, others sell from the rear end of a
wagon, and others again, from a box on the sidewalk. Sacks
of flour, sides of bacon, barrels of whisky, bars of steel, fuse,
blasting powder, sweet cider, fluid lightning, mining tools
and an endless variety of all kinds of traps can be bought
in the open air. . . . . Bootmakers work in tents and the
blacksmith sets up his forge in the open air. . . . Vast trains
of huge wagons file through the streets and discharge their
cargoes of merchandise, or pass on to the mountains with
ponderous machinery that soon will drive away forever the
solitude that so long has reigned."

The banks of the Platte are sprinkled with emigrant
tents and wagons and a whole village of Arapahoes have
set up their smoke-browned tepees among the large cottonwoods in the bottomland. In the opposite direction on the
Cherry Creek road, three miles southeast of the settlement,
the new cemetery caps the hill (present Cheesman Park)
which overlooks the city. Here are recent graves of several
men who died with their boots on.

But more interesting than the physical city are the
people who inhabit it. Pioneer Denver had an intriguing
variety of characters, a citizenry which one pioneer, Dr.
Willing, described in his diary as a mixed population of
"white, black, red and yellow." Among the men there were
all types, from the proud and pompous operator to the
shiftless street loafer. The pioneer newspaper in June, 1860,
gives this description of the general group of miners and

freighters: "Hardy, brown-faced, weatherbeaten sovereigns
from the plains, the mountains and the mines, with a pro-
fusion of buckskin patches, red shirts and hairy faces crowd
every corner, fill up the stores and thickly surround the auc-
tion stands."

But it was no longer wholly a man's town; the woman
in calico dress and sunbonnet was a familiar figure and
Dame Fashion had entered, dressed in shimmering crinoline
and expanding hoopskirt. The pioneer editor writes of two-
year-old Denver: "Ladies promenade its streets, arrayed in
the newest, costliest, silks from Stewart's, made up in strict
conformity with the latest Paris fashions. The daintiest bonnets are gracefully appended to the backs of their dear little
heads, and butterfly parasols have shielded them from the
ardent rays of 'old Sol' for months past; Keevil hats, Heenan
neckties, patent leather gaiters and the complete get up,
that goes to make up a dainty outfit, no longer look strange
to admiring savages."

And there really were "savages" to admire, who also
had styles of their own to display as they visited the Denver merchants to barter their buffalo robes and peltries for
blankets, trinkets, sugar and whisky. The squaw was dressed
in buckskin or calico dress or wrapped in a buffalo robe
or blanket, her face brilliantly painted and her arms and
dress bedecked in shining tinselry; the black-eyed papoose
was tied in its cradle on her back and little half-naked children followed at their mother's heels. The "bucks" were
dressed in a variety of clothes, from a pair of buckskin trousers to the cast off military uniform of some soldier.

Since Denver is built on a favorite camp ground of
the Arapahoes, these Indians continued to set up their village on the Platte bottoms just below the mouth of Cherry
Creek for some years after the white men came. They were

hereditary enemies of the Utes of the mountains and often
the Arapaho squaws and papooses were left at Denver while
the braves made a foray into the mountains against their
enemies. In May, 1860, such a war party returned to Denver with four Ute scalps and fifty horses, and straightway
the scalp dance commenced at their camp in present North
Denver where one thousand Indians were assembled under
Chief Little Raven. The *News* of May 23, 1860, records:

"On Friday there was a large accession to their numbers and a grand triumphal entry into the city, with music,
banners, and hundreds of gaily caparisoned horses and their
riders. During the day the scalp dance was performed several times in the principal streets, in the presence of hundreds of curious spectators.

"Never have we seen a more striking contrast between
savage and civilized life. Dusky warriors, bedizened with
paint and tinselry, dancing to their rude music, precisely
as their ancestors danced centuries ago in celebration of the
same barbarous rites, and on the same ground; but now
over their mystic circles falls the shadow of lofty buildings;
around them stand throngs of curious pale faces, and by
them—even turning out of the way to pass—rolls and
surges the ceaseless tide of advancing emigration—long lines
of tented wagons wending their way steadily toward the
setting sun, sure harbinger of the speedy disappearance of
the red man."

There were homes in the new "cities" of the Pike's
Peak region surprisingly well furnished, some of the more
prosperous families having brought their household furniture, silverware, china, linen, and the like to their new
homes in the West. Such were able to entertain in the approved style of the period, though the scarcity of domestic
help usually kept the hostess busy in the kitchen. As

early as January, 1860, ladies of Denver began social activity by forming the "Ladies' Union Aid Society," with
Mrs. W. N. Byers as president. There was a Library Association formed in February, a "Pioneer Club" in April,
and a "Literary and Historical Society" in December. Various fraternal organizations such as the Masons and Odd
Fellows were meeting regularly in this year.

Dances and the theater were the principal forms of
amusement. The violin, accordion, or mouth harp provided
the music for the dance and the guests disported themselves
in the Quadrille, Virginia Reel, the Schottische, and the
Waltz, often continuing their festivities to the "wee sma'
hours" of the morning.

Theatrical performances in Denver were given at the
Apollo Theater by a professional troupe and by local tal-
ent. Of his visit in 1860 Richardson writes: "Denver already boasted the Apollo Theater, neither ceiled nor plastered, illuminated by twelve candles and containing rough
benches for three hundred and fifty people. As it was the
upper story of a popular drinking saloon, clinking glasses,
rattling billiard balls and uproarious songs interfered with the
performances. The price of admission was one dollar; . . .
Among the spectators were several ladies, and despite the
boisterousness of the house there was no gross coarseness
and no profanity."

The "code of honor" was yet in vogue and several duels
were fought on the banks of Cherry Creek near present
Broadway, Denver, before large crowds in 1859 and 1860.
But when the pioneer editor, W. N. Byers, was challenged
because of some supposed insult, he gave the absurd practice a telling blow in his newspaper with a strong editorial
which ended thus: "You may murder us, but *never* on the
so-called field of honor under the *dignified* name of duel.

To this last we are conscientiously opposed, looking upon it as a relic of barbarism which has descended to us from the dark ages, and the man who upholds it is more fit to live among savages than under a government controlled by law."

Horse racing, foot racing and such outdoor sports were enjoyed. Horseback riding and buggy riding were common forms of recreation. Occasional prize fights were held. The saloon was as yet the poor man's club. Baseball was not introduced here until 1866 and the velocipede, forerunner of the bicycle, came about the same time.

There were considerable fluctuations in prices in pioneer Colorado, the chief determining factors being freight costs and supply and demand. Since most goods were freighted by ox teams across the plains from the Missouri River (at a cost of $4 to $6 per hundred pounds) it took weeks to obtain goods in quantity to supply the demand. In January, 1860, flour cost $25 per hundred pounds in Denver (and $30 to $40 in the mountain mining camps) whereas game was plentiful and venison sold at seven cents per pound, bear meat at thirty cents per pound and ducks sold at fifty cents per pair. As spring opened and freight trains arrived from the East, flour dropped to $12; then in the fall on arrival of a large supply from Utah it dropped to $8, and the following summer sold for $5 per hundred pounds. Prices of building materials showed great changes. In 1859 lumber brought $100 per thousand feet and the following year, after logs were floated down the Platte to the boom at Denver, it sold at $35 per thousand. Coal oil, or kerosene, was sold in the drug stores in the early sixties, at $3 per gallon.

Fresh fruit was almost unobtainable in Colorado in pioneer times, except the wild berries, plums and cherries which were gathered in the mountains and along the streams. Apples were shipped in and sold at ten to twenty-five cents apiece, and peaches are reported to have sold as high as $1 each. Dried apples was one of the staples for making pies. But since the art of canning had recently been put to practical use, fruits and vegetables preserved by this process could now be had.

Cows and chickens were brought to the Pike's Peak region by the '59ers, and butter, milk and eggs were usually to he had at fair prices. As early as 1860 Denver had the milk man, the ice man and the vender of vegetables. In 1861 a drove of 250 hogs was driven across the plains from Missouri, and bacon and ham soon showed a decline in price. Turkeys also were driven from Missouri in 1863. This complaint we read in the Denver *Commonwealth* of August 6, 1863: "A few people buy hogs in the spring, pasture them in the streets and grow rich out of the proceeds, but every housekeeper is daily pestered with them. Nothing but a sentry at the door keeps them out of the house. . . . Anything left for a moment out of doors is rooted over and eaten up. . . . Will not the Council take means to abate the nuisance."

Prior to 1860 gold dust was the money of the realm. It was usually carried in buckskin pouches and was weighed out on scales at the stores. In the absence of scales a "pinch" of dust (the amount normally taken up between the thumb and fore finger) was counted as twenty-five cents, and purchases were rarely made for less than that amount. The late Rev. Charles Marshall recalled that as a young boy he was provided by his parents with a pinch of dust wrapped in a paper to drop on the collection plate at church.

In July, 1860, the private mint of Clark, Gruber & Co. at Denver began turning out gold coins. Small change,

however, was scarce and paper currency, called "shin plas-
ters," was issued in small denominations by various banking
houses for the convenience of their patrons. The ordinary
interest rates in pioneer times would be declared outrageous
today, for the borrower paid from two to five per cent a
month to obtain a loan.

Life in the pioneer mining camps was picturesque and
fascinating. Mining was hard work. Wielding pick, shovel
and pan all day, or dragging ore from the hillside to a sluice
or rocker, took men of muscle and endurance. But that ever
present hope of "striking it rich" lured the miner on and
made him forget present labor in his anticipation of the
great strike he was one day to make. Always there was a
stream of hopeful miners journeying toward the diggings
and a similar stream of disappointed ones, who had failed
to find their fortune, wending their way back. Richardson
writes: "The newcomers going into the mines were sanguine and cheery, climbing with elastic step, and beguiling
the way with song and laughter. But the stampeders turning
homeward, convinced that gold digging was hard and un-
remunerative, left their packs and shovels behind, and
trudged mechanically with downcast woe-begone faces."

Men from all parts of the nation and from many foreign
countries were in the camps. There were men who had traveled around the world and boys who had never before left
their fathers' farms. There were doctors, lawyers, preachers
and farmers turned miners; there were unschooled lads and
university graduates jostling each other in the narrow gulches
and voting in mass meetings to make the laws for their district. The success of the day's panning, the news from
another gulch were usual topics of conversation, but dis-
cussions of Shakespeare, religion and philosophy were hardly
less common. Clothes did not distinguish the man, for all

wore substantial shirts, trousers and boots appropriate to their heavy work. Long whiskers often hid a youthful face. There were no old people in pioneer Colorado. One early comer declares that it was several years before he saw a person with gray hair. Young men and women laid the foundation of this State.

At first the miner did his own cooking; flapjacks, bacon, beans and coffee being the staples of his diet. These were often cooked over an open fire beside his tent or primitive log cabin. The frying pan, coffee pot, tin cup, tin plate, butcher knife and iron spoon were essential culinary wares, as the pick, shovel, pan and ax were the tools of his profession. Pine boughs were his mattress, and blankets and buffalo robes his cover at night. Writes one miner from the hills: "The sweetest of all rest is on the bosom of mother earth, watched by sentinel stars, lulled by the sad-hearted pine and falling water." Add to this, pure mountain air, the contentment of successful work, the fatigue of a hard day's labor—and the miner's sleep was blissful.

Gambling and drinking were the amusements of some, while others found ample recreation in the reading of books and magazines. And religion was not left at home. A visitor to one of the new diggings asked if there was a church in camp and a miner replied, "No; but we are going to build one before next Sunday." A. D. Richardson describes an interesting scene at one of the camps he visited near Gregory Gulch:

"On Sunday morning a walk through the diggings revealed nearly all the miners disguised in clean clothing. Some were reading and writing letters, some ministering to the sick, and some enacting the part of Every-man-his-own-washer-woman—rubbing valiantly away at the tub. Several hundred men, in the open air, were attending public re-

ligious worship. . . . They were roughly clad, displaying
weapons at their belts; and represented every section of the
Union and almost every nation of the earth. They sat upon
logs and stumps, a most attentive congregation, while the
clergyman upon a rude log platform, preached from the
text: 'Behold, I bring you good tidings of great joy.' It was
an impressive spectacle—that motley gathering of goldseekers among the mountains, a thousand miles from home
and civilization, to hear the 'good tidings' forever old and
yet forever new."

✦ ✦ ✦

SELECTED REFERENCES FOR FURTHER READING

A. D. Richardson, Beyond the Mississippi
L. R. Hafen, The Overland Mail (1926)
E. S. Hill, A Dangerous Crossing (1924)
E. S. Hill, Foundation Stones (1926)
Rocky Mountain News; Denver Commonwealth; Rocky Mountain Herald;
    Central City Register; Black Hawk Journal; Western Mountaineer
Colorado Magazine: "Early Days in Canon City and South Park" (May,
    1926); "Cabin Life in Colorado" (Mar., 1927); "Supplies and Market
    Prices in Pioneer Denver" (Aug., 1927); "Pioneer Life" (Dec., 1927);
    "Empire City in the Sixties" (Feb., 1928); "Experiences on the Platte
    River Route in the Sixties" (Aug., 1928); "Early Central City Theatri-
    cals" (Mar., 1929); "Life at Camp Weld and Fort Lyon, 1861-62"
    (July, 1930); "Old Julesburg and Fort Sedgwick" (July, 1930); "Pioneer
    Days on the Big Thompson" (Sept., 1930); "Reception of Colorado's
    First Governor" (Nov., 1930)

CHAPTER X

EARLY DAYS OF COLORADO TERRITORY

The Testing Time of the Sixties

TO Abraham Lincoln in 1861 fell the duty of appointing the first officers for Colorado Territory. For Governor he chose Major William Gilpin of Missouri, a Western enthusiast who knew the Rocky Mountain region as did few men of his day. Gilpin had accompanied Fremont to Oregon in 1843, had been a major in the War with Mexico, and had led a campaign against the plains Indians in 1848. He had lectured widely and had written a book upon the West, describing its resources and prophesying its great future. One historian has called him the "John the Baptist of the West." News of his appointment as Governor was received with evident satisfaction in Colorado, where he was well and favorably known among the pioneers. The other federal appointees as installed were: Lewis L. Weld, Secretary; James E. Dalliba, Attorney General; Copeland Townsend, Marshal; F. M. Case, Surveyor General; B. F. Hall, S. N. Pettis and C. L. Armour, Judges of the Supreme Court.

Two months elapsed after the appointment of the Governor before his arrival in the Territory, months fraught with portentous developments for the nation. The Southern States had announced their secession from the Union and following this came the firing on Fort Sumter (April 12th) which precipitated the great Civil War. News of these events were regretfully received in Colorado. Pioneers had gathered here from both North and South and their natural sympathies were not left behind. When the black cloud of war cast its shadow over the new-born Territory and let fall its rain of dissention, the seeds of conflict began to swell and burst.

On April 24th a Confederate flag was unfurled from one of the Denver stores, but was quickly torn down. The following day a mass meeting assembled for expression of Union sentiment. Before the leading hotel a huge bonfire was lighted, a band played patriotic airs, and speeches of fervid patriotism expressed the sentiments of the thousand assembled unionists. Resolutions of loyalty were adopted which stated that "as for Colorado, she, with willing hearts and ready feet, will follow the flag and keep step to the music of the Union." To President Lincoln this message was sent: "The eyes of the whole world are upon you—the sympathies of the American People are with you—and may the God of Battles sustain the *Stars and Stripes*."

Similar meetings in Boulder, Golden, Central City and other towns demonstrated the patriotic feelings of the majority of the pioneers for the Union cause. But the feeling was far from unanimous. As the calls came for troops, many true sons of the South and of the North, threw down the pick and pan, and retraced their steps across the plains to enlist in defense of their old homes. Others kept at their work, tried to remain calm, courting the hope that an amicable adjustment would be effected and the terrible conflict be averted.

On the afternoon of May 27th a cloud of dust along the road announced the coming of the overland mail. As the four-horse stage drew up before the hotel in Denver Governor Gilpin stepped from the crowded Concord coach. A spontaneous welcome greeted his arrival, followed by a more formal reception in the evening when cannon were fired, the band played, and speeches were delivered from the flag-decked balcony of the Tremont House. "Governor" Steele of "Jefferson Territory" now issued a proclamation declaring the provisional government at an end and call-ing on all good citizens to support the new executive and the government of Colorado.

Early in June Governor Gilpin made a tour of the set-tlements and mining camps to become acquainted with the people and local conditions. He had a census taken which revealed a population of but 25,331 for the Territory, while Denver, the largest town, contained less than 3,000 citi-zens. The war was having its effect, for not only had im-migration fallen off, but large numbers had returned to the East to participate in the armed conflict.

The Supreme Court of Colorado Territory was or-ganized July 10th. Two days later Governor Gilpin des-ignated the election districts, and announced a general elec-tion to choose a Delegate to Congress and members of the Territorial legislature. Conventions were held by the Re-publican and the Union parties to nominate candidates for the respective offices. At the election on August 19th Judge H. P. Bennet, the Republican candidate was chosen as Delegate to Congress, on a platform endorsing Lincoln and his war policy. B. D. Williams, who had been the Delegate from "Jefferson Territory," was defeated for the office largely because of his secessionist support.

To constitute the first legislature of the Territory nine Councilmen and thirteen Representatives were elected. They were men of superior caliber, two of whom—J. B. Chaffee and George M. Chilcott—subsequently found places in the United States Senate. The first legislature convened at Denver on September 9, 1861. It divided the Territory into seventeen Counties and provided for the selection of

County officers; enacted civil and criminal codes; recognized the records, decisions and practices of miners' courts, claim clubs and such tribunals which had existed in the region prior to the organization of the Territory; chartered the city of Denver; and enacted other general legislation. A resolution pledging the Territory to the cause of the Union, and memorials to Congress asking for improved mail service and the establishment of a branch mint at Denver were adopted. Many private acts were passed incorporating wagon road, ditch, and mining companies.

In the summer of 1861 United States troops were quartered at Fort Garland in the San Luis Valley and at Fort Wise (soon renamed Fort Lyon) on the Arkansas, but in the new towns and mining camps farther north no military units were stationed. There were Confederate sympathizers among the pioneers whom Union men distrusted. Especially did Governor Gilpin, a man of military training and staunch Union sentiment, feel the necessity for military measures to safeguard the Territory and assist the national cause. Accordingly, he appointed a military staff and began the purchase and collection of arms. He decided to raise a regiment of volunteer infantry and therefore commissioned officers who opened recruiting offices in the principal towns and camps during July and August. By the end of September, 1861, Colorado's First Regiment was practically filled and in October it was housed in "Camp Weld," within the present southern limits of Denver. John P. Slough was made Colonel of the regiment, with Samuel F. Tappan, Lieutenant Colonel and John M. Chivington, Major. Then the recruiting of a second regiment was begun.

For equipment and provisions for these troops no money had been provided by the federal or the Territorial government and Governor Gilpin was in a quandary. He decided

COL. WILLIAM GILPIN
First Governor of Colorado Territory

OVERLAND STAGE LINE RECEIPT, 1865

BLAKE STREET, DENVER (MATHEWS DRAWING, 1865)

to issue drafts on the national treasury in payment of his purchases, with the expectation that they would be honored and his actions upheld. His drafts were readily accepted by the Colorado merchants, but upon being presented at Washington were refused recognition. News of this situation caused a wave of consternation in Colorado. The Governor was roundly condemned for having assumed unwarranted authority and having involved citizens of the Territory in such difficult financial straits. In late December Gilpin set out for Washington to explain his actions and to seek recognition of his drafts. Opposition to the Governor crystallized, and aggrieved citizens of the Territory circulated a petition asking for his recall and the appointment of General William Larimer as Governor.

The mid-winter months of 1861-2 were hard for Colorado pioneers. With approximately $400,000 tied up in Gilpin drafts and with uncertainty existing as to whether they would ever be paid, the situation was well nigh disastrous to merchants and others who had accepted the drafts in good faith. At Washington, Gilpin's efforts were supplemented by those of Delegate Bennet and of representatives of Colorado business men. The matter was finally adjusted. Holders of the drafts submitted itemized statements of their claims, which were duly paid. But Gilpin's action was repudiated and he was presently removed from the governorship.

No one has questioned the Governor's motives nor his patriotism, only his assumption of authority and his emergency measures were criticised. And even these appear now to have justified themselves in view of their results. At the very time that the Governor's political enemies were asserting that the arming of troops in Colorado was the height of folly, there was being organized a Confederate army in Texas to conquer New Mexico, Colorado and the great

Southwest. It so happened that the Colorado troops recruited and equipped by the aggressive first Governor of
Colorado were destined to strike the decisive blow in
thwarting those well conceived plans of the South. Let us
follow the First Colorado Regiment on that brilliant campaign which was to reflect glory on the men and their Territory and give warrant to the action of the Governor who
assumed the authority to organize and equip them.

Texas early planned the invasion of New Mexico. From
the threatened territory came appeals to Colorado asking for
Union troops to meet the Texan advance. In response, two
companies, Ford's and Dodd's, were mustered into the federal service at Fort Garland in December, 1861, and dispatched to New Mexico. South of Santa Fe, one by one
the string of forts along the Rio Grande fell before the Confederate army, and as General Sibley pressed on to Al-
buquerque the federal troops retreated before him until
by March 10th Union forces had left Santa Fe and retired
to Fort Union, some ninety miles to the northeast.

In the meantime the Colorado troops, most of whom
were stationed at Camp Weld, near Denver, were growing
impatient for action. They had enlisted to do fighting, and
camp routine irked them. During the winter months they
fretted, almost to the verge of mutiny, for a chance to show
their mettle. At last the opportunity came, for orders were
received directing Colonel Slough to march his men to the
defense of northern New Mexico.

On February 22, 1862, they set forth from Camp Weld.
Near Trinidad, Slough was joined by three companies of
his regiment previously sent to Fort Wise (Fort Lyon) on
the Arkansas. Together the united companies continued
toward Fort Union. Near Raton Pass they were met by a
courier bearing news of Sibley's victorious advance and

carrying a plea for haste in their march to the rescue. By forced marches the Colorado troops hurried on, making a tramp of ninety-two miles in thirty-six hours.

Upon reaching Fort Union Colonel Slough assumed command. On March 22d, with over 1300 men, he set out toward Santa Fe. Marching toward him from the west came Colonel Scurry with a detachment of Sibley's victorious Texans. On the 26th, advance parties of the opposing forces met in Apache Canyon, a section of La Glorieta Pass, and fought the first engagement of the Battle of La Glorieta. Major Chivington, the "Fighting Parson," led the Colorado troops to victory in this engagment. After signing a truce for the next day to permit burial of the dead, he rejoined Slough's larger force and together they encamped near the eastern end of La Glorieta Pass. The Confederate troops at the same time made their camp near the western end of the pass. On the 28th the battle would be resumed.

The Union officers now planned a bold stroke. Major Chivington with about 400 men was to take a circuitous course to the south of the pass, clamber over the mountains, and attack the Confederates in the rear. The Confederates, confident of victory, left their camp equipment and supplies under a guard at the western end of the pass and boldly marched toward the enemy. At ten o'clock they met Colonel Slough near the eastern end of the pass and the bloody battle began. All through the afternoon it continued. Gradually the Union troops were being pushed back by the superior numbers of the Texans. Then unexpectedly the Confederates presented a flag of truce and the fighting ceased. Colonel Slough's forces had held the field long enough to permit Chivington's men to do their work. These latter had made their circuit to the rear of the Confederate troops, and there had completely destroyed the enemy's great supply

train and provisions. It was news of this disaster which induced the Confederates to ask for an armistice. That night,
under cover of the truce, their retreat began and it did not
end until after they had retraced their steps through New
Mexico and were safely back in Texas.

The Battle of La Glorieta has been called the "Gettys-
burg of the Southwest," for it marked the end of Confederate danger in this region and held the Southwest for the
Union. Beyond La Glorieta lay the wealth of Colorado and
of California, and who knows where the Southern conquest
would have ended had not Colorado volunteers stopped the
advancing tide with a victory at the pass?

Upon being prevented by a superior officer from following aggressively the defeated Texans, Colonel Slough resigned. Major Chivington was advanced to the colonelcy
to fill his place. During the greater part of 1862 the First
Colorado Regiment was retained in New Mexico, but finally
it was returned to Colorado, where it was converted into
a cavalry regiment. Colorado Territory was now made a
military district with Colonel Chivington in command. The
returning troops were distributed throughout the Territory
to guard against Indian depredations and to keep open the
routes of travel. In this important service they spent the
remaining period of the war.

The Second Colorado Regiment of infantry was recruited in 1862 with Ford's and Dodd's companies as a
nucleus. It was organized with Jesse H. Leavenworth as
Colonel, T. H. Dodd, Lieutenant Colonel, and J. M. Ford,
major. After spending some months at Fort Lyon on the
Arkansas, six companies of this regiment were sent east,
where they performed valuable service during 1863 in the
Oklahoma-Arkansas region.

During August, 1862, recruiting began for the Third

Colorado Regiment, with William Larimer, Denver pioneer, as Colonel. But available men were scarce and although a bounty of $25 and one month's pay were given each volun' teer, the enlistments were slow and the regiment was never recruited to full strength. The five companies raised for the Third Regiment marched to Missouri early in 1863 and during the summer served in General Schofield's Army of the Frontier. In October of this year the incomplete Second and Third Regiments of infantry were united and converted into the Second Colorado Volunteer Cavalry. This new regiment with J. H. Ford as colonel, was sent into eastern Kansas to combat Confederate guerrillas, and became a part of General Blunt's army fighting the Confederate General Price in 1864. The Colorado troops fought bravely and lost heavily, but they assisted in finally driving General Price from Kansas and Missouri.

Colorado made a large offering of men to the Union cause. It is stated that she furnished more volunteers in pro' portion to her population than did any other Territory or State. Her losses, too, were proportionately large.

Having briefly followed the Colorado soldiers through their campaigns in behalf of their country, let us return to the citizens at home to note other developments in the young commonwealth. We have already referred to the removal of Governor Gilpin in the spring of 1862. In his place was appointed Dr. John Evans of Chicago, a personal friend and supporter of Lincoln, a man destined to exhibit his strong character and sterling worth in the upbuilding of Colorado. The new governor arrived in the Territory in May, 1862. He was pleased with prospects here. Promising beginnings in agriculture were in evidence, large stores of mineral wealth had been revealed and he foretold the day when the plains to the eastward would be covered with farms and dotted with

cities. A bill had been passed by Congress for the building
of a railroad from the Missouri River to the Pacific Coast
and Coloradans expected this to traverse their Territory
and be a boon to the settlers here.

The second session of the Territorial legislature convened at Colorado City (present Colorado Springs) on
July 7, 1862, the first legislature having designated that city
as the seat of government. But the hopeful capital was small
and was unable to provide adequate accommodations for the
lawmakers. They became dissatisfied and after a few days
adjourned, took their horses and wagons and made the two-
day journey to Denver, where they completed the session.
The matter of the location of the capital was an important
political question during these first years, various towns
contending for this political preferment. The legislature in
its second session changed the capital from Colorado City
to Golden and this city retained the designation, in name
at least, until 1867, when Denver became the capital.

During the early and middle sixties the immigration
to the Territory was small and the population remained
about stationary. The war in the East and the opening
of mines in Montana, Idaho and Nevada partially account
for this condition. But the chief cause of stagnation in Colorado's affairs at this time was the slump in mining. The
placer deposits that had yielded the gold returns during the
first three years were largely worked out. The ores on the
gold lodes had become more and more refractory as the
workings penetrated farther beneath the surface, and from
the sulphide ores now being obtained no known process
would extract the rich gold values.

In the middle sixties many new "processes" were tried
and much expensive machinery was freighted by ox teams
across the plains only to be discarded after it was tested and

found unsuccessful. James E. Lyon built elaborate smelting works at Black Hawk in 1865, but while considerable quan' tities of gold and silver were extracted from refractory ores by his furnaces, the process was not financially successful. Silver ore was found near Georgetown in 1864 and rich silver veins were revealed in the years immediately follow' ing, but no satisfactory method was yet devised for ex' tracting the precious metal. By trial and error, however, processes were being discovered which were ultimately to succeed.

As heavy expenditures and the issuance of greenbacks during the Civil War inflated the currency and caused a rise in the price of gold, eastern capitalists were·inclined to in' vest in gold mines in the West. Then as the speculation fever grew, unscrupulous promoters "salted" mining claims with gold and used other dishonest methods to sell poor claims and worthless mining stocks to people in the East. Such actions gave Colorado mining property and prospects a bad name abroad, soon frightened away investors, and made it difficult to procure the capital needed to develop good properties and establish the mills and smelters required for treatment of the ores. It was not until the close of the sixties that new chemical processes were devised with which the refractory ores could be successfully treated. But prior to these discoveries the discouraging condition in the mining camps was reflected in the valley towns.

Denver, Golden, Colorado City and Boulder had smal' ler populations in the middle sixties than they had boasted in 1860. In addition to the business depression and a popu' lation decrease, Denver was visited by fire and flood in these years of discouragement. A large part of the business section was wiped out by a furious fire on April 19, 1863, and the following year a torrential flood swept down Cherry

Creek upon the unsuspecting citizens, carrying death and destruction before it. The City Hall with its records was
swept away, much property was destroyed, and eleven lives
were lost. But from charred ruins sprang better buildings
and the havoc of flood was repaired by far-seeing pioneers.

It was at this time also that the pioneers were called
upon to meet a widespread and threatening uprising of the
plains Indians. These lords of the plains had looked with
startled eyes upon the white men who came in an endless
chain of white-topped wagons, winding along the trails
through the Indian's country. White men's horses and
oxen cropped the grass and white hunters drove away and
killed the buffalo. The "Indian's cattle" were his food and
shelter and as he saw the buffalo slaughtered he read his
fate in the whitened bones on the prairie. The mining
camps, the farms along the streams and the clusters of white
men's tepees called cities, were crowding the red man from
the land of his fathers. He must rise up and fight or forever lose his heritage. Mayhap the Great Spirit, Manitou,
had caused the white men to war among themselves that the
Indians might the better drive the intruders back to the land
of the rising sun. Intelligent Indians saw in the Civil War
their opportunity and planned to make the most of it. Their
chief obstacle was the hereditary enmity existing between
the various tribes which made cooperation difficult. Despite
this, preparations were made.

In 1862 the Indians began the collection of firearms and
horses, and the white pioneers became alarmed at the possible
Indian danger. The whites made a move for peace in February, 1863, by sending delegations of Arapaho, Cheyenne
and Ute leaders to Washington to visit the Great Father,
Lincoln. It was hoped that when these painted war chiefs
saw the great cities and the mighty armies of the white

man they would see the futility of an Indian uprising. But the Indians were not overawed and the plains Indians, especially, continued their preparations in 1863.

In the fall of this year Governor Evans endeavored to arrange a peace meeting with the Indians of the Colorado plains, but they refused to meet him in council. With the Utes of the mountains he had better success, for they met him at Conejos in October and agreed to a treaty whereby they accepted a restricted reservation on the Western Slope and in payment were to receive $20,000 annually in goods and provisions. Chief Ouray, who had been to Washington in the preceding spring and had been impressed with the white man's power, exerted his great influence for peace. But among the plains Indians there was no Ouray to counsel discretion. In April, May and July of 1863, General Mitchell of Nebraska held councils with the Sioux on the Platte River, but each attempt to make a peace treaty ended in failure.

In the spring of 1864 detachments of Colorado troops had engagements with Cheyennes on the Arkansas River and on the South Platte. In early June horses were stampeded from freighters on the "cut-off" road between Denver and Fort Morgan and on the 11th an Indian assault was made on the Hungate ranch on Running Creek, thirty miles southeast of Denver. Mr. Hungate, his wife and two children were murdered and scalped. Their mutilated bodies were brought into Denver and when exhibited, horrified the citizens and called forth demands for revenge. Rumors spread that all the settlements were to be attacked and a feeling of panic prevailed. In Denver the people collected guns, prepared for defense, and some of the women gathered for safety in the second story of Kountze's bank, the U. S. Mint and what is now the Lindell Hotel at Larimer and 11th streets.

The Governor ordered all business houses closed at 6:30 P. M. and all able bodied citizens to meet for drill at seven o'clock. But the immediate danger to the settlement was more fancied than real, for no attacks were made upon the Colorado towns.

Along the stage line and immigrant road, however, matters were different. An attack was made upon the stage stations and freight trains between Fort Morgan and old Julesburg in mid July and most of the stations were burned, the stock run off, and a number of men killed. In early August a widespread outbreak occurred on the immigrant road in Kansas. Ranches were sacked and burned, men killed and women carried away captive.

Governor Evans issued a proclamation: "Patriotic citizens of Colorado: I again appeal to you to organize for defense of your homes and families against the merciless savages. . . . Any man who kills a hostile Indian is a patriot; but there are Indians who are friendly and to kill one of these will involve us in greater difficulty. It is important therefore to fight only the hostile, and no one has been or will be restrained from this." The *Rocky Mountain News* added: "A few months of active extermination against the red devils will bring quiet and nothing else will."

The Governor had sent messengers to the tribes thought to be friendly, directing them to rendezvous at Fort Lyon and Camp Collins where they would be protected. He now made an appeal to the War Department and was authorized to raise a regiment of "one hundred days men" to fight the Indians. All mail service with the East was interrupted by this summer uprising and for a time Colorado mail from the East was sent by way of Panama to California and thence eastward to the Rocky Mountain settlements. The freighting of merchandise and supplies was also stopped and soon

DR. JOHN EVANS
Second Territorial Governor of Colorado

INDIAN CHIEFTAINS ARRIVING IN DENVER FOR COUNCIL, SEPT., 1864

a scarcity of certain provisions existed in the Territory. Prices began to soar and there was danger of real suffering for want of food.

A secret, concerted attack upon Colorado settlements was planned by the Indians to take place about August 22d. But friendly Indians informed Elbridge Gerry (who lived with his Indian wife east of present Greeley) and he raced to Denver to warn the Governor. Thereupon messengers were sent to the other settlements and defensive prepara' tions were made. The Indians, finding that their secret had leaked out, refrained from the contemplated attack.

In late August, 1864, a letter from Black Kettle of the Cheyennes, and other chiefs proposed peace and exchange of prisoners. Major Wynkoop went to their village on the Smoky Hill, recovered four white prisoners and brought the chiefs to Denver for a parley. As winter was coming on, the chiefs were ready to sign a peace treaty and receive winter rations. But the young men of the tribes, who had been committing most of the depredations, were beyond control of the chiefs and the military men were unwilling to make peace until the Indians had been punished. Thus the council of the chiefs with the Governor and Colonel Chiv' ington at Denver accomplished nothing and the Indians re' turned to their tribes.

About the middle of October, Left Hand's band of Arapahoes came in to Fort Lyon, announced their peaceful intentions and turned over some of their summer's plunder. After being fed for some days at the fort the commandant sent them to establish camp on Sand Creek, some forty miles northeast of the fort. Here they were joined by Black Ket' tle's Cheyennes and together formed a village of six or seven hundred. They apparently considered themselves as having complied with the governor's directions and thus

secure from attack. But in the meantime plans were ma-
turing which were to make their position far from safe.

The regiment of "Hundred Days Men," recruited for
service against the Indians, having been fully equipped by
the middle of October, were anxious to execute some decisive
military action that would punish the Indian marauders
and make the homes and highways of the white men safe.
They had been patrolling the Platte River road but nothing
decisive had been done. General Curtis, in command of the
military department which included Colorado, had instructed
the Colorado officers to make no peace "till the Indians suffer
more." Colonel Chivington, in compliance with this policy,
decided to strike an effective blow. With most of the Hundred Days Men and several companies of the First Colorado
Regiment he set out for the Arapaho and Cheyenne village. Moving rapidly and cautiously he marched to Fort
Lyon and after receiving a reenforcement from this fort continued toward the Indian encampment on Sand Creek, taking special care that no news of his approach reach the Indian village.

The soldiers marched all night and at sunrise of November 29, 1864, made their attack upon the unsuspecting
camp. The greatest terror and confusion reigned among the
Indians as the soldiers opened fire upon them, while one
detachment of the troops cut off and stampeded the Indian's
horses. Some of the Indians protested friendship, but the
fight was already on and no effort was made to discriminate.
The slaughter was terrible, the fleeing men, women and
children being shot down as they ran. It is impossible to
determine the exact number of Indian losses, but there must
have been nearly 500 killed. The others escaped by flight.
Of the troops, ten were killed and thirty-eight wounded.

This Sand Creek Affair is the most controversial subject in Colorado history. Some have called it a "battle," in which the Indians got their just desserts, while others have condemned it as an unjustifiable "massacre" of peaceful Indians. Some white scalps in the wreckage of the camp indicated a connection of at least some of the occupants with recent depredations upon the whites. The presence of a white flag and of the United States flag over the chief's lodge, the absence of defensive precautions, and the peaceful demonstrations made by certain Indians at the time of the attack are cited in the red man's favor. But all in all the attack, with its attendant circumstances and methods was an unfortunate affair which we might well wish had never occurred. Instead of cowing the Indians, this blow stirred them to revenge.

The fugitives from the Sand Creek encounter reported the affair to other tribes. One thousand Indians joined together and moved northward to make a counter attack. Early in January they plundered the station and supply stores at old Julesburg, and a mile to the west killed a number of the soldiers at Camp Rankin (later known as Fort Sedgwick). Other stations and some emigrant trains along the road were plundered.

Again there was great excitement among Colorado settlers. Acting Governor Elbert telegraphed to Washington: "We must have five thousand troops to clean out these savages or the people of this territory will be compelled to leave it. Everything is already at starvation prices. The General Government must help us or give up the Territory to the Indians." Flour soared to $27 per hundred pounds and bacon and sugar rose to fifty cents per pound.

In early February the Indians returned to the south Platte road, burned Julesburg and plundered everything in sight. Two large supply trains were captured west of Julesburg and the Indian revelled in quantities of flour, sugar, rice, coffee, shoes and clothing. The Indians now moved northward to the Powder River country of Wyoming to enjoy their spoils.

Martial law was proclaimed in Colorado on February 8, 1865, and business houses were closed until 360 men were raised to open the road to Julesburg. Other troops were soon sent to the plains from the East. The Indian danger diminished, but there continued to be attacks on isolated stations and on the stagecoaches and freight trains traveling the Platte, the Arkansas and the Smoky Hill routes to Colorado. Finally, treaties were made with the Cheyennes and Arapahoes in 1865 and 1867 whereby they relinquished title to all their former territory in Colorado and accepted a reservation in Indian Territory, present Oklahoma, though permitted under certain restrictions to hunt upon their former territory. The Indians did not consider the treaties seriously and continued to make forays.

In the spring of 1867 they raided stage stations on both the Platte and the Smoky Hill routes. Governor Hunt became alarmed and telegraphed to General Sherman on June 3d: "Our people are too poor to offer anything but muscle—have plenty of that. Will the government back us in the expense of a campaign?" The next day twelve of the leading federal officers in the Territory wired President Johnson, saying in part: "In the name of God and humanity we make this appeal to you, and ask that the too long continued temporizing policy toward these merciless devils shall cease and that you will at once direct that prompt and decisive measures be taken for the protection of the country." Central City became aroused and announced that $5,000 had been raised to pay for Indian scalps at $20 apiece.

In response to the calls General Sherman came out with troops to Fort Sedgwick, Colorado, and General Hancock came to Denver. Troops were raised in the Territory and the Indians were dispersed. But the next year they came again. A band visited Colorado City in the summer of 1868 and in the vicinity killed several settlers. There were also raids on Plum Creek, south of Denver, and in the valley of the Cache la Poudre. Again troops went in pursuit but were unable to catch the marauders.

Although there were rumors in 1868 that the Utes of the mountains were going to join the Indians of the plains against the whites, the confederation did not materialize. Governor Hunt induced a band of Utes to come to the defense of the party of Schuyler Colfax (soon to become Vice President of the United States), who was at the time on a trip in South Park.

One of the most famous encounters with Indians in Colorado history occurred in September, 1868. Colonel Forsyth had organized a party of fifty experienced scouts to pursue Indians who had been pillaging in western Kansas. On September 16th the party encamped on the Arickaree river, about fifteen miles south of present Wray, Colorado. Here they were attacked the next morning by about one thousand Indians, led by the famous warrior, Roman Nose. The scouts moved onto a low sandy island in the river and scooped out holes in the sand in which to conceal themselves. The most heroic defense in Colorado history now followed. Charge after charge was repulsed, in one of which Roman Nose was shot down. On the first day Colonel Forsyth was severely wounded and Lieutenant Beecher was killed, but the scouts fought on. During the first night two scouts, Stilwell and Trudeau, volunteered to attempt to steal from their island prison and make their way to Fort Wallace,

Kansas, for help. Upon the success of their effort rested the fate of their companions.

Through nine long days the Indians continued the siege. Doggedly the scouts held on despite death, wounds and the stifling odor from their dead horses. At last as a troop of United States cavalry appeared, the besiegers suddenly vanished. Stilwell and Trudeau had reached Fort Wallace and their surviving companions were saved. Five of the scouts were dead, eighteen were wounded and the remainder were nearly exhausted. Beecher Island has been named for the brave lieutenant who lost his life upon it and a monument has been erected by Colorado and Kansas to the memory of the scouts who here fought their heroic fight.

During the following winter a number of vigorous campaigns, conducted in the Oklahoma region and elsewhere, dealt the red men some effective blows. Indian troubles for the eastern half of Colorado were practically over. There occurred but one further encounter worthy of mention. A band of Indians who had been raiding in western Kansas in the summer of 1869 were pursued by troops into northeastern Colorado. While the Indians were encamped at Summit Springs, about ten miles south of present Sterling, they were attacked by the troops and routed. Tall Bull, leader of the band, and fifty of his warriors were killed and over 300 horses and mules were captured. Two white women captives were in camp. One was killed and the other wounded by the Indians when the fight commenced. This was the last fight with the plains Indians on Colorado soil. The red man was driven from the land of his fathers and the vast herds of buffalo which had sustained him were being slaughtered to extinction. The white man had felt the need for more land and had taken it. The weak race gave way to the stronger.

Despite the Indian troubles, the slump in mining, and the demands of the Civil War—factors which retarded the development of Colorado in the sixties—there was progress in some directions. Farming was making gains and the areas producing crops were being gradually extended. In the spring of 1863 the Colorado Agricultural Society was organized and the following year was chartered by the Territorial legislature. It conducted the first Territorial Fair at Denver in 1866, at which the excellent exhibits of farm products were a standing wonder to new arrivals from the East. But the farmers were being pestered with grasshoppers, which in various sections ate the crops and left the fields bare. In the *News* (Oct. 9, 1865) we read: "It is generally conceded by Coloradoans that but for the grasshopper plague the territory would this year [1865] have produced its own supply of breadstuffs, vegetables, and feed for stock. They destroyed the crop totally in many places and injured it in all." In 1866 it was estimated that 100,000 acres were under cultivation. Today over 7,000,000 acres are producing crops.

Manufacturing was in its infancy in the sixties, but there were flour mills, saw mills, brick yards and breweries being operated in several parts of the state, salt works in South Park, a paper mill and fire brick and pottery works at Golden, and a stone quarry near present Morrison. Coal was being mined in a number of places, iron manufacturing was attempted, and oil was being obtained from the region about Canon City. This was in addition to the milling and smelting of ores from the mines.

Roads were gradually being built or improved between the towns and mining camps, and bridges were beginning to span the streams. Ditches for irrigation and for mining purposes were being constructed and water power was employed for running mining machinery and mills. The City Ditch was completed to Denver in 1866 and water was soon running in ditches along the sides of the streets. Dry yards were now converted into green lawns with flowers, shrubs and trees. Even a street sprinkler of home make was introduced in Denver in 1868. A Hook and Ladder Company was organized in Denver in 1866 and soon the volunteer firemen were performing good service as well as having occasional parades in their striking uniforms of fireman's hat, red shirt and black pants.

The daily stagecoach line running from the Missouri River to California was moved from the North Platte to the South Platte route in 1862 and presently was rerouted to include Denver. A weekly stage operated over the Santa Fe Trail up the Arkansas into southern Colorado at this time. The mountain camps were served by branch lines, some running daily and others on a weekly schedule. In 1865 D. A. Butterfield began the operation of a stagecoach line over the Smoky Hill route to Denver, which was in competition with Ben Holladay's great overland line along the Platte. In 1867 a stage line was established from Denver to Santa Fe, New Mexico, running by way of Trinidad.

During the sixties heavy freight from the East was being lugged across the plains by long trains of ox- and mule-drawn wagons. A freight train usually consisted of about twenty-five wagons and each wagon was drawn by two or three yokes of oxen or by four or six horses or mules. It was reported that 7,240 wagons, 57,002 oxen, 6,887 mules and horses, and 7,700 men were employed in freighting goods across the plains to Colorado in 1865 from the one shipping point of Plattsmouth on the Missouri River, while much was being shipped from other points. It was estimated that about 125,000,000 pounds of freight was shipped to Colorado during that year. The *News* tells of one shipment consisting of 1600 barrels of liquor and 2700 cases of champagne being transported in an eighty-wagon train.

The first transcontinental telegraph line, built in 1861, had followed the Oregon Trail and thus touched only the northeast corner of Colorado. Two years later a branch line was built from Julesburg station to Denver and this was extended to Central City in November, 1863. In 1868 a telegraph line was built from Denver to Santa Fe, New Mexico, going by way of Colorado City, Pueblo, and Trinidad. At the close of the same year a wire was stretched from Denver to the new town of Cheyenne, Wyoming.

Colorado was visited by a number of persons of prominence in the sixties. As guests of the Territory, Generals Grant, Sherman, Sheridan, Pope, Dodge, Dent, and Connor were entertained in true western style. Colfax and Blair, candidates for the Vice Presidency of the United States, came to Colorado in 1868 and Secretary William Seward came the following year. Bayard Taylor, A. D. Richardson, Samuel Bowles and Charles Kingsley, prominent writers who visited Colorado during this period, recorded their impressions of the people and the country.

Provision for free public education came slowly. The private schools instituted in 1859 and 1860, which were noted in a previous chapter, did not satisfy the citizenry of the Territory. An act was passed by the first legislature in 1861 providing for a "Common School System," but many districts, unwilling to vote the necessary taxes, remained without schools for several years. The first free public schools were begun in 1862. During the early years the support was meager, the facilities far from adequate. With crowded, poorly-equipped rooms, with no regulations

to enforce attendance, the system really served only part
of the school population. In the later sixties conditions improved somewhat. More money was provided and there was
a noticeable advance along educational lines.

Of the various attempts at education in the '60s, however, private and sectarian schools were most effective. They
were the first to give instruction of academic grade. Colorado Seminary, established by the Methodists, and St.
Mary's Academy by the Catholics, were begun at Denver
in 1864. The former was to develop into Denver University, and the latter into Loretto Heights Academy and Regis
College. In 1868 the Episcopal Church opened at Denver,
Wolfe Hall, a school for girls; and the following year commenced Jarvis Hall, a school for boys at Golden. The legislature in 1861 had passed an act establishing the University
of Colorado at Boulder, but it was more than a decade later
before the University was actually put into operation. During the sixties there was not yet a public high school in
the Territory.

Despite the small population of Colorado during the
middle sixties there were ambitious citizens who felt that
the Territory should throw off its swaddling clothes and
become a full-fledged State. Republican politicians in Washington were equally anxious for the creation of new states
where their own party was in control. Accordingly, Congress passed an Enabling Act in March, 1864, permitting
Colorado to form a constitution and become a state. During July a convention met to frame a state constitution,
but many Coloradans were opposed to statehood, with the
financial burdens it would bring. When the vote was
taken in September the constitution was defeated.

The following year another constitution was framed
and was adopted by a close margin. A set of officers was

elected with William Gilpin as governor, John Evans and
Jerome B. Chaffee as senators. But inasmuch as President
Johnson objected to the proceeding and refused to issue the
necessary proclamation, the movement for statehood failed.
In 1867 Congress again passed an act providing statehood
for Colorado but the measure was vetoed by President Johnson and failed of fruition. Enthusiasm now subsided somewhat and Colorado remained a Territory until the middle
of the following decade.

In October, 1865, John Evans was replaced as governor by Alexander Cummings, who remained the chief executive until 1867. He was superceded by Governor A. C.
Hunt, who was in turn replaced by Governor McCook in
1869. Three men served in the sixties as Delegates to Congress from Colorado. H. P. Bennet, the first Delegate, after
serving two terms was succeeded by Allen A. Bradford for
one term. George M. Chilcott followed Bradford in 1867
and was himself succeeded by Bradford two years later.
During these years there were many political bickerings and
fights, but none consequential to the Territory. Republicans
were generally in control in the elective offices, but being
a Territory, most of the important officials were appointed
by the President of the United States, the people of Colorado having no direct voice in their selection.

In the statehood fight of 1865 controversies rose as to
the actual population of the Territory. As a result, the
General Assembly made provision for the taking of a census
in 1866. The returns were rather disappointing, for they
revealed a population for the whole Territory of but 27,901
—less than one-tenth the population of present Denver.

During the decade of the sixties only two new counties
were created, Las Animas and Saguache, formed in 1866.
Las Animas was taken from the original Huerfano County,

and the town of Trinidad became its county seat. Saguache County was carved from Costilla, and the new town of Saguache City became its county seat. With the removal of the Cheyennes and Arapahoes to Indian Territory, and the cession of their former reservation in eastern Colorado to the United States, the Territorial legislature in 1868 extended the boundaries of existing counties to include the lands of this reservation.

When the first transcontinental railroad was chartered in 1862. Coloradans hoped and expected that it would traverse their territory. The year before, Berthoud Pass had been discovered by Captain E. L. Berthoud of Golden and the old scout Jim Bridger, and it was hoped that the Pacific railroad would cross the continental divide through this gateway. Surveys, however, revealed that the grade up Clear Creek was too steep for practical railroad building, that Berthoud Pass (11,315 feet) was much higher than South Pass or Bridger Pass in Wyoming. Finally the Union Pacific Company chose the route through southern Wyoming and left Colorado "high and dry."

With Indians on the warpath and crops being devoured by myriads of grasshoppers, with placer mines played out and the reduction of refractory ores hardly begun, with immigration fallen to low figures and statehood denied, it was almost "the last straw" on the backs of pioneers to have the railroad pass them by. These years in the sixties were probably the gloomiest ones in Colorado history, but "the darkest hours are just before the dawn," and so it proved to be for Colorado.

✦ ✦ ✦

SELECTED REFERENCES FOR FURTHER READING

Baker and Hafen, History of Colorado, 490-515, 792-816
J. C. Smiley, History of Colorado, 363-450

Frank Hall, History of Colorado, I, 258-464
Steinel and Working, History of Agriculture in Colorado
O. J. Hollister, The Mines of Colorado
Samuel Bowles, Across the Continent (1866)
Bayard Taylor, Colorado: A Summer Trip (1876)
M. O. Morris, Rambles in the Rocky Mountains (1864)
E. F. Ware, The Indian War of 1864 (1911)
W. C. Whitford, Colorado Volunteers in the Civil War (1906)
Ellen Williams, History of the Second Colorados (1885)
J. E. Wharton, History of the City of Denver (1866)
The Trail (1908-24)
Colorado Magazine: "Pioneer Struggles for a Colorado Road Across the
    Rockies" (Mar., 1926); "With the Troops in Colorado" (May, 1926);
    "Freighting and Merchandising in Early Denver" (Sept., 1929); "Army
    Life at Fort Sedgwick" (Sept., 1929); "Early Pueblo and the Men Who
    Made It" (Nov., 1929); "The Battle of Summit Springs" (Nov., 1929);
    "Life at Camp Weld and Fort Lyon" (July, 1930); "The Tyler Rang-
    ers" (July, 1930); "Pioneer Days on the Big Thompson" (Sept., 1930);
    "Colorado's First Fight for Statehood" (Jan., 1931); "The Second Colo-
    rado Cavalry in the Civil War" (May, 1931); "Early Denver History
    as Told by Contemporary Newspaper Advertisements" (Sept., 1931);
    "The Smoky Hill Trail" (Nov., 1932)
Rocky Mountain News; Colorado Tribune; Central City Register

CHAPTER XI

COLORADO BECOMES A STATE

Development in the Early Seventies

THE population of Colorado in 1870 was 39,864—considerably less than that of present Pueblo. Five years thereafter it had trebled. This remarkable growth, which was in such marked contrast to the slow development of the preceding decade, we shall attempt in the present chapter to explain.

The Civil War over, people in the East were now free to come west and build new homes. The Indians of the plains had been moved to reservations. Railroads were being extended into the West, affording swift and easy transportation for immigrants and their freight. Ways were being devised for the successful treatment of the refractory ores, which gave an impetus to mining development. The agricultural resources of the region had been demonstrated and now invited further development. All these factors increased the desirability of the region.

In the summer of 1867, when the Union Pacific was building through southern Wyoming, it was freely predicted that Colorado was bound to decline. With gloomy certainty, the self-appointed prophets declared that Denver was destined to fade away and to be supplanted by the new city of Cheyenne on the transcontinental railroad. Numbers of people pulled up their stakes in Colorado and moved out, but others sternly resolved to "bring the mountain to Mohammed."

A branch railroad line must be built to serve the pi-

oneers of Colorado. To effect this purpose the people turned
to the Colorado Central Railroad Company, which had been
previously organized and of which W. A. H. Loveland was
the promoter. But there now developed a rivalry between Golden and Denver which postponed the actual building of the road. Each of these ambitious cities.wanted to
be the terminus of the branch, to develop into the trade metropolis of the region. When the survey indicated that the
line was to run directly to Golden, Denver withdrew- her
support, and Arapahoe County bonds which were to have
aided the project were not issued.

In the meantime the Kansas Pacific Railroad Company,
building westward from Kansas City, held out the promise
of reaching Denver at an early date. But in November,
1867, it was learned that the building had come to a stand-
still in western Kansas, inasmuch as the government subsidy
was exhausted.

It was at this juncture, when the prospects for Denver were near eclipse, that her citizens made one of the
most heroic.efforts in the city's history. With property values falling, people leaving the city by the score, with many
men facing the loss of their possessions and the fading of
their hopes, the leaders of the city rose as a unit to meet the
great emergency. It was clear that the only safe dependence
was upon their own local efforts. Accordingly, they organized a "Board of Trade" and under its leadership launched
the Denver Pacific Railroad Company to build a line from
Cheyenne to Denver. Subscriptions of stock in the project
were solicited. The entire city was canvassed. It was
pointed out that in order to save the city and its property
values everyone must come to the rescue. "Pay or perish"
was the slogan. The response was remarkable, for in a single
day the subscriptions amounted to $225,000, and this from

a little frontier city of less than four thousand people. Some offered to pay for their stock by working on the roadbed; others agreed to furnish a certain number of ties. As enthusiasm increased it was planned not only to build a branch line but to make Denver a railroad center. In January, 1868, Arapahoe County voted $500,000 in bonds as a stock subscription to the Denver Pacific and in May the actual work of grading was begun with fitting ceremonies before a large and enthusiastic crowd.

Efforts were now made to induce Congress to grant a right of way and the customary land grant to aid the enterprise. Though rebuffs and delays were encountered, the objective was finally achieved. Additional money was raised by the sale of bonds. The laying of track was begun in 1869. By December of this year the railroad had reached the new town of Evans (named in honor of the leading spirit of the enterprise, Governor Evans), and by June 24, 1870, it was completed to Denver. The last spike, of solid silver, a gift from the city of Georgetown, was driven amid great rejoicing.

In the meantime the Kansas Pacific Railroad Company secured additional funds and resumed construction work toward Denver. The Indians objected to the building of this road through their favorite hunting grounds and came up from their reservation to make frequent attacks upon the construction crews. But their feeble efforts were futile. The iron horse nosed his way across the prairie and ignored the flights of arrows intended to cripple him or turn him back. In the spring of 1870 grading began on the Kansas Pacific from Denver eastward. As the crews working from the east and west ends of the line approached each other their rivalry increased. On the last day the remarkable record was made of laying $10\frac{1}{4}$ miles of track in ten hours. On

August 15th the first train over this road reached Denver.

Meanwhile the Golden-to-Cheyenne railroad project of the Colorado Central had encountered great difficulties, and although some little grading had been done in 1868, no track was laid prior to 1870. With two roads entering Denver in this year, the Colorado Central decided to link Golden with Denver. Accordingly, the short connecting link was constructed, the road being opened to traffic on September 23, 1870. By the close of 1872 this line had penetrated Clear Creek Canyon and reached Black Hawk.

The Denver and Boulder Valley Railroad Company was organized in October, 1870. Inmmediately, work was begun on a line running west from Hughes Station (later Brighton) on the Denver Pacific to the Erie coal fields. The town of Erie was laid out and the railroad reached this point in January, 1871. The line was subsequently pushed on to Boulder, reaching that city in September, 1873. Another railroad launched in the early seventies was the Denver and South Park. Its first section of road was built in 1874 from Denver to the mouth of Bear Creek Canyon, where the town of Morrison had been laid out in October, 1872. But no further building by this road was done until after the close of Colorado's Territorial period.

A railroad destined to be closely identified with the development of Colorado was launched under the leadership of W. J. Palmer in the fall of 1870. This was the Denver & Rio Grande, planned to run south from Colorado's capital city to El Paso, Texas, and ultimately to extend to Mexico City. Branches were to serve the mining camps and mountain districts as the need arose. Inasmuch as it was expected to traverse much mountain country, a narrow gauge (3 feet wide) was decided upon as the most practicable and economical gauge for this road.

It was an extremely venturesome undertaking to build a
railroad through this country of magnificent distances, in a
territory yet practically uninhabited. That there was little
traffic immediately in sight is evident from the fact that the
then existing stage line running between Denver and Pueblo
carried an average of but three passengers daily. If the railroad was to be constructed it must be built on faith—faith in
the latent resources of the region and with the expectation
that a railroad would quickly develop those resources. On
that rather intangible basis the enterprise was started.

The work of building began in March, 1871, and by
October following the road had reached the vicinity of Colorado City. Here the city of Colorado Springs was laid out
as a beautiful residence city, with the expectation that it
would become a fashionable summer resort. Profits from
the sale of lots were to be expended in public improvements,
the manufacture and sale of intoxicants were prohibited,
and various measures were taken to insure the development
of a desirable home city. By the end of the year 1871 there
were 150 buildings, with a population of nearly 800 in the
new town. The next year a hotel was built and a village
begun at the soda springs of Manitou. As Colorado Springs
continued to attract settlers by its scenic beauties and progressive spirit its growth was steady and substantial.

In 1872 the railroad was continued down Fountain
Creek and completed to Pueblo by the end of June. A large
group of excursionists from Denver, including the Governor, Territorial and City officials and many citizens, boarded
the train; and the quaint little engine "Ouray," which today would be taken for a toy, whirled the happy citizens
over the narrow track to their destination at the noteworthy
speed of twenty miles per hour. At Pueblo all joined in
celebrating the completion of the iron bands which tied

together the valleys of the Arkansas and the Platte. Speeches of congratulation and of prophesy bespoke the sentiment and the hopes of the assembled enthusiasts.

The railroad company, through a subsidiary development company, purchased a portion of the Nolan Land Grant (originally acquired from Mexico) and laid out the city of South Pueblo on the south side of the Arkansas. The two towns were later joined into one. Before the end of the year 1872 the railroad was extended from Pueblo to the coal fields near Florence, but not until 1875 was it continued to Canon City.

The coming of the railroad had a magic effect upon the quiet little village of Pueblo. The rows of primitive adobe houses gave way to impressive structures of brick and stone. Public schools and churches came to the fore and the city began to assume the appearance of growth. From a population of less than 700 in 1870 it increased to over 2,500 by 1875, while its greatest days were yet ahead.

A railroad that was to play a great part in the development of southern Colorado was the Atchison, Topeka & Santa Fe—commonly called the Santa Fe. This road had been launched as early as 1859, but not until 1873 did it reach the town of Granada, within the eastern borders of Colorado. Here, because of the road's financial difficulties, the end of track remained for two years. Then, with the aid of county bonds voted by Bent and Pueblo counties, construction was resumed and the road reached La Junta in December, 1875, and was completed to Pueblo in the following March. For a time the Santa Fe had a competitor for the Arkansas Valley trade and the freight destined for New Mexico. The Kansas Pacific railroad had built a branch from the town of Kit Carson on its main line to West Las Animas in 1873, and continued it to La Junta in 1875.

Three years later, however, this branch was abandoned and the rails were removed.

There had been many ranches and a number of towns begun in the valleys of the Arkansas and its tributaries before the railroads came. To protect these settlers and the traffic on the roads, Fort Lyon and Fort Reynolds were established in the sixties and garrisoned with United States troops. But the rise of present towns was due largely to the coming of the railroad. Las Animas and Rocky Ford moved bodily from their first locations to sites beside the rails and La Junta and other towns owe their origin to the railroad. Irrigation ditches were dug during the early seventies to supply the farms and early towns but the bigger irrigation projects in this region were to await development until after Colorado had become a state.

The advent of the railroad to Denver in 1870 and the development that immediately ensued, worked a marvelous transformation in the young metropolis. The citizens, now confident of a great future for their city and Territory, set about to build for that future. More people came in to make this their home. The population of approximately 5,000 in 1870 doubled in the two years following, and by 1874 had trebled. Business blocks and splendid residences sprang up. Real estate, which had been almost worthless, took on value and rose rapidly in price. Business increased amazingly, bank deposits and clearings were augmented, and an air of prosperity was everywhere evidenced. Denver began to provide the luxuries of the modern city with the municipal conveniences of the day. In 1870 gas works were built and the city was supplied with gas manufactured from coal. The following year water works were installed, the water being pumped from a well or "sump" near the Platte at the foot of 15th Street. The same year saw also the building of the first street railway in the city, horse-drawn cars being used for this service. The city was assuming the airs of an up-to-date metropolis.

Golden, Boulder and Canon City were growing, and the mining towns of Central City, Black Hawk, and Georgetown were showing new life and prosperity. This period of development saw not only the growth of existing towns but the beginning of new ones founded on agriculture.

One of the most striking features of the early seventies in Colorado was the establishment of agricultural colonies and "colony towns." The building of the railroads made it easy for settlers to reach the Territory. Already pioneers had demonstrated the agricultural possibilities of the region. The land grant railroads had large areas of land which they were anxious to sell, not only to obtain money but to bring in settlers who would develop business for the railroads. The Denver Pacific, the Kansas Pacific, and the Denver & Rio Grande railroads, with their subsidiary land companies or town development companies, advertised the region and stimulated its settlement.

The colony plan of settlement was well adapted to the conditions in Colorado, where agricultural communities must depend upon irrigation projects constructed through co-operative effort. The colony plan would also provide a community life with schools and churches from the outset, thus eliminating the loneliness of ranch life.

The first of the agricultural colonies to come to Colorado was the German Colonization Company organized in Chicago by Carl Wulsten in 1869. The Wet Mountain Valley south of the Arkansas was selected, and the colonists came out to the site in February, 1870. Dissension soon rose in the ranks. The colony plan proved a failure, but the settlers remained to take up land individually.

The most famous Colorado colony was the Union Colony which founded Greeley. Nathan C. Meeker, associated
with Horace Greeley on the New York *Tribune*, was or-
ganizer of this enterprise. A site in the Cache la Poudre
Valley was chosen. To this promising land the associated
colonists came in the spring of 1870. Thrifty, high-class settlers, they set about with energy and foresight to make the
project a success. A town was laid out, lots were distributed among the members, and irrigation ditches were constructed to supply the town and farms. There was hard
work and discouragement, but through cooperative effort
and persistence a thriving city and a productive agricultural
area were developed.

The Chicago-Colorado Colony, organized on the Greeley plan, founded the town of Longmont in the spring of
1871. By June there were over 400 colonists at Longmont
and fifty or sixty buildings, including a Town Hall and Library. A colony of the same pattern was launched at Evans,
near Greeley in 1871, but it did not prosper; and a similar
project at Green City, 25 miles farther down the Platte,
failed completely.

Promoters and town development companies took up
the colony idea and name, and launched a number of settlements. Platteville, some 35 miles north of Denver, was so
begun in 1871. The military reservation of Fort Collins,
abandoned in 1872, was taken over by a town company, organized by General Robert A. Cameron, and the foundations
of the present city of Fort Collins were laid.

Several groups of settlers who came to Colorado in
the early seventies were frequently spoken of as colonies,
though they were not cooperative societies in the full sense.
They were individual settlers who formed themselves into
groups in order to settle together. Green Russell, pioneer

prospector, led such a party from Georgia to settle about the town of Badito on the upper Huerfano. Other "colonies" came from Ohio, Kentucky, Michigan and other states of the East and Middle West. In addition there were hundreds of individual families that came independently and took up their residence in existing towns or on promising homesteads. Down the Platte Valley east of Greeley, where the stage stations of the sixties had been abandoned or converted into ranches, irrigation ditches were built and farms developed. The town of Sterling (three miles east of the present city of that name) was begun in 1874 and soon had its sod school house and community life. In a similar way the Arkansas Valley east of Pueblo began to be threaded with irrigation ditches and dotted with farms and towns.

Many agencies contributed to the rapid settlement of Colorado in the seventies. The railroads with their grants of land to dispose of, were energetic promoters of settlement. The colonies and town development companies issued pamphlets extolling the resources of the region. A Board of Immigration, created by the Territorial Legislature in February, 1872, began its work of disseminating information and encouraging immigration. Altogether the publicity campaign conducted by these various agencies brought thousands of settlers to Colorado and succeeded in giving the state a forward look.

While railroads were being built, while agricultural colonies were being founded in the early seventies, mining activity continued as new mineral discoveries were made in various parts of the Territory. One of the most important factors in promoting mining development was the perfecting of processes for treatment of refractory ores. Building on the experience of Lyons and other pioneer metallurgists, Professor N. P. Hill devised methods of reducing the ores

which met with marked success. He organized the Boston
& Colorado Smelting Co., and in 1867 built a plant at Black
Hawk. The works were added to and improved and together
with other mills and "process" plants promoted mining in
the region. The building of the Colorado Central railroad to Black
Hawk in 1872 aided mining development of that region by
affording cheaper transportation of supplies, including coal
for the mines and mills. The famous mines of Gilpin County
continued in the early seventies to produce between one and
two million dollars yearly. Central City was a bustling center, and though nearly completely razed by fire in 1874,
it rose from the ashes a new city with more houses of brick
and stone. Clear Creek County was thriving in the early
seventies, with rich silver mines giving forth their treasure
at the rate of from one to two million ounces per year. This
wealth of the white metal was reflected in the growth and
development of Georgetown, the prosperous leading city.

The famous Caribou mine in Boulder County, discovered in 1869, yielded its wealth of silver during the early
seventies, while the newly found telluride ores in the vicinity
gave forth their thousands in gold. In the Wet Mountain
region south of Canon City rich mines were discovered.
As a result, in 1873 the town of Rosita sprang into life.

The most striking development of this period occurred
in the San Juan country of southwestern Colorado. We
have already mentioned the fruitless and tragic Baker expedition of 1860 into this region. In the late sixties other
prosepectors penetrated the area, one of the largest parties
coming all the way from Prescott, Arizona. When some
minor finds were made in 1870 and 1871, the news spread,
and a rush into the region began. These prospectors were
intruders into territory reserved for the Utes. By treaty

of 1868 the greater part of the Western Slope had been set aside as a Ute reservation. But when veins of gold and silver beckoned, treaties were powerless to hold back the miners. The whites began to advocate a new treaty. They explained that the mountain area so valuable to themselves was practically worthless to the Indians. The machinery of negotiation was set in motion and in September, 1873, the Brunot Treaty with the Utes was signed. By it the Indians relinquished their rights to the San Juan Mountains area, and in return received certain annuities of money and goods from the government.

But even before the signing of the treaty the rush was on to the San Juan mines. As the principal trail led through the San Luis Valley, there sprang up in 1872 the town of Del Norte, "Gateway to the San Juan," to serve as an out' fitting and supply depot. More rich veins were discovered in the area, mining districts were organized, and towns sprouted in the picturesque mountain valleys. Lake City and Silverton were founded in 1874, and Ouray in the fol' lowing year. To reach the centers of mining activity trails had to be blazed and roads built over high mountains and through precipitous canyons. Long trains of humble burros and pack mules climbed the steep and dangerous paths to carry in supplies, and to transport the ore to points within reach of wagons. Then came the building of wagon roads farther into the mountains by such men as Otto Mears. Later these crude roads were to be succeeded by rails of steel.

In other portions of the Western Slope some begin' nings were being made. After miners had prospected the re' gion of the upper waters of the Gunnison, Dr. Sylvester Richardson and others in 1874 attempted to found the town of Gunnison a few miles east of the Ute reservation. Though

a number of people moved into Middle Park and some few
into North Park in the early seventies, the development
was as yet very slow.

While miners were prospecting the mountain ranges
for the precious metals, the United States government, under the supervision of Professor F. V. Hayden, was conducting an important scientific survey, which revealed the geography and geological structure of the mountain region of
Colorado. The Hayden maps and reports, immediately published, were of great value in directing and encouraging the
development of the Territory. After fifty years the work of
the Hayden surveys remains the standard authority as regards most of Colorado.

The growth of population and the rapid development
of certain sections of the Territory were reflected in the
creation of new counties during the early seventies. From
the eastern portion of Pueblo County the new County of
Bent, extending to the Kansas border, was created in 1870.
In 1874 the legislature created five new counties: Elbert, on
the east central plains; Grand, in the northwestern section
of the Territory; and Rio Grande, Hinsdale, and La Plata
in the San Juan country. In 1876 La Plata County was
divided to give rise to the county of San Juan. This gave
Colorado at the end of her Territorial period a total of
twenty-six counties instead of the seventeen with which
she had begun her career.

Although the period of the early seventies was one
primarily of development and growth, it was not a period
entirely devoid of trials. The financial panic of 1873 which
worked such havoc in the nation as a whole, had its effects in Colorado. Especially was railroad development
halted by the money stringency. Real estate values in the
larger towns also took a decided slump.

The other principal ordeal of the period was the grasshopper visitation. Swarms of the Rocky Mountain locusts,
commonly called grasshoppers, had invaded Colorado farms
in 1864 and in 1867, but their most serious invasion was
in the middle seventies. Forerunning swarms of the pests
did considerable damage in 1874, but the greatest devasta-
tion came the following year. Myriads were hatched on
local farms, while millions of others came in as migrating
clouds that nearly darkened the sun. The Central City
Register says of one such incursion:

"As the sun reached the meridian today, countless millions of grasshoppers were seen in the air while the atmosphere for miles high was literally crammed with them. They
sailed by under the pressure of a light east wind in vast bil-
lowy clouds, the lower strata falling in a ceaseless shower
on the ground, covering the streets, sidewalks, the exterior
of buildings, jumping, crawling, crushed by every passing
foot, filling the eyes and ears, and covering the garments
of pedestrians, swarming everywhere in irrespressible cur-
rents."

The hosts of hungry insects invaded the fields and ate
them bare. Many farmers were left bankrupt, business was
struck a heavy blow, and had it not been for the product
of the mines the Territory would have been in desperate
straits. Colorado was not the only victim of the grasshopper
plague. Kansas, Nebraska and other states to the eastward
suffered as much or more and the federal government even
made a "grasshopper appropriation" for feeding and clothing the destitute farmers.

Politically, Colorado's history during the early seventies
was not unlike that of the period of the sixties. As all important appointments were made by the President of the
United States, factions within the Territory sparred for

advantage and for Presidential favor. Edward McCook, who succeeded A. C. Hunt as governor in 1869, retained the position until 1873. Then President Grant was induced to remove him and to appoint Samuel H. Elbert as chief executive. McCook, humiliated at his removal, went to Washington to present his case. The President, a former military associate of the aggrieved ex-governor, lent a sympathetic ear, removed Elbert, and reappointed McCook in 1874. But the factional contest had now become so intense that the people of Colorado were divided into two hostile political camps that gave the President no peace. Finally President Grant withdrew support from both factions and appointed Colonel John L. Routt as Governor in 1875. As Territorial days were now drawing to a close the new Governor was able to win the support of the great majority of the people and to manage affairs to their satisfaction during the remaining days of the pre-state period.

We have noted in the previous chapter the efforts made in the sixties to obtain statehood for Colorado. The meager population, however, along with the opposition to statehood at home and in Washington resulted in the continuance of the Territorial status. But with the rapid increase in population, the general development, and the improved outlook for the Territory in the early seventies the movement for statehood grew in favor.

In 1872 the Territorial legislature adopted a memorial asking Congress for statehood. The following year President Grant recommended to Congress the passage of an enabling act for Colorado. During his four years as Delegate of the Territory in Congress (1871-1875), Jerome B. Chaffee worked incessantly toward this end, and his efforts were supplemented during the winter of 1874-5 by those of Delegate-elect T. M. Patterson. Together they were able to pilot

GOVERNORS OF COLORADO TERRITORY, 1865-75
1. Alexander Cummings.   2. A. Cameron Hunt
3. Edward McCook.   4. Samuel H. Elbert

COLUMBIA WELCOMES COLORADO TO THE SISTERHOOD OF
STATES, 1876

through Congress an enabling act which became a law on March 3, 1875.

It was now Colorado's privilege to make a state constitution for herself. The best legal minds of the Territory were searched out and sent to the convention which convened at Denver in December, 1875. A great duty and opportunity confronted these thirty-nine delegates. Sinking partisanship, they set to work with energy to draft the fundamental law of a great commonwealth. Taking the United States constitution as a pattern and drawing from the experience and laws of older states they framed a constitution of great merit, embodying the most progressive thought of the day. It was a long document of nineteen articles, which set up the framework of government and laid down the general principles of state policy and legislation. When finally completed, the constitution was submitted to the citizens of the Territory on July 1, 1876, and by a majority vote of nearly four to one was adopted.

On the Fourth of July, following, a grand celebration was staged in honor of the statehood which was now assured. A colorful parade through the streets of the capital and a patriotic program in the cottonwood grove on the west bank of the Platte were the chief features of the day. The principal attraction among the marching columns, waving flags and decorated floats was the "Grand Car of the Union," consisting of two flat wagons joined together and drawn by six white horses. On the first of these rode thirteen comely matrons representing the original thirteen states, while on the rear float a charming, native-born girl as "Miss Colorado," was accorded homage by girls representing each of the thirty-seven sister states.

The parade ended at the cottonwood grove where the citizens assembled to hear the program and enjoy a picnic.

A spirit of good will and of hopefulness pervaded the crowd. Former political enemies met, shook hands and for, got their quarrels. Pioneers gathered in groups beneath the trees to chat of ox trains and Indian scares, miners' courts and vigilance committees, gold diggins' and first cabins, floods and grasshoppers. Happy boys and girls waded in the shal, low portions of the river and sported in swings hanging from the cottonwood limbs. It was a day long anticipated and one thoroughly enjoyed.

On the first of August, 1876, President Grant issued the proclamation declaring Colorado admitted to the union of states. It was the one hundredth anniversary of American Independence, and by popular acclaim the new common, wealth was appropriately called the "Centennial State." The dream of pioneers and state builders had been realized; the Territorial days were over. With head erect Colorado took her place in the sisterhood of states and gazed with confidence into the future.

◆ ◆ ◆

SELECTED REFERENCES FOR FURTHER READING

J. C. Smiley, History of Colorado, 450-520
Frank Hall, History of Colorado, I, 464-549; II, 91-226, 268-321
Baker and Hafen, History of Colorado, 442-456, 515-523
Steinel and Working, History of Agriculture in Colorado
Willard and Goodykoontz, Experiments in Colorado Colonization (1926)
J. F. Willard, The Union Colony at Greeley (1918)
Frank Fossett, Colorado (1876)
The Trail (1908-1924)
Colorado Magazine: "Pioneer Days in Sterling" (Mar., 1927); "Early Days in the Arkansas Valley" (Dec., 1927); "Trinidad and Its Environs" (Sept., 1929); "Building the Narrow Gauge from Denver to Pueblo" (Nov., 1931)
Rocky Mountain News; Denver Tribune; Central City Register; Colorado Transcript

CHAPTER XII

THE YOUNG STATE ADVANCES

The Days of the Leadville Boom

WITH statehood achieved, steps were immediately taken to put the new political machinery into motion. The Republicans and the Democrats rallied their forces, held their conventions and made up tickets headed by John L. Routt and Bela M. Hughes, respectively. The campaign, brief but spirited, resulted on October 3, 1876, in a slender majority for the Republicans. Routt, the last Territorial governor, became the first state executive; Henry C. Thatcher, Samuel H. Elbert, and Ebenezer T. Wells became Justices of the Supreme Court; James B. Belford was elected to Congress; and fifty of the seventy-five members of the General Assembly were Republicans.

The first state legislature convened at Denver on November 1, 1876. It was empowered by the constitution to choose presidential electors and United States senators (selections which today are made by popular vote). Naturally, Republicans were chosen. In the close presidential contest that ensued (Hayes-Tilden) the Colorado vote was decisive for Hayes. For the United States senate two distinguished statesmen were selected—Henry M. Teller and Jerome B. Chaffee—who were ably to represent the new state.

The General Assembly provided for a complete revision of the Territorial laws, enacted new measures, and set in motion the machinery of state government. Governor Routt took the helm of the ship of state and launched it on a successful course.

During the first years of statehood Colorado's development continued on a rather even tenor. The grasshopper
plague was not repeated after 1875, and agricultural returns
were more secure. Productive new mines were opened in
the San Juan country and the outflow of the precious metals
was reflected in the building of roads, towns and mills in
that region. The older mining camps of Gilpin, Clear Creek
and other counties continued to produce extensively, and
more and better smelters were erected to extract the metals
from the ores.

But the outstanding feature of the early days of statehood was the discovery of silver-bearing carbonate-of-lead
ores at the headwaters of the Arkansas. The development
which created Leadville and centered about that magic city
spread its beneficence abroad and gave new tone and vigor
to the whole state. For a decade or more Leadville was the
most important influence in Colorado.

Early placer miners in California Gulch had been an-
noyed by a black sand almost as heavy as gold, which clut-
tered up their sluices and made difficult the separation of gold
from the gravel. Heavy, dark boulders had given additional
trouble. In the middle seventies, Alvinus B. Wood, a partner
of W. H. Stevens, both experienced and critical miners, an-
alyzed this disturbing substance and found it to be a rich
carbonate of lead, carrying silver. They worked quietly to
discover the ore-body source of this mineral and in the winter of 1874-5 located an outcrop on the crest of a heavily
wooded hill to the north of the gulch, which they named
Iron Hill. They located claims on this outcrop for more than
a mile, north and south and kept their discovery to themselves as long as possible. But the secret was out in the
winter of 1876.

During the spring of 1877 miners began to flock in

and new ore bodies of great extent and richness were rapidly discovered. By fall several hundred men were in the carbo-nate district, ore shipments were increasing and promising mines were being opened. By mid-January, 1878, a town was organized under the name of "Leadville." News of the richness of the district was broadcast and the great rush set in with the early spring.

Machinery by the carload had been shipped from the East to the nearest railroad termini and as soon as moun-tain roads were passable great freighting outfits began the work of transporting it to the new mines. Immense quan-tities of merchandise and supplies were added to other freight demanding shipment, and freighters received from five to ten cents per pound plus bonuses to get the goods to the new bonanza. Long trains of mule teams struggled through the mud and snow and hurried on to their goal amid the shouts of muleteers and the crack of whips. Hundreds of passengers demanded immediate transportation. Stagecoach lines were multiplied, private hacks were requisitioned, and many of the poor and hopeful trudged on foot with their packs on their backs. All roads led to Leadville — from Canon City up the Arkansas, from Colorado Springs by way of Ute Pass and South Park, from Denver via Turkey Creek road or from the terminus of the South Park rail-road in Platte Canyon.

The discoveries of 1878 and 1879 exceeded all pre-vious finds. Destitute prospectors became wealthy over night and men of moderate means became bonanza kings. One of the most famous of the latter was H. A. W. Tabor, keeper of a small store at Oro City when the first dis-coveries were made. To Tabor's store in 1877 came two shoemakers, Rische and Hook, who had turned prospectors. On finding them without supplies to continue their search

for "carbonates," Tabor agreed to "grubstake" them and
to share in any discovery they might make. The shoemakers
went to the top of Fryer hill, considered an unpromising
location by the wise ones, and began to dig. Industrious
and persevering, they labored on; and Tabor stood by them
with additional supplies. Finally they struck the great ore
body of the Little Pittsburgh mine and wealth was theirs.
One year from the date of discovery the holdings were cap-
italized at $20,000,000. Tabor bought Hook's interest and
purchased new claims in the vicinity. It seemed that everything he touched turned to silver. With bewildering sud-
denness he was elevated to wealth and power, and millions
came to him as if by magic. He was elected Lieutenant
Governor of Colorado in 1878 and United States Senator
in 1883. But smiling fortune turned her face and the famous bonanza king died a poor man in 1899.

Among scores of notable mines the Robert E. Lee was
perhaps the most famous to be opened at Leadville. Discovered by an obscure prospector, it poured forth its silver
lavishly, reaching the peak of $118,500 in a single day. The
Morning Star made Governor Routt his fortune, but only
after his resources were exhausted and his credit was at
the breaking point. The Matchless mine added to Tabor's
wealth, while the Chrysolite, the Little Chief and others
produced their millions. Smelters sprang up to handle the
rich ores, Berdell & Witherell, the Harrison Reduction
Works, and the Grant Smelter being the first.

Leadville grew as by magic. Writes Helen Hunt (Jackson) of the town in 1878: "In six months a tract of dense,
spruce forest had been converted into a bustling village.
To be sure, the upturned roots and the freshly hacked
stumps of many of the spruce trees are still in the streets.
. . . The houses are all log cabins, or else plain unpainted

McCLELLAN AND SPOTSWOOD STAGE, DENVER TO LEADVILLE, 1880

HARRISON AVENUE, LEADVILLE, 1880

RAILROAD IN THE ROYAL GORGE

board shanties. . . . The Leadville places of business are another thing; there is one compact, straight street, running
east and west, in the center of this medley of sage brush,
spruce stumps, cabins and shanties. . . . The middle of the
street was always filled with groups of men talking. Wagons
were driven up and down as fast as if the street were clear.
It looked all the time as if there had been a fire, and the
people were just dispersing, or as if town meeting were
just over. Everybody was talking, nearly everybody gesticu-
lating. All faces looked restless, eager, fierce. It was a
Monaco gambling room emptied into a Colorado spruce
clearing."

Shelter was at a premium in the new town and the
man was fortunate who secured a bed on the floor of a
boarding house tent. Saw mills hummed, and the green
boards were jerked away to be nailed into shanties, hotels
and business houses. The sound of hammer and saw continued by day and night and yet the supply was not equal
to the need. Real estate vaulted skyward and business
sites were grabbed up at amazing figures. Lot jumping became common; mine owners maintained armed guards at
their mines. There was a frenzy for buying and selling,
bonding and leasing, with speculators in city lots and mining shares conducting a lively business. Crime was of daily
occurrence and vice was open and blatant. Saloons and
gambling dens drew great crowds eager for excitement. Everyone seemed impatient for wealth and many were unscrupulous as to the methods of gaining it.

The rush to Leadville continued through 1878; the
following year witnessed an even greater flood; and the third
year saw no slackening. Leadville was the busiest and most
talked of city in the nation. The wealth of her mines was
unprecedented and her meteoric rise unrivaled. To her

came all classes—capitalists, eager to invest in the mines; miners and prospectors intent on finding their fortune; business and professional men anxious to reap the by-products of the mining prosperity; day laborers attracted by high wages; and gamblers, thugs and other parasitic dregs of society who cluster about the sources of newly-won wealth. The daytime bustle in the chief business streets was exceeded by the jostle at night. The historian, Fossett, gives this contemporary picture: "Difficult as it is to make one's way along the main thoroughfares by day, it is still more so just before and after nightfall. Leadville by lamp-light fairly 'booms' with excitement and life. The miners then drift into town in swarms; a dozen bands are drumming up audiences for the theatres and variety shows, scores of saloons and numerous gambling-houses are in full blast and the entire scene gives the town and place the appearance of one grand holiday."

But amid the wild excitement there were forces working for law, order and stability. The criminal element was somewhat cowed by two timely lynchings by vigilance committees in 1879. A regular city government was established the same year, replacing the town organization of 1878. Streets and alleys were laid out and graded, a water system and gas works were installed, a fire department was organized, and a police force established. A telegraph line connected Leadville with the outside world in 1878 and a telephone exchange was organized the following year. Daily newspapers were established and received a liberal patronage. Substantial stone business houses were built, hotels erected, and banks founded. The Clarendon Hotel and the Tabor Opera House were worthy examples of such structures. Churches and schools were early introduced and civic, military, and fraternal societies were formed.

By 1880 Leadville was "settling down." The boom of the preceding two years had led to overcapitalization of certain mining properties. Collapses came which induced more conservative financing and more consistent development. A widespread strike of miners occurred in the spring of 1880, which for a time threatened dire consequences; but after martial law was proclaimed the strike finally collapsed. By the end of 1880 the city had become a well-ordered municipality with the typical features of a new metropolis.

The mines of Leadville inaugurated an era of prosperity for Colorado. The millions in silver poured from these mines quickened business in all its branches and reflected prosperity throughout the state. Denver was especially affected by Leadville's bounty. Business was stimulated and real estate began to boom. Leadville fortunes were invested in Denver property and bonanza kings built palatial homes in the capital city. Tabor expressed his faith by heavy investments in Denver, erecting with Leadville silver the Tabor Block and the Tabor Grand Opera House. The latter, one of the finest theaters in the world at the time, was opened in September, 1881, by Emma Abbott and her opera company. Eugene Field, then employed on the *Denver Tribune*, wrote the dramatic criticism for his paper.

The remarkable discoveries of carbonates at Leadville stimulated the search for similar ore elsewhere. Prospectors spread in all directions and noteworthy discoveries were made. Kokomo and Robinson, eighteen miles north of Leadville were promising camps on the headwaters of the Blue River; the Eagle River and the Holy Cross districts about Red Cliff showed rich ores; while Aspen on the Roaring Fork was to develop into a rival of Leadville itself. On the headwaters of the Gunnison the Tin Cup mining district was revealed, and carbonate ore found about the town of Gunnison started a heavy emigration to that section. A correspondent of the Pueblo *Chieftain* writes from Parlin's ranch on May 17, 1880, that on the day previous he counted 250 teams bound for Gunnison, Ruby and Gothic. "One would think," he says, "that there must be an end to this procession, but the end is not yet, for far away on the Saguache road there is a long line of white wagon covers." The discovery of carbonate ore in the Wet Mountain Valley near Rosita in 1878 caused a rush to the region and created the town of Silver Cliff, which for a time was the third city of the state, ranking next after Denver and Leadville in population.

To each newly discovered district a mad rush was made, and the towns and camps which sprang up reenacted on a smaller stage the tumultuous life of Leadville. Some camps faded almost as quickly as they rose, while others continued for years as rich producers of the precious metals.

The new mining camps attracted the railroads. The heavy traffic to Leadville was a prize for which the Denver and South Park, the Denver and Rio Grande, and the Santa Fe railroads contended. The first of these roads began building up Platte Canyon toward South Park in 1877, little dreaming of Leadville and its boom. The great traffic of 1878 was an unexpected windfall for the road and vigorously the track was pushed toward the new Eldorado. The road had more traffic than it could handle. The business was so profitable that the cost of new construction was paid for from current earnings. With each advance of the railhead the route was shortened for the big freight outfits and for the numerous stagecoaches connecting with the end of the track. The rails crossed South Park in 1879 and descended Trout Creek to the Arkansas early the next spring.

In the meantime a portentous struggle was on between the Denver and Rio Grande and the Santa Fe. The logical and most feasible route to Leadville was up the valley of the Arkansas, with the Royal Gorge as the key to the route. Each of these railroads was determined to secure the right of way through this deep and vital gorge, for there was room for but one road and hardly that through this scenic chasm.

Both railroads had good claims to the canyon. Each began the work of grading its road bed. The question of right of way was presented to the courts, and while the legal battle raged, the construction gangs were armed camps ready to turn their picks and crowbars to the defense of their company's claims. Some clashes between rival camps of workmen actually took place, but no lives were lost. The legal fight was long and bitter and the lower courts ruled for one and then for the other of the claimants. Finally the case was carried to the United States Supreme Court which decided in favor of the Denver and Rio Grande. A working arrangement was made by the rival roads whereby the Denver and Rio Grande agreed not to build south to El Paso, Texas, and the Santa Fe promised not to build to Leadville.

With the legal question settled, the Rio Grande made all haste to complete its road to booming Leadville. Shifts of men were kept at work day and night, ties and rails were laid with the utmost dispatch, and early in July, 1880, the first passenger train was welcomed in Malta, reaching Leadville the following September. The Denver and South Park road, which had reached the Arkansas near Buena Vista in the spring, now made an arrangement with the Denver and Rio Grande to run its trains the remaining distance to Leadville over the latter's track.

As the opening of remote mining camps created an urgent need for transportation facilities before the railroad could be expected, there developed a most remarkable system of trails and roads, of pack trains, stagecoaches and freight outfits, all adapted to the rugged mountain region of Colorado. Prospectors blazed the trails; and the pack mule or the foot-sure burro—sometimes called the Rocky Mountain canary—usually carried in the first supplies and returned with the first ore. Wagon roads were the next need. In the absence of county and state funds for road building, the chief reliance was on the toll road. Companies were formed, roads were built, and tolls were collected from users of the road to pay the cost of construction. The rugged San Juan country saw the most extensive development of these transportation features. The outstanding leader in this movement was Otto Mears, known as "The Pathfinder of the San Juan." He piloted pack trains, he built toll roads, maintained freighting outfits, and ultimately became a railroad builder. Perhaps his most spectacular accomplishment was the construction in 1882 and 1883 of the famous Ouray-Silverton road over Red Mountain, which today as the "Million Dollar Highway," is perhaps the most scenic highway in Colorado.

In the late seventies, packing and wagon freighting were at their height and thousands of men and animals were employed in the business. The typical freight outfit consisted of three spans of mules and two heavy wagons. The "skinner" was an expert teamster. He rode the left wheel mule and drove with a jerk line running to the bridle of the left leader. On dangerous dugways, around sharp curves and down steep grades his skill was put to the test. Brakes were of the utmost importance, each wagon being equipped with heavy brake blocks and a wooden pole extension of the lever arm. A rope, extending from the top of the pole to the teamster's saddle, was used to operate the brake. The toll charge varied with the length and character of the road but was usually from $1 to $5 per team.

At the end of the wagon road, pack animals were employed for the remaining distance to the mines. Packing was an art in itself, for the load must be properly balanced and securely tied on the back of the animal. All shapes and sizes of articles were transported up the steep and narrow trails to the mines, and the patient little burro was often almost hidden in his bulging load. One end of timbers or other such long pieces was fastened to the pack saddle while the other end was allowed to trail on the ground at the back of the animal. Pack mules were usually hitched tandem and led by the driver, while burros were herded loose and driven from the rear. Packing rates varied with the grade and the distance, but were approximately $2.50 per hundred pounds for ten miles.

It was a picturesque life in the San Juan country of the '70s and '80s. Jolly mule skinners, arrogant stagedrivers, and skillful packers thronged the toll roads and trails. Hopeful prospectors wandered over the hills while successful miners scooped the silver and gold from rich veins in the ribbed mountains. The bustling mining towns with their saloons, stores and miner's cabins clung to mountain sides, squeezed themselves into narrow canyons, or nestled serenely in enchanting, mountain-walled valleys. Buried treasure was the lure that brought this new life to the "Silver San Juan."

One of the most important developments of the early years of statehood was the expulsion of the Utes and the opening of the Western Slope. Forces had been working toward that end from the first coming of the white settler to

Colorado, but the process was brought to a climax by a tragedy at the White River Agency in 1879.

In accordance with treaty provisions and United States policy, there were maintained among the Ute Indians, agents who distributed the annuities and worked as best they could to direct the Indians into the ways of civilization. Occasionally, red tape in the Indian Bureau at Washington delayed the delivery of goods and the government was not always prompt in keeping its promises. This caused mutterings among the Indians, but Ouray, chief of the Southern Utes, was able to explain delays and calm his people. Among the Northern Utes, however, murmurs were more frequent and persistent.

Early in 1878 Nathan Meeker, principal founder of the town of Greeley, was appointed Indian agent for the White River Utes. He took up his work with the zeal of a missionary, eager to turn the wandering Utes to agricultural pursuits and the ways of settled life. But these Indians had a strong dislike for agriculture and for white education. The school, the plow and the barbed wire fences were hated institutions, and the more Meeker persisted in his efforts to introduce them the wider became the gap between the agent and his wards. The Indians began to oppose and then to defy him. In the summer of 1879 Indians left their agency, contrary to orders, burned some houses on the Yampa and set fire to forests in several directions. Meeker lost all control of the Indians. To a friend he said:

"I came to this Agency in the full belief that I could civilize these Utes; that I could teach them to work and become self-supporting. I thought that I could establish schools, and interest both Indians and their children in learning. I have given my best efforts to this end, always treating them kindly but firmly. They have eaten at my table and have received continued kindness from my wife and daughter and all the employees about the Agency."

But what the kindly agent exhibited in determination he lacked in diplomacy. He was unable to win the confidence or love of the Indians. Finally he acknowledged his plight and called upon the government for military protection. After some delays Major Thornburg was ordered from Fort Fred Steele in southern Wyoming to the White River Agency. While on the march to the agency Thornburg was met by Captain Jack, chief leader of the Northern Utes, who urged him not to bring his soldiers on to the reservation but to go to the agency himself and attempt to fix up matters. Thornburg replied that his orders were to march to the agency and he must go.

The troops reached the Milk Creek branch of the Yampa near the boundary line of the reservation on September 29th and here the advance troops ran into an ambush in the canyon. Major Thornburg found himself nearly surrounded by well-armed Indians under Captain Jack. After a brief resistance the advance troops, being greatly outnumbered, dashed for the wagon train in their rear, but Thornburg and thirteen of his men were killed in the action. The troops corraled the train, made breastworks of wagons and supplies and prepared to withstand a siege. From behind the cedar trees and rocks the Indians kept up a fire at the forted troops and with their Sharps and Winchester rifles succeeded in wounding or killing several men, and in slaughtering nearly 200 mules.

During the first night of the siege Joe Rankin, the scout, made his way from the besieged camp and dashed away on his heroic 160-mile ride for reenforcements. Twenty-eight hours later he drew up at Rawlins, where General Merritt received the word and soon mustered his troops to begin a march to the rescue. In the meantime a courier had been sent out to Captain Dodge and his company of colored troops who had been sent up from Fort Garland to guard the set' tlers in Middle Park. These "buffalo soldiers," as the Indians called the colored troops, arrived on the third day of the siege but were too few in number to bring relief.

General Merritt's command arrived on the sixth day and were prepared to force their way through. But the advance had hardly begun when a man appeared among the Indians with a white flag. He was a messenger from Chief Ouray of the Southern Utes, who upon hearing of the battle and massacre had sent a runner to tell the Utes to stop fighting. The firing now ceased and the Indians scat' tered and fled. General Merritt returned to the wagon train camp and after caring for the dead and wounded continued his march toward the White River.

In the meantime death had stalked at the agency. The Indians, who blamed Meeker for the coming of the troops, had made an attack on the agency within a few hours after the beginning of the Thornburg battle and had wreaked their vengeance upon the agent and his employes. Meeker and eleven other men were killed, the three women and two chil' dren were taken captive and most of the buildings were pil' laged and burned.

When news of the Thornburg battle and the Meeker massacre reached the people of Colorado there was a bitter outcry against the Utes and a demand for their prompt punishment. But to safeguard the lives of the captives the troops were ordered to cease their farther advance while commissioners negotiated with the Indians for the release of the captive women and children. Through the praise' worthy efforts of Ouray and General Charles Adams this release was finally effected. Though the soldiers and most

of Colorado's citizens demanded thorough punishment of
the Utes, military action against them was refused by the
Washington authorities while a commission and a Congressional committee investigated and took testimony to determine the causes of the outbreak.

As weeks passed and it became evident that no Indians
were to be punished, the demand arose for expulsion of the
Utes from the state to avoid the recurrence of similar trage-
dies. The Colorado Senators and Congressmen introduced
bills in Congress aiming at such a consummation; the Commissioner of Indian Affairs began negotiations and finally a
treaty was agreed upon, which provided for the removal of
the White River Utes to a Utah Reservation. The removal
was promptly effected, being encouraged by the pressure
of United States troops. Throughout the state there was
rejoicing at the withdrawal of the Utes. The Ouray *Times*
thus expressed itself:

"Sunday morning the Utes bid adieu to their old hunting grounds and folded their tents, rounded up their dogs,
sheep, goats, ponies and traps, and took up the line of
march for their new reservation, followed by General Mc-
Kenzie and his troops. This is an event that has been long
and devoutly prayed for by our people. How joyful it
sounds and with what satisfaction one can say, 'The Utes
have gone'."

As the Indian tragedy was coming to its last act on
the Western Slope, while Leadville and the San Juan country were experiencing their boom days and the valley towns
were basking in reflections of mining splendor, there was
being enacted on the wide plains of eastern Colorado a
drama of the open range.

Great herds of longhorn cattle were grazing on the un-

fenced prairie and cowboys were living the life which growing boys vision as the ideal. It was a life prosaic enough
to those who lived it, but to those who see it through the
eyes of the writers of "Western stories," and as portrayed
on the movie screen, its glamour is engaging.

Horses, cattle and sheep had come to America with
the early Spaniards and rapidly had worked their way
far into the interior. When the first Anglo-Saxon pioneers
crossed the prairies to the Rocky Mountains the Indians
of the plains were already on horseback. Cattle gradually
worked their way up from Mexico into Texas and New
Mexico and were ready to advance upon the northern plains
when Colorado was born.

Ox teams drawing the pioneers and their freight to
Colorado had subsisted on the grass of the plains, and the
milch cows brought by the Pike's Peakers had done the
same. Soon the settlers realized that the "Great American
Desert" was a great pastoral domain beckoning to the cat-
tleman. Small herds of cattle were developed in the valleys of the Rio Grande, the Arkansas and the Platte in
the early sixties, but on the plains the buffalo still dominated;
though his day was drawing to its close. The slaughter of
the buffalo had already begun, and in the early seventies
reached the vast proportions of a million a year. Most of
these were killed for the hides and tongues only, and carloads of tongues and train loads of hides were shipped east
on the newly constructed railroads. In the wake of the
hunters came the bone gatherers, and carloads of buffalo
bones were gathered up and shipped to eastern markets to
be ground into fertilizer.

Then onto the trails of the vanishing buffalo came the
Texas longhorns, hardy scions of the wiry stock from old
Spain. They came by the thousands, long winding "trail

EARLY TOLL ROAD IN SAN JUAN MOUNTAINS

PACK TRAIN LOADED WITH CABLE AT TELLURIDE

HEREFORD CATTLE ON COLORADO RANGE
INSERT—A TEXAS LONGHORN

herds" working their way northward. Soon the prairie was again covered, rivers and lakes of shining, widespread horns replacing the dark sea of massive humps that once had blackened the landscape. Home ranches were taken up on creek and river, springs and water holes were appropriated, and the reign of the "cattle kings" began.

One of the earliest and perhaps the most famous of the "cattle kings" in Colorado was John W. Iliff, who began raising cattle in the sixties. By 1877 he had 35,000 head, owned 15,000 acres of land in the South Platte Valley and by his ownership of water frontage practically controlled thousands of acres more running back from the river onto the prairie. He not only bought thousands of Texas cattle each year, but built up his herds by the introduction of Shorthorn blood. Forty cowboys with two hundred horses were required during the summer season for his roundups and drives.

During the eighties large cattle companies were formed, several of these corporations being owned and directed from Great Britain. Perhaps the largest of these operating in Colorado was the Prairie Cattle Company, which came to hold over two million acres of Colorado land, on which were run over 50,000 cattle. Beside the large companies and the big cattle men were many small owners who cooperated with each other in the conduct of their business.

One of the noteworthy features of the industry was the roundup. All the men running cattle on the range of a given district would assemble in the spring at a designated place to begin the roundup. For instance, the cattlemen of the South Platte gathered near Julesburg, cattlemen and companies providing cowboys in proportion to the number of cattle they owned. A boss was appointed who directed the movements of the 100 to 150 cowboys employed. From

Julesburg they worked their way up the river, rounding up the cattle, branding the calves, and cutting out and segre' gating the cattle according to ownership. Up the valley they moved at the rate of five to ten miles a day. "Moving camp was quite a spectacle;" writes one of the early day cowboys. "With all the wagons, hundreds of horses and thousands of cattle moving along in clouds of dust it was a busy time for all concerned." A similar roundup took place along the Arkansas, usually beginning at Colorado's eastern boundary and working up the river. Others were conducted in various parts of the state. In the fall, round' ups somewhat different in character took place, the beef cattle being gathered for market.

The life of the cowboy was strenuous. Often in the saddle from daylight till dark for months at a time, drink' ing filthy water from shallow water holes, breathing the thick dust from wheeling herds, straining patience with footsore laggards or curbing the will of bull'headed steers, he was so tired when night came that he forgot the bumps under his blankets and the hardness of his bed.

But there was the brighter side—the thrill of new adventure, the consciousness of power over the herd, the response of his horse to the move of the rein or the touch of the spur, the exhibition of skill in roping and throwing a steer, plenty of hard work and a good appetite, the fellow' ship of jolly cowboys around the campfire with their songs and pranks and stories, and at close of day tranquil sleep beneath the stars.

At times the cowboy was the tired laborer, serf of his lord; again he was the mounted knight riding his steed in a blaze of glory.

The cowboy's dress and equipment were borrowed largely from old Spain and in many cases retain their Span' ish names. The sombrero, bandanna, chaps, boots, spurs, quirt and lasso, though picturesque, were admirably adapted to their uses. Utility and protection were primary consider-ations, but color and ornament were not ignored. Excellent equipment, especially a high class saddle, was the cowboy's pride, while a highly trained bronco, or cow pony, that re-sponded to his every move and signal was a constant joy. The agile cowboy, the wiry bronco and the wild steer were complements to each other. Together they comprised a com-plete show.

The cattle industry on the open range of Colorado was short-lived. Two decades saw its rise and fall. In part it fell of its own weight through overstocking of the range. But more especially was it pushed aside by the need for higher usage of the land, for farming ever replaces grazing as population increases. The domain of the cattle kings in Colorado was conquered in the late eighties by the humble "nesters," who gradually pushed across the plains and took possession of the soil for their homesteads. The farmers claimed the streams and the waterholes and ran their wire fences across the deep worn cattle trails. Cattlemen swore, sometimes fought, and occasionally murdered. They ap-pealed to the government, but all was in vain; they were pushed from the plains by the growth of the nation.

The early years of statehood saw noteworthy develop-ment in Colorado along educational lines under such able leaders as Aaron Gove, Horace M. Hale and James H. Baker. The public schools, founded in the sixties, were ex-panding and improving, and high schools were being estab-lished in the cities. The Denver High School graduated its first class in 1877 and thereafter high schools sprang up rap-idly in the different cities of the state.

In December, 1875, the Colorado Teachers Association was formed and committees were appointed which worked out school system provisions to be incorporated into the state constitution and into legislative statutes. The teachers association has continued since its inception to work for the professional improvement of its members and for the general cause of education in the state.

Higher education received attention during the early years of statehood. The state University of Boulder, which had been created on paper in 1861, opened its doors in September, 1877, with Joseph A. Sewell as president. The School of Mines, which had its meager beginning in the early seventies in connection with the Jarvis Hall School for Boys at Golden, developed into a collegiate institution of merit. The Agricultural College at Fort Collins received some small appropriations during the Territorial period and was able to begin instruction in September, 1879. Colorado Seminary, founded in 1864, was reorganized as Denver University in 1880. Colorado College opened with a preparatory department at Colorado Springs in 1874 and soon developed into an institution of collegiate rank. These higher educational institutions, from humble beginnings were to grow in size and service and other schools were later to rise to supplement their efforts in the educational field.

While educational facilities were being afforded for the fortunate normal members of society, institutions for the less fortunate were being provided. A penitentiary at Canon City had been established by law in 1868 and was opened in 1871. The institution was enlarged as the need arose. The State Insane Asylum was established at Pueblo in 1879. In 1881 the State Industrial School for Boys was opened at Golden. Other correctional and charitable institutions were to be created as the population increased.

Political events during the first years of statehood were overshadowed by the more important developments of mine and farm and range. Though campaigns were conducted with vigor and debates were often heated, the rank and file of the citizenry were not greatly disturbed. Governor Routt's administration passed smoothly, with no political develop-ments of unusual character. The second state election (1878) resulted in a Republican victory, with Frederick W. Pitkin, a lawyer and mining operator from Ouray, chosen governor and James B. Belford elected to Congress. The Republicans secured also a majority of the members of the legislature and thus were able to control the election of a United States Senator. For this coveted honor Professor Nathaniel P. Hill, a prominent metallurgist and founder of the smelter at Black Hawk, was chosen to succeed Senator Chaffee in the upper house of Congress.

The growth of the new state was reflected somewhat in county formation. Four new counties were created by the first General Assembly of the state (1877). The south-ern part of Fremont County was formed into Custer County, taking the name of the famous General Custer who had been killed by the Indians the year before. The western por-tion of Grand County became Routt County, christened for the first State Governor. Chief Ouray's name was given to the new county created from San Juan, while Gunnison County was formed on the western slope, taking the name of the intrepid explorer who had surveyed that region in 1853. The rapid growth of population in and about Lead-ville induced the second state assembly (1879) to divide Lake County, and Chaffee County was created from its southern portion.

The first years of statehood saw a heavy immigration into Colorado, induced to a large extent by the Leadville boom. When the enumerators took the census in 1880 they found a population of 194,327, which was almost five times the number reported a decade before (39,864). And of this remarkable increase approximately half had been acquired after statehood was achieved in 1876.

✦ ✦ ✦

SELECTED REFERENCES FOR FURTHER READING

J. C. Smiley, History of Colorado, 685-693
Frank Hall, History of Colorado, II, 363-513
Baker and Hafen, History of Colorado, 901-907
C. C. Davis, Olden Times in Colorado (1916)
Steinel and Working, History of Agriculture in Colorado
Dawson and Skiff, The Ute War (1879)
H. M. Hale, Education in Colorado, 1861-1885 (1885)
Sidney Jocknick, Early Days on the Western Slope (1913)
Andy Adams, The Log of a Cowboy (1903)
G. F. Willison, Here They Dug the Gold (1931)
History of the Arkansas Valley (Baskin, 1881), 122-178
Colorado Magazine: "Butchering Buffalo" (April, 1928); "The Cattle Round-
    up" (Oct., 1928); "Early Cowboy Life in the Arkansas Valley" (Sept.,
    1930)
The Trail (1908-1924)
Denver Tribune; Rocky Mountain News; Denver Times

CHAPTER XIII

THE PROSPEROUS EIGHTIES

The Era of Great Expansion

THE rapid growth so noticeable in Colorado during the seventies continued unabated through the succeeding decade. Mines continued to give forth their wealth, and ever-extending farms produced the crops necessary to sustain the increasing population. Cities were growing, wealth was increasing; it was indeed the period of the "prosperous eighties."

Perhaps no better index to the development of the state could be found than in the railroad building that was pushed to completion during this decade. The heavy traffic to Leadville, the opening of new mines elsewhere, and the growth of the state generally, stimulated railroad construction in the '80s to an extent never before nor since witnessed in Colorado. The Denver and Rio Grande was the most active Colorado road, building an average of over 300 miles of track each year from 1880 to 1882. In 1881 the Rio Grande continued its line from Leadville over Tennessee Pass to Red Cliff, and built its line from Salida over Marshall Pass to Gunnison and Crested Butte, while a branch line was pushed to the vicinity of Silver Cliff. The line to Gunnison was built westward to the Utah line in 1882 and the following year was joined to a Utah subsidiary which carried it on to Salt Lake City.

Even before the Leadville development, the Rio Grande had begun building toward the San Juan country. It started from Pueblo in 1876, crossed Veta Pass the following year and reached Alamosa in 1878. Then working westward it crossed Cumbres Pass and reached Durango in 1881, continuing up the Animas to Silverton the following year. Towns sprang up at strategic points along these routes, many becoming important trade centers. Salida and Buena Vista in the upper Arkansas Valley rose from a railroad foundation; Alamosa became an important center for the productive San Luis Valley immediately upon its founding in 1878; Durango developed at once into a trade and smelting center when the railroad reached the Animas. Other towns and stations too numerous to mention here owe their existence to the railroad.

But the Denver and Rio Grande, running wild over the Colorado Rockies, was not alone in the field during this period of remarkable railroad expansion. Its closest competitor in the mountain area was the Denver and South Park, which we have mentioned as having built from Denver to the Arkansas Valley below Leadville in 1880. This, like the Rio Grande, was a narrow gauge road that could climb mountains like a burro. It raced the Rio Grande to the Gunnison country in 1881, building via Chalk Creek and Alpine Pass, a road that has since been abandoned. After being acquired by the Union Pacific the South Park road built via Boreas Pass, Breckenridge, and Fremont Pass to Leadville, a line operated today by the Colorado and Southern.

The Santa Fe railroad, which had reached Pueblo in 1876, built its line from La Junta to Trinidad and crossed the Colorado-New Mexico line via Raton Pass in November, 1878, from whence it continued on to the New Mexico capital. In 1887 it completed its road from Pueblo to Denver.

Denver railroad builders conceived great plans for making their city a railroad center. Lines were projected in all directions—one to Duluth on the Great Lakes, one to Puget Sound, one to New Orleans and one to Galveston on the Gulf. Only one part of the plan materialized, that realized by the Denver and New Orleans Railway Company. This road reached Pueblo in 1882, but financial difficulties stop' ped it there until reorganizations were made which effected completion of the line to Texas and New Orleans in 1888. This was later to become a part of the Colorado and South' ern system.

The Colorado Midland Railway Company was organ' ized in 1883 and began building its standard gauge line in 1885. Its route westward from Colorado Springs was via Ute Pass, South Park, and Buena Vista to Leadville. Thence it crossed the continental divide by a tunnel under Hagerman Pass, ran a branch to Aspen, and its main line to Glenwood Springs and Newcastle. The road operated for a number of years, but later much of its road bed was abandoned and the remainder was incorporated with the Denver and Rio Grande.

The Colorado Central built its line to Georgetown in 1877 and to Silver Plume via the famous Georgetown Loop in 1884. Its line from Golden to Longmont was extended to Cheyenne in 1877 and the towns of Loveland and Ber' thoud sprang up along the road. The Julesburg Cutoff of the present Union Pacific was completed in 1882, giving for the first time to the valley of the South Platte east of Greeley the advantages of rail transportation.

The prosperous eighties saw the building of three new trunk railroad lines across the plains to Colorado. The Bur' lington came in from Nebraska and reached Denver in 1882. The Missouri Pacific built along the Arkansas Valley, some distance to the north of the river, and reached Pueblo in

1887. The Rock Island pushed across the central plains to Colorado Springs in 1888 and was soon operating trains from Limon to Denver over the Union Pacific track. This was the last of the main lines built to Colorado from the East. The state at the close of the eighties was served by six eastern lines—the Union Pacific, the Burlington, the Rock Island, the Kansas Pacific, the Missouri Pacific and the Santa Fe. The railroad facilities from this direction remain the same today. Other minor railroads and extensions of existing lines, too numerous to mention here, were built in all parts of Colorado during the eighties, each adding its bit to the upbuilding of the state. The decade witnessed almost a trebling of railroad mileage in Colorado, the length of track increasing from 1,570 miles in 1880 to 4,176 miles in 1890.

The early eighties saw important developments in western Colorado. The removal of the Utes from the west central portion of the state made possible the white settlement of their former reservation. When the lands were formally thrown open to occupation on September 4, 1881, there was a rush to the choice locations within the area. Homeseekers, prospectors and townsite promoters made up the pioneer bands. Within a few months many farms and grazing claims were taken up, and the beginnings were made of the leading cities of the Western Slope.

To the site of Grand Junction went George A. Crawford and some associates, who on September 26, 1881, duly claimed a 640-acre tract for a townsite. A town company was organized and settlers began to arrive. The town was incorporated in 1882. One of the first community enterprises was the opening of a public school in a rude picket cabin. The coming of the Denver and Rio Grande railroad, toward the end of 1882, heightened the prospects of the settlement. While the foundations of the city were being laid, ranch claims were taken up in the valley and irrigation can-als were built for the development of agriculture. The pi-oneer settlers planted vines and fruit trees and found the region admirably adapted to horticulture. The fame of Western Slope fruit was destined to spread throughout the country.

The junction of the Gunnison and Uncompahgre rivers was chosen as a suitable site for a settlement and a town company was organized. Settlers came in and the town of Delta was incorporated in the spring of 1882. Above the town, on the North Fork of the Gunnison, important be-ginnings were made in the fall of 1881. The ranch claims of Samuel Wade and Enos Hotchkiss were to develop into the towns of Paonia and Hotchkiss respectively. Orchards were planted and herds of cattle introduced.

Montrose was located as a townsite in January, 1882, and was incorporated the following spring. The building of irrigation canals, of homes and business houses empha-sized the permanence of the settlement.

The three cities of Grand Junction, Delta and Montrose possess much in common as to their origin and early history. Springing simultaneously, almost as by magic, from the aban-doned hunting grounds of the Utes, they present striking examples of the fruits of American vigor. The establishment of smaller towns, of farms and ranches in their neighbor-hoods was no less important for the development of the state. The General Assembly took note of the growth of this sec-tion of the Western Slope and in 1883 created from the western portion of Gunnison County, the new counties of Mesa, Delta, and Montrose, designating the cities of Grand Junction, Delta, and Montrose respectively as the county seats. This political arrangement remains unaltered today.

At the junction of the Roaring Fork with the Colorado River, the Defiance Town and Land Company laid out a town in 1882, which the following year took the name of Glenwood Springs. Garfield County, named for the martyred President, was organized in 1883, and Glenwood Springs soon became the county seat. The mineral springs and the natural scenic beauty of the region were attractions destined to make Glenwood Springs famous. In the vicinity, along the valleys of the Colorado River and the Roaring Fork, farming and fruit growing were successfully developed.

Following the Meeker massacre of 1879 General Merritt established a military camp on White River, some four miles above the ruined agency. Buildings of adobe, brick and logs were built around a square parade ground. After the removal of the Utes, the post was abandoned, and residents of the valley purchased the property. The military post became a town, which was christened Meeker in honor of the murdered Indian agent. The town was incorporated in 1885, and when Rio Blanco County was organized in 1889, Meeker was chosen as the county seat.

The site of Steamboat Springs lay beyond the boundary of the Ute Reservation and the beginnings of a town were made at this point before the Ute removal. James H. Crawford was the pioneer of Steamboat Springs, having claimed the site in 1874. The promising location and the presence of hot mineral springs that suggested the name for the town, attracted settlers who developed the agricultural and stock raising resources of the region. Down the Yampa Valley to the westward, ranches were taken up, some of which were to develop into important towns such as Craig and Hayden.

In southwestern Colorado important changes were occurring in the eighties. Ranch claims had been taken up on the Animas River and other branches of the San Juan during the middle seventies, at the time when mining development was attracting such great attention to the mountains of that region. But during the seventies, little progress was made in the La Plata County region because of its remoteness and inaccessibility. The coming of the Denver and Rio Grande railroad speeded developments. Durango was founded in September, 1880. The railroad reached the new town in July, 1881. The presence of large coal veins and the favorable location of the city in reference to the mines of Silverton, Ouray, Rico, and Telluride led to the erection of important smelting works at Durango.

To the eastward, on the upper reaches of the Rio San Juan, the Pagosa hot springs early attracted attention. First settlers came in 1876 and the town of Pagosa Springs soon developed. In 1885 the region was formed by the legislature into Archuleta County.

The Montezuma Valley of far southwestern Colorado, which had first been occupied as a winter grazing range for cattle herds, received its first actual settlers in 1881. On the Mancos and Dolores, ranches were developed at about the same time. The greater growth of the Montezuma Valley awaited construction of large irrigation canals to bring water from the Dolores River. Cortez was founded in 1886, and when Montezuma County was established in 1889, this city became the county seat.

While the valleys of western Colorado were blossoming forth with farms and cities, other sections of the state were advancing with equal strides. The construction of large-scale irrigation projects was one of the factors which accounts for much of this improvement. In fact, the development of large irrigation projects was one of the chief features of the period of the eighties. Irrigation had been the basis for farming in the valleys of the Rio Grande, the Arkansas and the Platte since the days of first settlement, but the early developments were on a small scale. In the first period—during the fifties and sixties—the irrigation ditches were generally built by individual farmers to water small claims on the bottom lands beside the streams. The second period—in the seventies—witnessed the cooperative effort of members of a community uniting to build larger ditches to supply their own district. The canals built by the Greeley colony and others were typical of such community enterprises. Then followed the third period of irrigation development, characterized by the building of great projects by corporations. Although a number of fairly large canals had been constructed previously under the leadership of such men as George W. Swink, Benjamin H. Eaton and others, it was the decade of the eighties which saw the greatest activity in the development of the large irrigation projects.

In the Cache la Poudre valley several important canals were built in this period.* The North Poudre ditch was begun in 1880 and the Larimer County Canal the following year. These canals supply 35,000 and 52,000 acres respectively. From the South Platte proper a number of large irrigation canals were taken during this decade. Famous among these was the Highline Canal, which draws its water from the Platte near the mouth of Platte Canyon and meandered originally for 95 miles out onto the high plains to the east of the river. It commands nearly 100,000 acres, but receives insufficient water for the full area. Just north of Denver is the headgate of the 80-mile Burlington Ditch,

*The data here given was furnished by the State Engineer's office.

built in the middle eighties and enlarged in 1908, which supplies 75,000 acres. Farther down the river are the Fort Morgan and the Bijou canals, built in the eighties.

The valley of the Arkansas witnessed great irrigation development during the same period. In 1884 the Fort Lyon Canal was begun. It is the longest in the state—105 miles long—and is capable of irrigating 120,000 acres. The 48-mile Catlin Ditch, built the same year, carries water to the Rocky Ford region. The Bessemer Ditch, heading west of Pueblo, and the Amity Canal, with headgate near Manzanola, were begun in 1887.

The waters of the Rio Grande are carried to the level acres of the San Luis Valley by large canals built in the eighties. About 1881 the largest canal in the valley and one of the largest in the state was begun. This ditch, which has come to be known as the Rio Grande Canal, heads at the town of Del Norte and carries water to 120,000 acres. The Monte Vista Canal was begun in 1882 and the San Luis and Empire canals in 1885. Two years later the Farmers' Union Canal was constructed to cover an area of 76,000 acres.

The Montrose and Delta Canal of 1883, diverting water from the Uncompahgre, and the Grand Valley Canal of 1888, leading water from the Colorado, were large canals built on the Western Slope during this period. Each was capable of watering about 35,000 acres. A large project was launched by J. W. Hanna in the Montezuma Valley of southwestern Colorado in 1885, water being diverted from the Dolores River through tunnel and ditch into the Montezuma Valley about Cortez.

Some of these large irrigation systems of the eighties were entirely new constructions, while others represented the enlargement and extension of existing canals or the consolidation of several minor ditches. In any case these projects entailed large investments, and the bringing in of capital from outside of Colorado was in most cases necessary.

Prominent among the corporations building irrigation systems was the Northern Colorado Irrigation Company, commonly known as the "English Company," which constructed the Highline Canal and others from the South Platte and its affluents. T. C. Henry promoted irrigation development and induced a subsidiary of the Travelers Insurance Company to make investments in irrigation projects in the Arkansas, Rio Grande, and Uncompahgre valleys. Many of these large enterprises were not at first financially successful, but the projects were fundamentally sound and almost without exception ultimately justified the investments. And regardless of immediate returns, they rank in Colorado history as projects of great importance to the state.

The irrigation projects of the eighties brought about the development of hundreds of new farms, and the influx of settlers gave rise to towns and cities. In the valley of the Platte east of Greeley and on the Arkansas below Pueblo, this development was most noticeable and far reaching.

At the site of Camp Wardwell (later Fort Morgan) a number of ranches had been taken up in the '70s, but it was not unitl 1884 that the town of Fort Morgan was begun on the site of the abandoned United States military post. The city was incorporated in 1887 and as the surrounding territory developed, the improvement was reflected in the growth of the new city. Upon the creation of Morgan County in 1889, Fort Morgan was chosen as the county seat. Brush was begun in 1882. At first it was but a station on the newly built Burlington railroad, but irrigation development made it the center of a productive agricultural area.

We have noted in a previous chapter the beginnings of Old Sterling in the early seventies. The present Sterling, on a new site, owes its founding to the coming of the railroad and the building of irrigation canals. The site was laid out and platted by M. C. King in 1881 and the city was incor'porated three years later. Being a railroad division point and located in a rich agricultural and grazing area, it soon developed into an important business center. It was chosen the county seat of Logan County when this county was created in 1887.

The present town of Julesburg arose at the railroad junction where the Denver branch of the Union Pacific takes off from the main line. The site was platted in 1884, the city incorporated two years later. When Sedgwick County was formed in 1889, Julesburg was made county seat.

The founding and growth of cities and towns along the Arkansas correspond with irrigation development in this river valley. In 1877 the first Rocky Ford, near the river, had been replaced and largely transferred to its present site on the railroad line. The town remained little more than a station until 1886, when George W. Swink platted a larger area and attracted incoming settlers.

Although La Junta had been founded in 1875, upon the coming of the Santa Fe railroad, its first years witnessed but halting progress. When the railroad was extended to Trinidad and New Mexico, however, La Junta became an important junction point. The town was incorporated in 1881. When Otero County was created in 1889 La Junta became the county seat.

Las Animas, one of the oldest towns of the Arkansas Valley, had gained its first prominence as a stock center and had developed into an important shipping point during the middle seventies. Agricultural activity during the following decade furthered the growth of the city and the development of the surrounding country.

Lamar is one of the youngest important cities of the state. It was founded in 1886 and incorporated the next year. Prior to the middle eighties the Arkansas Valley in the Lamar district was practically undeveloped, but the building of large irrigation projects changed all this and converted the region into one of the most productive areas of the state. It also led to the formation in 1889 of Prowers County, of which Lamar became the county seat.

While the development of large irrigation projects was transforming the river valleys of the state and giving rise to new towns and counties, a somewhat different type of development was begun on the non-irrigable plains of eastern Colorado. Onto this region, now known as the dry farm area, came homesteaders during the middle eighties. The choicest lands of Kansas and Nebraska had been taken up and as the frontier moved westward the land-hungry farmers advanced into Colorado.

For a time the big cattle companies tried to keep them out. In fact the cattle owners had fenced large tracts of the public land in their effort to hold it as grazing country. But when the farmers appealed to President Cleveland he responded in April, 1885, by issuing an executive order requiring all persons and corporations to remove their fences from the public domain. The order, though grudgingly complied with, threw open the land for occupation by the homesteaders. The president's order had an important effect in promoting the development of the dry farm area of Colorado.

The newcomers fenced their homesteads, built primitive sod houses or board shanties, and turned with their plows the virgin prairie sod. Most of the homesteaders came from the Middle West, bringing with them the farming methods of that area of ample rainfall. They were ill-prepared to deal with the new conditions of a semi-arid region, but fate was at first kind, the years of the middle eighties being blessed with an unusual abundance of rain.

Farmers were encouraged. Land speculators and promoters sang with ample voice their songs in praise of the new "rainbelt." The railroads joined heartily in the chorus, and newspapers published the libretto. In a Burlington railroad pamphlet of 1887 we read: "The rain belt has moved westward to within less than eighty miles of Denver. . . . So much rain now falls in the eastern portions of Colorado that it is no longer fit for a winter range for cattle. . . . What has brought about this great change cannot be accurately determined." In the same year a representative of a Denver newspaper visited the "rainbelt" and reported the region filling up rapidly. "The condition of the people in these new sections is gratifying in the extreme," he writes. "They have raised sufficient to feed them through the winter and have some to sell. The corn and all else was grown upon the sod but with results that far exceeded the most sanguine anticipations of the veterans who have seen the development of Kansas and Nebraska."

The influx of homesteaders created a need for trade centers and the new settlers were anxious for community life. Townsite companies responded to the situation, platting towns at suitable intervals along the railroad lines. Water tank stations grew into villages; hopeful towns sprang from the prairie.

In the northeastern section of the state some promising towns were founded along the Burlington railroad. Akron had been surveyed and laid off by the Lincoln Land Company in 1882, but the site was practically vacant until 1886,

when the general immigration began. The town was incorporated in 1888. Yuma was surveyed in 1885 and a town
grew up about the water tank and station house. Wray
was laid off the following year. Laird was begun in 1887
and Eckley two years later.

The Lincoln Land Company surveyed and platted
Holyoke in 1887 and the town was incorporated the following year. Haxtun was begun in 1888. Cheyenne Wells
had been a stage station on the old Smoky Hill route, and
became a railroad station when the Kansas Pacific crossed
the plains in 1870. Kit Carson and Hugo owe their rise
to the railroad, the former being an important shipping point
for the southern Colorado and New Mexico trade in the
early seventies.

Eads, Arlington and other towns were begun in 1887
along the newly built track of the Missouri Pacific. To the
northward, on the route of the Rock Island, the town of
Burlington was laid off the same year by the Lowell Town-
site Company. Other towns sprang up along the track as
the Rock Island rails were pushed across the plains in 1888.
When farmers began to crowd in upon the cattlemen on the
plains to the south of the Arkansas, the beginnings of Spring-
field and other towns were made in this far southeastern
portion of the state.

Surrounding these various prairie towns and constitut-
ing the chief excuse for their existence, were the farm houses
and plowed acres of the homesteaders. The plains were being fenced and converted into farms at an amazing rate and
a general hopefulness prevailed in the plains country. With
the large immigration of farmers, the abundance of rainfall,
and the coming of new railroads, an optimism developed
which carried the legislature with it and resulted in the
creation of eight new counties on the eastern plains of the

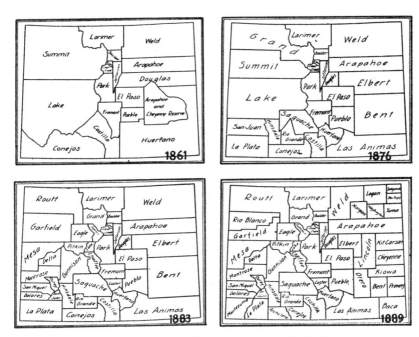

STAGES IN THE CREATION OF COUNTIES

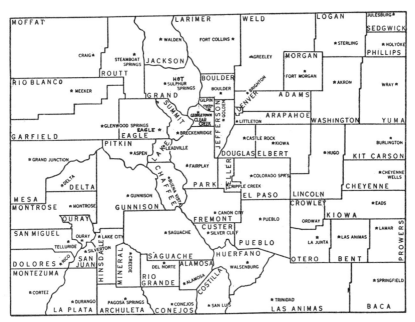

COLORADO'S SIXTY-THREE COUNTIES IN 1932

1. IRRIGATING AN ORCHARD IN MESA COUNTY
2. IRRIGATION CHECK ON RIO GRANDE, SAN LUIS VALLEY

state. Washington County was formed in 1887, the other
seven—Phillips, Yuma, Lincoln, Kit Carson, Cheyenne, Kiowa, and Baca—were created in 1889. These counties (with
the exception of Baca, which had no railroad) were so
carved as to secure a distribution of the railroad mileage,
for upon the railroad the new counties were expected to
lean heavily in carrying the tax burden of schools and county
administration. Dry farming development, so promisingly
begun in the middle eighties, was soon, however, to meet
with discouragement and even disaster.

Although agriculture during the eighties was rapidly
coming to the fore in Colorado, it had not yet displaced
mining as the leading industry of the state. Gold continued
to be mined in slightly larger quantities than in the previous
decades but the amount of this precious metal was being
dwarfed by the greater production of silver. Even the value
of the lead produced was exceeding that of gold, the average
value of lead being over five million dollars per year, while
that of gold was less than four millions. But during this
decade of the eighties silver had an undisputed preeminence,
the value of the output averaging over $14,000,000 per
year. With silver as king, Colorado was coming to be
known as the "Silver State."

The pioneer mining counties of the state, Gilpin and
Clear Creek, continued through the '80s as consistent producers of the precious metals, each contributing approximately two million dollars per year. Leadville continued
through the decade as the principal mining center of the
state, although its production gradually diminished, Lake
County's total decreasing from approximately fifteen millions in 1880 to eight millions in 1890. To the older mining
districts of the '60s and '70s, there were added fresh sources

of wealth by the opening of new mines in the '80s. This development resulted in the rise of new cities and the formation of four additional mining counties during this decade. In 1869 some good prospects had been opened at the present site of Rico, but there was little development during the succeeding decade. When in 1879 ore from the famous Nigger Baby Hill proved to be lead carbonate, bearing silver, an important camp developed and the town of Rico was begun. The first freight brought by wagon to the new town was a saw mill and the press for the *Rico News,* which arrived in the fall of 1879. The Grand View smelter began operations the following year. The development of this locality brought about the creation of Dolores County in 1881 and Rico became the county seat.

Some placer mining had been done on the San Miguel River in the middle seventies and prospectors from Ouray and Lake City soon discovered rich lodes in the rugged mountains at the sources of the stream. Telluride, beautifully nestled in the lap of these high mountains, was begun in 1878 and developed into the center of mining activity of the region. It was designated the county seat when San Miguel County was organized in 1883.

Mining claims were staked at various points along the Eagle River in 1879. The town of Red Cliff was begun in July of that year, George Stevens opening one of the first stores with a jackload of goods brought from Leadville. The following year a smelter was built by the Battle Mountain Mining and Smelting Company. Eagle County was created in 1883 and Red Cliff was made the county seat.

Encouraged by the rich finds at Leadville, miners prospected on the Roaring Fork of the Colorado in 1879 and made important mineral discoveries. The following year when development of the mines began, the city of Aspen was founded. The next year Pitkin County was created with Aspen as county seat. During 1880-81 ore from some of the mines was transported to Leadville by pack trains at a cost of four cents per pound. With freight costs so high and the region so inaccessible, no extended progress was made until 1887, when the first railroad was completed to Aspen. This important event was duly celebrated with a parade and with fireworks and huge bonfires on the neighboring moun-tain peaks. By the close of the year Aspen had a population of 5,000, which continued to mount as the mines poured forth their wealth of silver. Says the historian, Frank Hall, "It became the handsomest, most substantial and attractive mining town in the Rocky Mountains, and gave promise of surpassing all others in the aggregate value of its mineral yields."

Large well-equipped school buildings, fine churches, an opera house, excellent hotels, three banks, three daily and three weekly newspapers, and water and electric light sys-tems reflected the wealth and progress of the city. The min-eral belt extended from the Taylor Range on the south to the Frying Pan Gulch on the north, the principal mines being located on Aspen and Smuggler mountains. The re-nowned Mollie Gibson mine was one of the richest prop-erties, the average yield of its ore being 600 ounces of sil-ver per ton. One 24-ton car of ore yielded $76,500. Dur-ing the last years of the eighties the mines of Pitkin County were producing over $6,000,000 per year. As Leadville production decreased, that of Aspen increased, until in 1892 the production of Pitkin County exceeded that of Lake County and trebled that of any other county in the state. Prosperity reigned in the district, and Aspen boomed until silver received its body blow in 1893.

Closely associated with mining progress was the development of smelting works in Colorado. Leadville, Denver, Pueblo, and Durango became the chief smelting points, but many plants were operated at other places during the '80s. In 1878 the Grant Smelter and the Harrison Reduction Works had been built at Leadville and during the same year the Hill smelter at Black Hawk was moved to Argo Junction near Denver. In 1880 ten or twelve smelters were operating at Leadville, three at Golden, the Greene smelter at Silverton, the Crooke at Lake City, the Grand View at Rico, and small plants at Tin Cup, Gothic, and other camps.

In 1882 the present Durango smelter was opened; the Grant smelter was built at Denver, the Mather and Geist plant at Pueblo, and a lead smelter at Aspen. The Eilers plant was built at Pueblo in 1883, the Globe smelter at Denver in 1886, and the Philadelphia plant of the Guggenheim brothers at Pueblo in 1888. Dr. Richard Pearce and others invented new methods and devices to improve smelting methods. The old arrastre and stamp mill of the pioneer years was replaced by complicated machinery and elaborate chemical processes.

The earliest smelters had burned charcoal in their furnaces, but as this fuel became scarce and expensive, coal took its place. The excellent coking coals of the Trinidad region were found to be especially suitable for use in the smelters. Although coal had been found and used by the early settlers, the output was small during the first years. With the coming of the railroads in the seventies, the production of coal rose with the increased demand, from 13,500 tons in 1870 to 462,000 in 1880. In 1882 it passed the million mark, and by 1890 over 3,000,000 tons of coal were being mined per year. This was worth approximately $2 per ton at the mine during the '70s and '80s. Las Animas County was the largest producer, about 1,000,000 tons per year being mined in this county during the late '80s. At the same period, Boulder, Fremont, and Huerfano counties were contending for second place, as each produced more than 300,000 tons per year. The Walsenburg and Trinidad regions, now so important in coal production, had gained their first prominence as cattle and sheep country. A few farmers had settled in the upper valleys of the Purgatoire, Huerfano, and on the various affluents of these streams during the sixties and early seventies, and some of the ranches had developed into towns. With the coming of the Denver and Rio Grande and the Santa Fe railroads in the late seventies, the large coal deposits were made available, and coal production began to assume great proportions.

Trinidad had been founded in the early sixties, but its growth was very slow for more than a decade. The town was organized in 1877. With the coming of the Santa Fe railroad in 1878, marked development began and continued during the eighties. Substantial residences and business houses were built; banks and newspapers were established; a water system, gas works, and a street car system were instituted.

The coming of the Denver and Rio Grande railroad in the middle seventies was a great boon to Huerfano County. The rich coal fields were developed. Walsenburg sprang into life and became the business center of the region. In Fremont County, Rockvale and Coal Creek supplied coal for the needs of Pueblo. In the region north of Denver, the towns of Lafayette, Louisville, Marshall, and Erie developed during this period as a result of coal mining activity. Anthracite coal beds, about Crested Butte in the Gunnison country, were opened in the eighties.

Closely associated with coal is the manufacture of iron

and steel, which has come to be of considerable importance in Colorado. There had been some little manufacture of iron in Colorado in the sixties, but the important develop' ment began at Pueblo in 1880. In this year the Colorado Coal and Iron Company (later the C. F. & I.) began con' struction of the Minnequa Steel Plant at Pueblo. A num' ber of coal mines were acquired and operated by this com' pany, which was to develop into the largest producer of coal and steel west of the Mississippi River.

The steel plant, the smelters, and the railroad connec' tion with Leadville transformed the little town of Pueblo into a thriving industrial city, and brought about nearly an eight fold increase of population from 1880 to 1890.

The political history of Colorado during the eighties was not particularly unlike that of the preceding decade. The Republican party was normally in control, but a schism developed in its ranks between the adherents of Senator Teller and Senator Hill which occasionally enabled Demo' crats to win over the divided opposition. The Greenback Party appeared in the state during this decade and though never strong enough to elect its nominees, sometimes held the balance of power between the two major parties.

In the election of 1880 Governor Pitkin was reelected and Congressman Belford, the brilliant orator, was returned to Washington. Senator Teller resigned his seat in the senate in April, 1882, to accept the position of Secretary of the Interior in President Arthur's cabinet. He was the first Coloradan to be honored by a place in the President's Cabinet. To succeed Teller in the senate Governor Pitkin appointed George M. Chilcott of Pueblo, a former Dele' gate to Congress for Colorado Territory. He held the of' fice until the state legislature took action at its next session.

In the election of 1882, the highly-esteemed Democratic nominee for governor, James B. Grant of Leadville, was elected, but the Republicans won the other state offices and secured a majority in the General Assembly. Horace A. W. Tabor, the wealthy mining man and philanthropist, was finally chosen by this Assembly to succeed Senator Chilcott for the remainder of the term (about thirty days) and Judge Thomas M. Bowen of Del Norte was elected for the full term beginning March 4, 1883.

Although the Democrats were successful nationally in 1884, and elected Grover Cleveland president, the Republicans won in Colorado. Benjamin H. Eaton, of Weld County, a farmer and a builder of great irrigation canals in northern Colorado, was elected governor and George G. Symes, a prominent attorney of Denver, was sent to Congress. In the General Assembly, convening in January, 1885, a contest between Teller and Hill for the senatorship was decided in favor of Senator Teller. The schism between these two outstanding leaders continued, and contributed in 1886 to the defeat of the Republican candidate for governor and the election of Alva Adams of Pueblo as chief executive of the state. Governor Adams was a young man of thirty-six, whose industry and integrity brought him to public favor. Congressman Symes was returned to Washington. The Republicans recaptured control of the state in 1888; Job A. Cooper, a banker of Denver, being elected governor, and Hosea Townsend of Custer County, Congressman. When the legislature convened in January, 1889, Edward O. Wolcott, destined for a brilliant career in the Senate, was elected to succeed Senator Bowen in the upper house of Congress.

The remarkable growth of Colorado during the '80s was apparent on every hand. From 1880 to 1890 the value

of assessed property in the state had trebled, the number
of farms had quadrupled, railroad mileage had almost trebled,
and capital invested in manufacturing had increased six
fold. The population of the state increased from 194,327
in 1880, to 413,249 in ·1890, or well over 100 per cent.
The growth of the larger cities was even in excess of that
of the state at large. Denver increased from 35,629 to 106,-
713—three fold; Pueblo from 3,217 to 24,588—nearly eight
fold; and Colorado Springs, Trinidad, Greeley, and Fort
Collins approximately doubled in population. A number of
cities, such as Salida, Durango, Grand Junction, Montrose,
Glenwood Springs, Aspen and others had come into a thriving existence. The growth of the state was also reflected
in the new counties created. Twenty-four counties came
into being during the decade, to be added to the thirty-one
already in existence. The state was forging rapidly ahead
and the future looked promising.

✦ ✦ ✦

SELECTED REFERENCES FOR FURTHER READING

J. C. Smiley, History of Colorado, 693-710.
Frank Hall, History of Colorado, III, 33-130.
Baker and Hafen, History of Colorado, 698-711, 907-915.
Steinel and Working, History of Agriculture in Colorado.
C. W. Henderson, Mining in Colorado (1926)
The Trail (1908-1924)
Colorado Magazine: "Early Days at Paonia" (Mar., 1927); "Early Days of
    the Telephone in Colorado" (Aug., 1928); "Yuma" (April, 1928);
    "The Founding of Dolores" (April, 1928); "A Sketch of Delta County
    History" (Oct., 1928); "The Founding and Early Days of Grand Junc-
    tion" (March, 1929); "The Founding of Steamboat Springs" (May,
    1929); "Early History of Lamar" (July, 1929); "The Founding of Du-
    rango" (May, 1930); "An Argonaut of the Roaring Fork" (Nov.,
    1930); "Denver Fifty Years Ago" (March, 1931); "History of Fort
    Lewis" (May, 1931); "Gunnison in Early Days" (July, 1931); "Pa-
    gosa Springs, Colorado" (May, 1932); "The Mission of Colorado Toll
    Roads" (Sept., 1932); "Pioneer Days in the Upper Arkansas Valley"
    (Sept., 1932); "Gunnison in the Early Eighties" (Nov., 1932); "Pio-
    neering at Akron" (Sept., 1931); "Trekking to the Grand River Valley
    in 1882" (Sept., 1931)
Rocky Mountain News; Denver Republican; Denver Tribune

CHAPTER XIV

DAYS OF DISTRESS

Panic and Hard Times of the Early Nineties

THE decade of the nineties opened with apparent promise. The production of the silver mines was greater than ever before, averaging over $20,000,000 per year from 1890 to 1893. Though the price of silver had been gradually declining during the eighties the large bodies of rich ore unearthed at Aspen, Leadville, and elsewhere enabled mining to be carried on at a profit. Then the passage in 1890 of the Sherman Act with its provision for large purchases of the white metal by the Government, temporarily brought up the price of silver.

There occurred at this time one of the important silver discoveries of Colorado, one which inaugurated a spectacular rush and mining boom. N. C. Creede, an old-time prospector, struck a promising mineral vein on the headwaters of the Rio Grande in the spring of 1890. Further development and additional discoveries revealed a rich field, and a new mining camp burst upon the world with all the vigor of a bonanza.

The town of Creede squeezed itself into the narrow winding canyon of Willow Creek. Fresh pine-board shanties sprouted up from the base of the rock cliffs, clinging like lichens to the solid rock walls. Furniture and kegs of beer, hauled in by big freight wagons, were dumped in the new camp; mining tools and drygoods boxes, ore wagons, and men jostled each other for space in the crowded, winding street.

The great rush which began in 1891 continued with boom proportions for two years. "The Last Chance" and "The Amethyst" were among the rich properties which yielded their millions. The extension of the Denver and Rio Grande railroad was built to the camp in the fall of 1891. One observer wrote in January, 1892: "The train when it comes is a sight to behold, the smoking car being an especial marvel. It is jammed. Men sit on one another, and on the arms of the seats, stand in the aisles and hang on the platforms. Pipes, blankets, satchels form the major part of their equipment. . . . The saloons and dance houses are in full blast and *such* dance houses as they are, and *such* discarded remnants as the old fairies who flaunt around them never were seen before. Along in the morning when the wheezy accordion lets up, the time is occupied by a riot. . . . There are a few bad men in Creede and many who are reckless."

Cy Warman, "the poet of the Rockies," launched his newspaper, the *Creede Chronicle,* in the roaring camp. In one of the issues he ran this famous descriptive stanza:

> Here the meek and mild-eyed burros
> On mineral mountains feed—
> It's day all day in the daytime,
> And there is no night in Creede.

Business generally throughout the state appeared to be thriving at the beginning of the '90s. Trade was active, money plentiful, prices were stable. Several large manufacturing undertakings were being launched. The Hitchcock Woolen Mills began operating at Denver in May, 1891; the Overland Cotton Mills set its spindles to play in July; and the Denver Paper Mills started operations in August. The Denver Steel Company was organized during the same year with an imposing directorate and elaborate plans for a great enterprise. In Denver the real estate business was flourishing in 1891; building was being pushed with vigor. Large business structures and handsome homes were giving the capital city an air of metropolitan stateliness. The Brown Palace Hotel and the Equitable Building, with architectural magnificence that was the pride of Denver, were occupied in August, 1892. Numerous palatial residences raised their imposing forms on Capitol Hill.

Pueblo was becoming the thriving metropolis of the southern portion of the state. There, on July 4, 1891, the dazzling Mineral Palace was formally opened. This was designed to house a permanent exhibit of Colorado minerals and also to furnish a place of public entertainment.

The early nineties saw a monumental State Capitol rise on Capitol Hill, Denver. The initial steps for such a building had been taken some years before. In 1868 Henry C. Brown had deeded to Colorado the two city blocks on which the capitol now stands. Upon admission to statehood Colorado had received fifty sections of land from the federal government as an aid to the erection of state buildings at its capital. Various private donations were received and in 1881 the state legislature established a mill levy to create a building fund for a capitol building.

By popular vote in the same year Denver was definitely fixed as the state capital. A Board was appointed. Legislation enacted in 1885 provided that a capitol be built of stone at a cost of not more than $1,000,000. A contract was made and some preliminary work was begun, but when difficulties arose the contract was cancelled. White sandstone had at first been chosen for the structure, but popular protest against this material induced the legislature in 1889 to decide in favor of granite. With plans settled and ob-

stacles removed, construction began. The cornerstone was
laid with due ceremony on July 4, 1890. The building was
occupied by the Governor in 1894 and by the legislature
the following January, though it was not fully completed
until 1900. The ultimate cost of the capitol was about $3,-
000,000.

The building is of Corinthian style, with ground plan
in the form of a Greek cross. The massive walls are of
solid, gray granite, quarried near Gunnison, and the imposing dome is covered with genuine gold leaf. The interior
trimmings are of lacquered brass, and of rare Colorado onyx
resplendent in unique and variegated colors. Sitting on the
brow of a low hill the capitol overlooks the business section
of Denver and dominates the entire city.

The seeming prosperity at the beginning of the nineties
did not extend to all portions of the state nor to all classes.
The cloud of misfortune rested most heavily over the eastern
plains of Colorado. We have related in the preceding chapter how hopeful farmers had flocked onto those plains in the
middle eighties, how unusually abundant rains during two
or three seasons had elated the new homesteaders and led to
the establishment of aspiring towns and the creation of numerous counties in the "rainbelt" area.

But, as in Pharaoh's dream, the fat years were followed
by lean. Summers of extreme drought succeeded the seasons
of abundant rainfall. Crops shriveled and died, as hot dry
winds scorched the prairie. A second, a third season of
drought brought disaster and financial ruin to the dry farmers. Many deserted their homesteads and left the state.
The young, recently-hopeful towns dwindled in size until
whole counties were almost depopulated. The future looked
dark indeed for the farmer on the plains.

Although the dry farmers were Colorado's most unfortunate class as the decade of the nineties began, there were other elements in the population with grievances. The boom of the eighties with its enlarged profits for business, had led to undue speculation and extravagant expenditures. Men borrowed beyond all reasonable expectations of their ability to repay. During the same period improved methods of pro' duction and the use of new inventions led to over-production and brought on a gradual decline in prices of commodities. The man in debt, receiving a decreasing price for his product, became discouraged or angered and began to demand relief. This was especially noticeable in the new agricultural West. A tariff wall afforded some protection to manufacturers, but the farmers, who had been taking up western land at a rapid rate, were producing more of the staple foods than the country could consume. Prices for agricultural products dropped to unheard-of levels and the farmers who had bor' rowed capital to provide buildings, machinery, fencing, and such needs, found themselves in straitened circumstances. Facing financial ruin they were in a mood to listen to any plan advanced as a panacea for their economic ills.

Farmers' Alliances, organized during the eighties, to labor for some form of relief, grew and spread rapidly. All over the country discontented farmers aired their grievances and voiced their demands in a series of meetings which cul' minated in the formation of the "People's Party," or "Popu' lists," at Cincinnati, Ohio, in 1891. A call was then issued for a regular national convention to meet at Omaha the following year to launch a political campaign.

In the meantime the silver question was pushing itself to the fore. In order to understand the problem, so momen' tous in Colorado history, one must know something of its historical background. Our currency system, devised in the days of President Washington, had provided for bimetallism, i.e., the coinage of both gold and silver. Free and unlimited coinage had continued until 1873, when the government stopped the coinage of silver dollars. (This act was in later years called "the Crime of 1873"). About this time the output of silver in the United States increased. The market price of the white metal began to drop. The western mining states demanded "free coinage" of silver—the right to have coined into money all the silver they might bring to the mint. They wanted the old ratio of sixteen ounces of silver to one of gold to be restored and fixed. Western Congressman fought for free coinage but secured only a compromise measure, the Bland-Allison Act of 1878, whereby the Secretary of the Treasury was directed to buy from two million to four million dollars' worth of silver and to coin it into dollars. This helped the price of silver somewhat, but the great output from Colorado, supplemented by that from other silver-producing states, so increased the supply that the price gradually declined despite the government purchases.

During the eighties silver was Colorado's most important product. The prosperity of the state was largely built upon it. Further decrease in price, which would mean the shutting down of mines and a consequent blow to the prosperity of the state, therefore was of serious concern to Colorado. Agitation continued for free coinage of silver. Colorado newspapers advocated the cause; speeches were made and pamphlets issued in its favor. A silver Convention met at Denver in 1885. Soon thereafter the Colorado Silver Alliance was formed. The National Silver Convention met at St. Louis in 1889, at which Colorado was represented by a large and aggressive delegation. Free coinage should be given precedence over all other political questions and over party fealty, the delegates contended. Representatives in

Congress from western silver-producing states formed a bloc in behalf of silver. They threatened in 1890 to kill the Mc-Kinley Tariff Bill unless Congress granted them free coinage of silver. Senator Sherman and other Congressional leaders, while opposed to free silver, realized that concessions must be made. The outcome was another compromise measure, known as the Sherman Act of 1890. This provided for the purchase of 4,500,000 ounces of silver per month by the United States Government, which amount was thought to be about the aggregate production of the mines of the coun-try. The passage of the Sherman Act, to the joy of Colo-radans, immediately sent up the price of silver to over a dollar an ounce, but a decline soon set in again when the supply was found to exceed the government purchases and the demands of private business.

As the price of the white metal again began to fall, silver advocates renewed their efforts. Silver clubs were formed throughout Colorado until they numbered over two hundred in 1892. These were federated into the Colorado State Sil-ver League, with its members including adherents of all parties.

As the political pot began to boil in 1892 it became evi-dent that many Coloradans were far more interested in free coinage of silver than in the success of any particular party. The state delegations to both major national conven-tions in the summer of 1892 worked strenuously to place strong silver planks in the party platforms, but both the Re-publicans and Democrats sidestepped the issue with evasive statements. However, the Populist Convention, meeting at Omaha July 2, 1892, came out with a vigorous free silver plank in its militant platform which bristled with all the mooted reforms of the day. Thus the party that had origi-nated with Farmers' Alliances and discontented laborites

made a successful bid for the support of the growing partisans of free silver.

Late in July a State Convention of the new-born Populist Party met in Denver and placed in the field a ticket
headed by Davis H. Waite of Pitkin County for Governor.
Most of the Silver League men went over to the Populists,
some of the silver Republicans followed, and an open rift
in the Democratic ranks ultimately resulted in the majority
of that party going over to the Populists. The Denver *News*
and a large proportion of the state press supported the new
party. The regular Democrats, or "White Wings," being
without an organ started the Denver *Evening Post*, which
two years later was to be taken over by Messrs. Bonfils and
Tammen who were to build it into the most widely circulated paper of the state.

The fact that both Benjamin Harrison and Grover
Cleveland, Republican and Democratic presidential candidates respectively, were opposed to free silver induced many
voters to turn to the new third party. Thus it was that the
radical Populists, through espousal of free silver and because of disaffection in the ranks of the major parties were
swept into political control of Colorado by the election of
1892. The Populist triumph was complete. For the first
time in its history the Republican ticket in Colorado was
defeated in *toto*. John C. Bell and Lafe Pence were sent to
Congress by the new party.

When John L. Routt gave over the Governor's chair
to Davis H. Waite in January, 1893, the price of silver was
still on the decline and business was in a dangerous condition. Over-expenditure during the preceding decade had produced an unsound economic condition in the country generally, and added to this was a financial apprehension on the
part of the moneyed classes that the heavy government pur-

chases of silver and the popular demands for cheap money would result in a replacement of the gold dollar by a depreciated silver dollar or by another issue of greenbacks. Invested capital would thus lose a part of its value.

As spring advanced, business began to tighten; uneasiness became more apparent. The gold reserve in the United States Treasury sank to the danger point. President Cleveland fought frantically to maintain it at the accustomed figure of $100,000,000. Commercial houses began to fail, banks contracted their loans, speculators dumped their holdings on the falling market. In May there was a stampede for safety. In June the report that the mints of India had ceased the coinage of silver sent the price of that metal to new depths. In four days silver dropped from 83 cents an ounce to 62. This was a great blow to Colorado. The leading mine and smelter owners of the state announced that they must close their mines and smelters until a recovery in the silver price would permit profitable operations.

A monster mass meeting convened at Denver July 11th and 12th to discuss the situation. Speakers painted lurid pictures of the disastrous results that would follow the crisis. Shrinkage of property values and the plight of debtors were especially alarming. Governor Waite, imbued with Populist principles, spoke vigorously as champion of the poor man. One of his sentences received widespread notoriety: "It is infinitely better that blood should flow to our horses' bridles rather than our national liberties should be destroyed." (Thereafter some referred to the Governor as "Bloody Bridles" Waite.) This and other immoderate utterances when circulated through the press gave the impression in some quarters that wholesale repudiation of debts or revolution threatened in Colorado.

The panic broke in full fury in mid July. People

swarmed the streets. They stormed the banks amid scenes of wild disorder. In three days ten banks closed in Denver alone, while throughout the state banks came down with a crash. Numbers of other business houses went to the wall. The real estate bubble in Denver burst, and building and loan associations went bankrupt. Men who were considered wealthy suddenly found themselves empty-handed. The goods of the merchant and the manufacturer were in small demand. Economy was forced upon households that had almost forgotten its meaning.

The closing of mines and the contraction of business resulted in the discharge of thousands of workers. These began to drift into Denver and soon the army of unemployed and money-less men brought serious public concern. Robberies and holdups were common; a brutal murder and a lynching in Denver gave rise to further apprehensions. Various bodies joined to take organized measures; a relief camp was established under military regulations, where tents, bedding and food were provided for the 10,000 destitute men. Gradually detachments of the jobless entrained to seek employment in the East.

The Panic of 1893 was general throughout the United States and the world. It closed one of those recurring economic cycles that have punctuated our history at approximately twenty-year intervals. While various factors already mentioned contributed to the unhappy result, Easterners quite generally pounced upon the Sherman Silver Purchase Act as the chief cause of the debacle. President Cleveland called a special session of Congress for August 7, 1893, to repeal the measure. This made matters look darker still for Colorado, the chief silver-producing state. Senators Teller and Wolcott exerted themselves to the utmost to stem the tide, but to no avail. (The law was repealed Nov. 1, 1893.)

In a final speech, when his cause was lost, Senator Teller said to the Senate: "We do not disguise the fact that we are to go through the valley of the shadow of death. We know what it means to turn out our 20,000 silver min' ers in the fall of the year. We know what it means when every man in the state who has a little money saved, must put his hand in his pocket and draw it forth to keep from starving." This gloomy forecast did not fully materialize but it was not far from the truth.

The first shock of the panic was followed during the autumn by continued depression. Unemployment persisted, business was at low ebb, and the processes of foreclosures and attachment were oppressing their victims. Governor Waite decided to call an extra session of the legislature in an attempt to devise some remedy. But the legislature could do little to help. It passed measures reducing the legal rate of interest and the penalties on delinquent taxes; extended the time for redemption on foreclosures; and exempted cer' tain wages and earnings from attachment for debt. Most of the Governor's recommendations were not enacted. The most notorious of these was that the State purchase the out' put of Colorado silver mines, ship it into Mexico, and there have it coined into dollars which were to be returned to Colorado and here be placed in circulation. But the scheme for "Fandango Dollars" was not adopted.

The Populist Governor, honest, sincere and headstrong, was thoroughly distrusted by many and was looked upon as radical and erratic. His political career was hectic, his diffi' culties legion. No sooner had the legislature adjourned (March 2), than he became embroiled in a conflict with the Fire and Police Board of Denver. Both sides resorted to armed enforcements, cannon were trained on the City Hall, and there was grave danger of a clash of rival forces. Fed'

eral troops from Fort Logan were brought upon the scene.
Business men and the courts intervened and finally put an
end to this "City Hall War" before actual bloodshed occurred.

At the same time a strike was on in the new mining
camp of Cripple Creek. (The rise and development of this
camp will be discussed in the next chapter.) Miners struck
against the lowering of wages, demanded an eight-hour day
and recognition of their Union. The first difficulties occurred
in February and March but broke out again in May. The
sheriff of El Paso County with a posse of deputy sheriffs
attempted to arrest some of the leaders of the strike. The
Governor, whose sympathy was with the striking miners,
sent detachments of the State militia to the scene and for a
time a clash was imminent between the militia and the sheriff's posse. There were charges and counter charges, demonstrations by miners and by the sheriffs, and attempts at ar-
bitration by public spirited citizens. The troubles continued with some acts of violence until in June, when the miners' demands were finally acceded to.

In late June, 1894, the Pullman Strike, begun near
Chicago, extended to the railroads of the country. When it
took effect in Colorado, transportation was largely para-
lyzed for about two weeks. Injunctions were issued by the
Federal Court. All the United States troops in Colorado
and a large force of deputy marshalls were on duty to bring
the strikers to trial and prevent the interruption of the mails.
While this was going on there was a widespread strike
among coal miners of the state, who attempted to join with
the railway strikers. In Pueblo and Trinidad these troubles
were most serious.

Hard times continued throughout 1894 for practically
all classes in Colorado. Business failed to show material

GOVERNORS OF COLORADO, 1876-1901
1. John L. Routt.   2. Frederick W. Pitkin.   3. James B. Grant.   4. Benjamin H.
Eaton.   5. Alva Adams.   6. Job A. Cooper.   7. Davis H. Waite.
8. Albert W. McIntyre.   9. Charles S. Thomas.

COLORADO WOMEN PROMINENT IN THE 1890s
Upper: Mrs. W. N. Byers, Mrs. H. A. W. Tabor, Mrs. N. P. Hill
Middle: Mrs. Frances Jacobs, Mrs. J. B. Belford
Lower: Mrs. Sarah Platt Decker, Mrs. M. D. Thatcher, Mrs. E. M. Ashley

improvement and unemployment continued. There was much unrest and considerable lawlessness, for men hungry and idle are not inclined to be peaceful. Some of the unem-ployed suggested a general march on Washington to demand relief, the most famous embodiment of the proposal being the organization and march of "Coxey's Army." Contin-gents to aid in this demonstration were formed in Colorado. Some constructed boats and attempted to float down the Platte River, but the venture ended in failure. Other par-ties went east by the railroads. Nothing, however, came of their efforts for national relief.

As the year 1894 wore on and the political campaign in Colorado got under way it was evident that Governor Waite and Populism were being roundly blamed for the bad state of affairs. A vigorous campaign was waged both for and against the Governor. The Republicans, declaring they would "redeem the State from the odium and evil conse-quences of Populist misrule," won most of the offices on elec-tion day, naming Albert W. McIntyre, Governor and send-ing John F. Shafroth to Congress.

In this election the women of Colorado exercised for the first time the elective franchise, and placed three of their number in the General Assembly. A large majority of the women voted the Republican ticket, which they looked upon as favoring law and order. Woman suffrage had come in Colorado only after long and continuous labor in its behalf. The early efforts in Colorado date back to the sixties. Governor Evans in 1868 and Governor and Mrs. McCook in 1869-70, worked for equal suffrage, but the Territorial legislature after some consideration refused to adopt it. The state constitution, adopted in 1876, made provision whereby women might vote in school elections. The first General Assembly of the State submitted the suffrage question to the voters at the general election of 1878, but it was defeated. The question was revived in the 1880s and gradually gained in favor. Sarah Platt Decker and others active in woman's club work and the equal suffrage movement, worked for the reform. The proposal, again submitted to the voters, was adopted in 1893. Colorado was the second state in the Union to admit women to political equality, Wyoming having been the first.

Practically every Colorado legislature since has had one or more woman members; the Superintendent of Public Instruction has uniformly been a woman; but otherwise women have occupied but few state offices. In general the woman vote has not been cast as a unit but has divided itself in about the same proportion as has the male vote. In humanitarian and welfare legislation, however, women's influence has been felt; the creation of the State Home for Dependent and Neglected Children, the State Industrial School for Girls, the Workshop for the Blind, the Training School for Mental Defectives, the Child Welfare Bureau, the State Bureau for Child and Animal Protection, has come largely through woman's activity.

The inauguration of Governor McIntyre in January, 1895, put an end to the Populist state government, but this remarkable third party elected a plurality to the State Senate and maintained control of several counties. The Populists continued to be an influence in the state and played a prominent part in the notable silver campaign of 1896.

In general, Governor McIntyre's administration was one of reconstruction and was free from friction. The most serious problem with which he had to deal was the Leadville Strike of 1896. The Western Federation of Miners attempted to secure the adoption of a $3.00 wage scale for the Leadville district, and upon refusal of the mine operators to concede, a strike was called on June 19th. Over two thousand miners left work, mining was suspended, the pumps stopped, and many valuable properties were flooded. Negotiations were opened between the two parties but no agreement was reached. At first there was no lawlessness nor disorder, but by August trouble was brewing. The mine managers began to negotiate for new men to take the places of the strikers, while the latter began to picket the roads and the mines and intimidate "scabs" who were willing to work.

In late August work was resumed at the Coronado Mine, despite the attempts of striking miners to prevent it. On September 21st a mob of strikers attacked this mine with rifles and bombs and set fire to the buildings. Several men were killed in the fighting. The Emmett Mine was then attacked. Mine owners appealed to the Governor and the entire National Guard was sent to the scene. This had an immediate quieting effect, but the troops were retained to prevent further outbreaks. The strike continued, but gradually, under protection of the troops, the owners were able to employ new men. Finally, after nine months' duration, the strike collapsed on March 9th. It had resulted in a loss to the state in wages, production, and business generally of several million dollars.

The continuance of hard times that followed the panic of 1893 caused many to turn to free silver as a panacea. The movement was given great impetus by the publication and wide circulation of W. H. Harvey's *Coin's Financial School*. This unique little volume of imaginary lectures and telling illustrations presented the case of bimetallism simply and in a way that appealed strongly to those who had little of this world's goods. It made hundreds of thousands of converts to the silver cause. A series of conferences throughout the country in behalf of silver culminated in the creation of the National Silver Party in 1896. Coloradans took a prominent part in the movement.

In the meantime the Democratic and Republican parties were being rent by the silver issue. When the National Republican Convention, meeting at St. Louis in June, 1896, nominated McKinley for President and placed a gold plank in its platform, an open breach developed in the party. Senator Teller, leader of the Colorado delegation, bolted, and followed by 34 other delegates from western states, walked out of the convention. In the National Democratic Convention in Chicago, partisans of bimetallism were in the majority and forced the adoption of a platform declaring for free coinage of silver at the ratio of 16 to 1. The "silver-tongued orator from the Platte," young William Jennings Bryan, swept the delegates into raptures with his famous "cross of gold" speech and received the nomination for president. Democrats favoring the gold standard re-assembled and placed another ticket in the field. The Populists and the National Silver parties in their national conventions endorsed Bryan and free silver. The campaign began at once; the great "Battle of the Standards" was on.

In Colorado the silver issue disrupted the major parties. Senator Teller and his supporters refused to follow the national Republican party, and organized the Silver Republican Party. Various attempts at cooperation among the parties finally resulted in the fusion of the Democrats and Silver Republicans on the one hand and the Populists and National Silver parties on the other, both combinations, however, endorsing Bryan and free silver. The McKinley Republicans placed a ticket in the field but it received slight support. The main fight in the state was between the Democratic-Silver Republican ticket headed by Alva Adams for

Governor and the Populist-National Silver party with M. S. Bailey for Governor. Adams and his entire state ticket were elected.

Although Colorado went almost solidly for Bryan and free silver, McKinley and the gold standard won in the nation at large. This defeat appeared as the death knell of free silver. Some of the more optimistic continued to hope for a return of bimetallism, but their hopes were destined to dwindle or die. Colorado, struck down by the blow to silver, had to struggle to her feet and achieve a reconstruction without dependence on the stimulus of an attractive silver market.

✦ ✦ ✦

SELECTED REFERENCES FOR FURTHER READING

Frank Hall, History of Colorado, IV; 360-468
Baker and Hafen, History of Colorado, 887-893, 915-924
J. C. Smiley, History of Colorado, 710-727
W. F. Stone, History of Colorado, 840-847
Charles Hartzell, History of Colorado During the Reign of "Davis the First" (1894)
W. H. Harvey, Coin's Financial School (1894)
J. W. Bookwalter, If Not Silver What? (1896)
O. C. Lightner, History of Business Depressions
Colorado Magazine: "A Populist Newspaper of the Nineties" (May, 1932)
Rocky Mountain News; Denver Post; Denver Republican; Denver Times

CHAPTER XV

THE TURN OF THE CENTURY

Recovery and Reorganization

THERE was one bright spot in the shadow that rested over Colorado in the early nineties—Cripple Creek. The site of the future great gold camp, a little south-west of Pikes Peak, had been previously prospected at various times but nothing promising had been revealed. In the late eighties it was a lonely cattle ranch. Robert Womack, one of the cowboys, did a little prospecting as he rode the range. His companions laughed at his persistent searching, but off and on he picked up pieces of float rock that encouraged him and finally, early in January, 1891, he discovered a promising vein. The find set him wild. He rode to Colorado Springs to celebrate his success and proclaim his discovery.

The early spring of 1891 saw many prospectors on the ground, and summer brought speculators and town-site promoters. On July 4th W. S. Stratton staked out the Independence claim, which was to raise him from poverty to affluence. Other mines were discovered. A mining district was organized in the fall. Bennett and Myers platted a town-site in October, calling it Fremont. The next year it was incorporated under the name of Cripple Creek. Other camps, later to become towns, sprang up in the region. The gold production from the district passed the half million mark in 1892 but this was only the beginning. Each of the two succeeding years saw over two million gold dollars poured into the channels of trade to absorb some of the shock from the disastrous panic and the silver collapse. Even yet the district had not found its full stride. The output trebled in 1895. This stream of gold was a potent factor in starting rehabilitation and producing a hopeful outlook for Colorado. The wealth from this richest gold camp in the United States continued to mount. The totals climbed in the succeeding years by millions, from seven to ten, thirteen, sixteen, and then to eighteen million dollars in 1900. During the succeeding decade an average of about $15,-000,000 in gold was mined annually. The Independence and the Portland mines and the Mary McKenny holdings were among the richest and most far-famed properties, each giving forth its millions. The rich ground of the district was soon honeycombed with miles of tunnels; with drifts and crosscuts. The latest and most improved machinery was employed and smelters were kept busy handling the ore.

During these years Cripple Creek was a bustling metropolis. From the disastrous fires of 1896 she quickly emerged on a grander scale. Handsome business blocks, hotels, banks and all the features of a modern city soon appeared. Newspapers and telegraph and telephone lines carried the news of the camp's development to an anxious world. Mills and smelters were built at Florence, at Colorado City, and at Victor; while Colorado Springs, Pueblo, and Denver began to reflect the luster of Cripple Creek gold.

Although the production from Cripple Creek district eclipsed that from other sections of the state, the other mining regions are by no means to be ignored during the late nineties. Deeper mining and the completion of large tunnels helped the old districts. New mines were discovered and worked. During the five year period preceding 1900 the mines of Lake County, with their gold, silver, lead and copper produced on the average nine million dollars per year, while those of Pitkin County averaged about four millions. During the same period Clear Creek, Gilpin, Mineral, Ouray, San Juan and San Miguel counties were each producing precious metals valued at from one to four million dollars annually. The total annual metal production of the state mounted from 32 millions in 1895 to 50 millions in 1900—the figure for 1900 being the highest in the history of the state.

During the late nineties there was a noticeable improvement in nearly all lines of endeavor. People were regaining their confidence and launching new enterprises. Crops generally were bountiful. Prices improved. Fruit production on the Western Slope was assuming large proportions. As reservoirs were constructed to store water for irrigation purposes, more land was brought under cultivation. Farmers were cautiously beginning to reoccupy the deserted dry farms on the eastern plains. Real estate in the cities and towns was beginning to recover its lost value, and business generally was showing signs of prosperity.

The inventory of Colorado as revealed in the census of 1900 was encouraging. As regards population, Colorado made a rather notable showing. Despite the losses through migration from the state during the hard times of 1893-5 the population showed an increase of 30 per cent over that of 1890, the figure rising from 413,249 to 539,700. The country at large in the same period had made an increase of but 20 per cent. During the decade the farms of the state had doubled their irrigated acreage, the value of livestock on the farms, the amount of capital invested in manufacturing, and the output of the factories had each more than doubled. In practically all lines, except silver production, substantial gains were shown for the decade.

Upper: BIRD'S-EYE VIEW OF CRIPPLE CREEK
Lower: BENNETT AVENUE, CRIPPLE CREEK, JULY 4, 1895

COLORADO GOVERNORS, 1901-1915
1. James B. Orman.   2. James H. Peabody.   3. Jesse F. McDonald.
4. Henry A. Buchtel.   5. John F. Shafroth.   6. Elias M. Ammons

The great free silver issue during the early nineties, as noted previously, had brought about new political alignments in Colorado. It caused rifts in parties and made fusion of factions necessary for victory at the polls. It resulted in the switching of many Republicans—including such leaders as Teller, Shafroth, and Ammons—to the Democratic Party.

The successive fusion tickets which centered upon the Democratic Party as a core, won political supremacy in Colorado in the elections from 1896 to 1902, naming three Democratic governors in turn—Alva Adams, Charles S. Thomas, and James B. Orman. Then in 1902, with the disappearance of the Silver Republicans and the separation of the diminishing Populists, the two old parties faced each other again. The Republicans now proved themselves the stronger and elected James H. Peabody as Governor. Henry M. Teller, veteran Colorado senator, continued through these years to represent Colorado in the Senate. Edward O. Wolcott, distinguished Republican senator, ended his second term in 1901, when the Democrats succeeded in replacing him with Senator Thomas M. Patterson. In the lower House of Congress John F. Shafroth and John C. Bell, Democrats, represented Colorado until 1903 when they were replaced by three Republicans—Robert W. Bonynge, Herschel M. Hogg and Franklin E. Brooks.

Politically, the course of events during these years maintained a fairly even tenor. There were vigorous campaigns and heated contests to be sure, but no far-reaching upheavals such as characterized the period of the middle nineties. The outstanding occurrence of Governor Alva Adams' administration was the Spanish War. Upon receiving news of the declaration of war with Spain the Governor organized a regiment of Colorado volunteers under

command of Colonel Irving Hale—Colorado's first gradu-
ate from West Point (where his record is exceeded only
by that of Robert E. Lee). These troops were soon sent to
the Philippines, where they distinguished themselves in engagements with both the Spanish troops and the Filipinos.
Some Colorado men joined the "Rough Riders" and saw
action in Cuba, while others who were sent east failed of an
opportunity to participate in the fighting. Upon returning from the Philippines in the fall of 1899 the Colorado
troops were met by Governor Thomas in San Francisco, and
received a rousing welcome upon their return to Colorado.

Public interest in the money question waned at the
close of the nineties. Not only was Cripple Creek sending
forth its millions in gold but the discoveries of the yellow
metal in South Africa and the Klondike were so augment-
ing the volume of the world's gold supply that money became more plentiful and prices rose. This condition took
the wind out of the sails of silver advocates to such an extent that when the United States passed the Gold Standard
Act of 1900 there was comparatively little protest. Even
Colorado appeared reconciled to the gold standard.

For years Denver had been a pawn in state politics,
the governor and legislature having direct control of its
municipal affairs. This condition was unfortunate both for
the state and its capital city, and to abolish it "Home Rule"
was advocated. The proposal also included the consolidation of city and county government, permitting the abol-
ishment of duplicate offices, and provided for annexation of
Berkeley, Montclair, and other small adjacent municipalities to Denver. The plan was adopted as an amendment to
the state constitution— Article XX—which created the
"City and County of Denver," and gave it political independence in municipal matters.

After a charter was framed and accepted, the new form of government went into effect in 1904. The election of Robert W. Speer as the first mayor under the new arrangement, inaugurated a period of a decade or more of great achievement and outstanding improvements for Denver. Parks were expanded and beautified, a boulevard and parkway system created, modern playgrounds established, the number of shade trees greatly increased, streets improved, viaducts constructed and storm and sanitary sewers extended. The ugly bed of Cherry Creek, long used as a dumping ground for rubbish, was walled and parked, and converted into the most beautiful boulevard of the city. A great auditorium was built, an impressive civic center created, while sculptured monuments and decorative fountains rose to grace the city. Reaching westward into the hills, she acquired an extensive area of beautiful mountain parks and made them accessible by winding roads and pleasure drives.

Other cities of the state were made more attractive and substantial by public and private improvements too numerous to detail here. Most of the cities showed marked growth during the decade ending in 1910. Although Leadville dropped from 12,455 to 7,508 and Cripple Creek from 10,147 to 6,206 the cities dependent primarily upon agriculture and manufacturing showed encouraging increases. The population of Denver rose from 133,859 in 1900 to 213,381 in 1910; Pueblo from 28,157 to 44,395; Colorado Springs from 21,085 to 29,078; Trinidad from 5,345 to 10,205; Boulder from 6,150 to 9,539; Fort Collins from 3,053 to 8,210; Greeley from 3,023 to 8,179; Grand Junction from 3,503 to 7,754.

The early years of the 20th century saw serious and widespread labor troubles in Colorado. A strike of gold miners at Telluride began in May, 1901, the strikers' object being to abolish the contract system by which wages were being reduced. The contest developed in July into a conflict between the Western Federation of Miners and the non-union men. Blood was shed and the non-union men were driven from Telluride. A settlement was effected which provided for an eight-hour day and for abolition of the contract system.

Discrimination against union men in the ore-reduction plants in Colorado City brought about a strike in March, 1903. This in turn led to a sympathetic strike of miners in Cripple Creek. After a month's interruption, negotiations resulted in a settlement on March 31st. In May, 1903, gold miners at Idaho Springs struck for an eight-hour day. About the same time a fruitless strike for an eight-hour day occurred at the Grant and Globe smelters at Denver. In San Miguel County in September a strike brought about an eight-hour day but with reduced wages.

A strike was declared at Cripple Creek on August 10, 1903, which took more than 3,500 men from work and developed into the most serious labor trouble of the period. Charles H. Moyer and William D. Haywood, officers of the then powerful Western Federation of Miners, directed the strikers' activity. The strike was to extend to most of the metal and coal mines of the state and result in a general tie-up of the mining industry. As destruction of property and outrages to persons continued, the National Guard was called to Cripple Creek in early September.

Troubles continued through the winter and spring of 1904, culminating in a dynamite explosion at Independence station in the Cripple Creek District on June 6th. Thirteen non-union men were killed and others badly wounded. This horrible deed, attributed to the strikers, wrought the community and state into a frenzy of excitement and brought about a demand for retaliation. The state militia under Adjutant General Sherman Bell, again assumed control of the district. All the prominent leaders of the strike and many of the rank and file were rounded up, placed in railroad cars and deported to Kansas or New Mexico with a warning never to return. Though the deportations gave the strikers a public sympathy they had not before enjoyed, the strike was broken by the forced exodus of union men and the control by the military. The open shop and the card system were established. During the same months of 1903-4 similar troubles had occurred in Telluride. There were clashes, arrests, and deportations before peace was finally restored in November, 1904.

In November, 1903, a strike occurred in the coal fields of the state, over 10,000 miners leaving their work. Through the "United Mine Workers of America," their union organization, they were asking for an eight-hour day and for the correction of certain grievances. The strike in the northern field (Boulder County) was settled November 28th, but in the southern field (Las Animas and Huerfano Counties) it continued to grow more serious. Clashes between the strikers and the deputy sheriffs guarding the mines resulted in a number of casualties. In March, 1904, Governor Peabody sent in troops of the National Guard. Deportations of strike leaders followed during April and May and the strike collapsed.

The strikes and Governor Peabody's handling of the resulting problems became the political issues in the campaign of 1904. Peabody was renominated by his party and Alva Adams was placed in opposition by the Democrats. Adams apparently won, and duly assumed his office as governor. But the election was contested by the Republicans. The fight was carried to the General Assembly. To end the contest a peculiar compromise was arranged. Peabody was to be seated on condition that he immediately resign and thus be succeeded by Lieutenant Governor Jesse F. McDonald, Republican. By this unusual settlement Colorado had three different governors within twenty-four hours.

A schism in the Democratic party between the adherents of Senator Patterson and of Mayor Speer of Denver, resulted in a Democratic defeat in the campaign of 1906 and the election of Henry A. Buchtel, Chancellor of Denver University, as Governor on the Republican ticket. The General Assembly, overwhelmingly Republican, retired Senator Patterson and sent Simon Guggenheim to the Senate. The course of Governor Buchtel's administration was smooth and without extraordinary events. The "Wall Street Panic" of 1907 led to a currency shortage in Colorado and to a slowing up of business activity, but the effects were comparatively slight in this state. In the same year a law was passed requiring the examination of state banks and the submission of reports to the State Bank Commissioner. Under the stabilizing influence of the measure the State banks showed rapid growth.

In the election of 1908 the Democrats elected John F. Shafroth governor, secured control of the General Assembly, and were thus enabled to elect their candidate, Charles J. Hughes, to the United States Senate. Senator Hughes succeeded Senator Teller, who now (1909) retired from political life after a long and honored career of public service. Governor Shafroth was re-elected in 1910 and his party retained control of the General Assembly. Under Governor Shafroth's administration the state constitution was amended (1910) to provide for the Initiative and Referendum, which gives the people the power of direct legislation. A primary election law also was passed (1910), which was designed to cure the abuses of the prevailing convention system. Neither of these reform measures, however, proved to be quite the panacea its advocates promised. One of the outstanding achievements in Colorado during the first decade of the 20th century was the development of the beet sugar industry. Back in the days before there was a Colorado, petitioners for a Mexican land grant in 1841 advocated the growing of sugar beets on the land they asked for—the Maxwell Grant in present New Mexico and Colorado. But after getting the land they appear to have made no effort to grow beets. In the middle sixties Peter Magnes of Littleton and L. K. Perrin on Clear Creek planted the first sugar beets in Colorado. They were enthusiastic about the possibilities of the new crop. J. F. L. Schirmer made laboratory tests of the beets and found the quality and the sugar content high. Agitation followed for the building of a sugar factory, but the necessary capital was not forthcoming. A bill in the Territorial legislature of 1872, providing a subsidy of $10,000 to the first sugar factory in Colorado, failed of enactment by one vote.

During the '80s the Agricultural College joined in the movement for sugar beet development. In 1892 a sugar convention was held in Denver. On the Western Slope Charles E. Mitchell advocated the building of a factory at Grand Junction. Charles M. Cox promoted this enterprise, the Mesa County Commissioners voted a subsidy, John F. Campion, Charles Boettcher and others gave financial support, and the first sugar factory in Colorado was erected and put into operation at Grand Junction in 1899. The following year factories were established at Rocky Ford and Sugar City. The factory erected at Loveland in 1901 was followed the next year by plants at Greeley and Eaton and in 1903 by factories at Fort Collins, Longmont and Windsor. The industry was now on its feet and well on the way to remarkable success. Six of these factories were consolidated in 1905 as the Great Western Sugar Company, destined to be the largest operator in Colorado. (It controls in 1933 thirteen of the eighteen factories in the state.)

The sugar beet industry was a great boon to Colorado. It diversified and intensified agriculture. Its by-product, pulp, promoted the business of livestock feeding and indirectly improved the market for hay and grain. Sugar beets yielded profitable returns to the farmer, furnished employment for laborers, and produced a good income to the owners of factories. The sugar industry brought new money from the outside and promoted the general prosperity of the state.

The introduction of the sugar beet crop promoted development in irrigation engineering. Sugar beets, like potatoes, require irrigation in the late summer when the natural streams are running low. The acreage of such crops being limited by the water supply, it was necessary to secure more water before extensive production could take place. The demands of the situation resulted in the building of many reservoirs to impound the high water of early spring and permit release of it in time of need in the late summer.

The reservoir development had begun in the eighties and nineties, prompted by the need for late water in the growing of alfalfa and potatoes. After 1900 it was greatly extended. An aid in the process was the enactment, by the General Assembly, of the "District Irrigation Law" of 1901. This authorized land owners to establish irrigation districts whereby canal systems could be jointly purchased, and reservoirs and ditches be constructed for the irrigation

of their land. They were empowered to issue bonds to obtain money for these joint projects, and to levy a tax on the
land to pay the interest and principal. Under this law the
water users in many districts have purchased their large irrigation systems.

Many of the private irrigation projects put through
in the eighties had gone bankrupt during the hard times of
the nineties. Practically all of these large projects constructed by outside capital have passed into the hands of
the owners of the lands served by these systems. "These
now are operated by mutual ditch companies formed by the
landowners, who obtain water for irrigation at cost, while
their canals are exempt from taxation."

To regulate the distribution of water for irrigation the
General Assembly provided for the appointment of a State
Engineer and subordinate engineers and divided the state
into Irrigation Divisions and numerous water districts.
Through this system priority rights to water are strictly
enforced and its equitable distribution safeguarded.

Among the first large reservoirs in Colorado were the
Terry Lake, the Windsor, Long Pond, Lake Loveland—all
constructed in the Greeley-Fort Collins region during the
nineties. Since 1900 the South Platte drainage area has
witnessed construction of the Fossil Creek, Union, Jackson
Lake, Riverside, Empire, Jumbo, Standley Lake, Antero,
and other such reservoirs which impound millions of cubic
feet of water for the irrigation of thousands of acres of
new land.

In the Arkansas Valley the "Great Plains Storage System" with a capacity of nearly 300,000 acre feet was constructed in the late nineties by W. M. Wiley. Since 1900
the Horse Creek, Adobe Creek, and other reservoirs have
greatly increased the available water supply of the region.

The big Rio Grande Reservoir on the headwaters of the Rio Grande, with a capacity of 46,000 acre feet, was completed in 1913. In addition, there were completed in the San Luis Valley, between 1911 and 1914, other reservoirs with an aggregate capacity of 220,000 acre feet. On the Western Slope, irrigation projects have been completed which have reclaimed thousands of acres. Waters from the Colorado, Gunnison, White, Yampa, Dolores and various affluents of the San Juan are being impounded for the thirsty acres of western Colorado. Perhaps the most famous project in this region is the Gunnison Tunnel, which carries water from the Gunnison River through the Vernal Mesa to the Uncompahgre Valley by a six-mile tunnel. The plan for such a tunnel was broached in the early nineties. In 1901 the General Assembly appropriated $25,000, with which a line for the tunnel was located and the work initiated. The Federal Reclamation Service, established in 1903, made a study of the proposed tunnel which resulted in the taking over of the project by the Reclamation Service. The drilling of the long bore was begun from each side of the mesa in 1905. In 1909 the two crews met. On September 22d of that year the tunnel was formally opened by President Taft. The water from this tunnel irrigates about 80,-000 acres in the Uncompahgre Valley. The project cost approximately $3,000,000.

The census of 1910 showed that during the preceding decade the value of investments in irrigation works in Colorado had multiplied five fold and the irrigated area had been increased by over one million acres, or nearly 75 per cent.

An interesting phase of recent irrigation development is the utilization of the "return water" which seeps from irrigated uplands back into the main stream beds. One of the ill effects of this seepage was to make swampy certain bot-tom lands near the streams, but subsequent drainage sys-tems have reclaimed much of this "sour" land. The return water has come to be a considerable item, and special can-als and reservoir systems have been built to utilize it. This is especially noticeable and duly taken advantage of in the valleys of the Platte and the Arkansas. It is estimated by John E. Field, C.E., that the water of the Platte is used three times in Colorado and once in Nebraska before it reaches the Missouri.

The dryfarming area of eastern Colorado was the scene of renewed activity in the first decade of the 20th century. Farms deserted in the late eighties, some of which had been reoccupied and again forsaken in the nineties, were again put under cultivation. Pioneering on the plains had been hard and disheartening and while a few sturdy and perse-vering homesteaders had managed to sustain themselves through the years of drought, a majority in many sections had given up in despair, left their farms to revert to open range and their shanties to tumble and decay.

But through trial and error, through experiments con-ducted by the Agricultural College and the Federal Govern-ment, knowledge was gradually gained. Certain drought-resisting crops were found and evolved; a system of tillage was developed which conserved the moisture. Fortified with this knowledge, and furnishing themselves with dairy cows, poultry, and hogs for the utilization of their crops, these farmers mixed "brains with their soil" and won a measure of success.

An indication of the development in the dry farm region is given by comparing the population statistics of the 1910 census with those of 1900. For example, Kiowa, Kit Carson, Washington, Yuma, Lincoln, and Cheyenne Counties showed increases ranging in an ascending scale from 313 per cent in Kiowa to 635 per cent in Cheyenne for the ten year period. The remaining agricultural sections of the state also showed very substantial growth. In the valley of the South Platte the population increases for Larimer, Weld, Morgan, Logan and Sedgwick Counties ranged from 107 to 215 per cent; in the Arkansas Valley, for Bent, Otero, and Prowers Counties, from 60 to 153 per cent; and on the Western Slope, in Montrose, Mesa, and Delta Counties, from 126 to 149 per cent for the decade.

For the state as a whole the value of farm property trebled in those ten years and the annual value of farm products (exclusive of livestock) increased from less than seventeen million dollars in 1900 to over fifty millions in 1910. The population of the state rose from 539,700 to 799,024, an increase of 48 per cent. The net increase of 259,324 was greater than for any other decade in the history of the state. The decade 1870-80, with an increase from 39,864 to 194,327 showed a greater proportional increase but a smaller net gain than did the first decade of the 20th century.

With the formation of the Progressive Party and the consequent split in the Republican ranks in the nation, the Democratic ticket in Colorado, headed by E. M. Ammons for Governor, won an easy victory in 1912. Ex-Governors Shafroth and Charles S. Thomas were elected United States Senators (Senator Hughes having died in January, 1911), and Edward T. Taylor, Edward Keating, George J. Kindel and H. H. Seldomridge were elected Congressmen.

Governor Ammons' administration was tormented throughout with turbulent strikes in the coal mining districts of the state. The strikers demanded recognition of

their union, a wage increase, and certain reforms. The miners formed tent colonies in which they and their families
lived. Mining property and railway stations were picketed,
assaults and assassinations occurred and the Governor, re-
sponding to numerous requests, mobilized the National
Guard and sent detachments to the disturbed areas. As time
passed the situation grew more tense, both sides more determined to win.

Several collisions occurred between strikers and detachments of soldiers, the most notorious taking place at
Ludlow station, eighteen miles from Trinidad. Here was
a strikers' colony housing about 900 men, women and children. On April 20, 1914, a clash occurred between the
militia and the camp and a number of persons were killed.
The incident was most unfortunate. Magnified or misrep-
resented in various quarters throughout the country, described as a massacre of women and children, it brought
appeals to organized workmen to rescue the imperiled miners.
The whole country, greatly disturbed, watched developments with the keenest interest. As difficulties continued,
the distraught Governor finally appealed to President Wilson for federal troops to take control of the situation. With
the arrival of the United States soldiers the tension was immediately relieved, law and order were re-established and
the mines gradually assumed their normal activities.

The strike and liquor prohibition were the paramount
issues in the fall campaign of 1914. The Republicans succeeded in electing George A. Carlson as governor and in
winning most of the state offices. The Democratic national
ticket was successful except for Congressman in the 2d
District. The prohibition amendment to the State Constitution was ratified, the measure to take effect January 1,
1916.

With the inauguration of Governor Carlson's administration, strike conditions virtually ceased and the federal
troops were soon withdrawn from Colorado. Laws were
passed by the General Assembly early in 1915 designed to
aid the cause of labor and prevent strikes. The "Industrial
Commission of Colorado" was created. It was instructed to
investigate the causes that lead to strikes, was given regula-
tory power intended to improve the conditions of labor, and
was authorized to arbitrate in cases of disputes between em-
ployers and employes, with a view to preventing strikes or
lockouts. A Workmen's Compensation law was passed, providing for laborers' insurance against accidents or death.

John D. Rockefeller Jr., one of the large owners of
property in the field where the principal strikes had occurred,
made an inquiry into the causes of the strike difficulties.
After considerable investigation he evolved a policy whereby
all interests were given representation, unions were not an-
tagonized, and non-union men were safeguarded.

One of the notable recent changes in Colorado has
been brought about by the introduction and rapidly growing use of the automobile. The odd looking horseless bug-
gies that began to appear in Colorado in 1900 were at first
looked upon as curiosities rather than as vehicles of practical use. The earliest of these carriages that frightened the
horses and amused the children were propelled by electric
storage batteries or by steam, but very soon gasoline-burn-
ing motors came into use and this type gained rapidly in
favor. They were to develop into our automobile of today.
They were to bring an end to the big horse-ranches so numerous and prominent in Colorado. They were largely to replace the bicycles then so popular with all classes. Soon
the bicycle clubs, the impressive bicycle parades and excit-
ing races would pass from the scene.

COLORADO'S FIRST AUTOMOBILE SALESROOM, 1900
The Locomobiles and Bicycles shared space in Felker's Display
Room, 16th Street, Denver

AUTOMOBILE PARADE AT MOUNTAIN AND PLAIN FESTIVAL,
DENVER, 1901

BEET SUGAR FACTORY AT BRIGHTON

By 1902 complaints were being made that the new-
fangled automobiles were being driven recklessly about the
city streets. On January 15th of this year, the first arrest
in Denver for speeding was made. Although the automo-
bilist said he was traveling but eight miles an hour, the po-
liceman protested that he must have been going at the rate
of forty miles. The motorist was fined $25 and costs. Thus
was inaugurated the now flourishing business of traffic
control.

In 1903 the first endurance automobile race in Colorado was held. The run was from Denver to Colorado
Springs. Eighteen cars entered the race and six were able
to finish. During the summer of this year the first transcontinental automobile trip was accomplished, two months
being required for the trip from the Pacific to the Atlantic
coast. Following trails and making roads over mountain
ranges and sand deserts was then a feat of skill and perse-
verance. When the twelve horse-power, one-cylinder tour-
ing car reached Littleton it was met by a cavalcade of fifteen automobiles and escorted into Denver. "The ride into
Denver was a corker," says a newspaper of the day. "As
the roads were rather dusty, the appearance was of a drove
of cattle hustling along the highway. . . . A local car took
the lead for the passage through the city, having a man
standing up and shouting: 'There they are—the across-the-
continent wagon'."

During the succeeding decade the increase in the number of automobiles was comparatively slow. The exact figures for early years are not available, but when the first
state registration took place in 1913 there were found to be
but 13,135 automobiles in the state. Today the number is
well over 300,000.

In 1902, forty-two automobilists met in Denver, formed

the Colorado Automobile Club, and launched a campaign for better roads. Pursuant to a call of Governor McDonald a convention met in July, 1905, and organized the Colorado Good Roads Association. At the meeting of the Associa' tion the following year a bill was drawn up for a State Highway Commission, but such a measure was not enacted by the General Assembly until 1909. This first highway law provided only a meager appropriation of $50,000 per year. But in 1913 the accumulated Internal Improvement Fund of $766,311 was given to the Highway Commission. Then too the first law was passed providing for the licensing of cars, and the resultant fees were made available for road improvements. A new Highway Act reorganized the de' partment and provided more funds. The great period of highway construction and improvement was now ushered in.

✦ ✦ ✦

SELECTED REFERENCES FOR FURTHER READING

J. C. Smiley, History of Colorado, 728-758
Frank Hall, History of Colorado, IV, 102-107, 468-476
Baker and Hafen, History of Colorado, 734-739, 924-947
W. F. Stone, History of Colorado, 533-545, 579-584, 847-876
E. F. Langdon, The Cripple Creek Strike (1904)
E. D. Wright, A Report on Labor Disturbances in Colorado, 1880-1904
    (1905)
Colorado Magazine: "The Coming of the Automobile and Improved Roads
    to Colorado" (Jan., 1931); "The Story of Cameron" (Sept., 1932);
    "Raising the Stars and Stripes Over Manila" (Mar., 1932)
Denver Post; Rocky Mountain News; Denver Republican; Denver Times

CHAPTER XVI

THE WORLD WAR AND AFTER

War-Time Conditions and the Reconstruction Period

THE World War, outstanding event of the first quarter of the nineteenth century, had its effect on Colorado. Within a few months after its outbreak, while prices rose, money flowed freely, and wages mounted, while farmers, stockmen and manufacturers reaped rich profits, Colorado was basking in a new and bountiful prosperity.

Along with the re-election of Woodrow Wilson to the Presidency in 1916, the Democratic party was victorious in Colorado. Judge Julius C. Gunter was elected Governor, while the state's delegation in Washington remained unchanged. Governor Gunter, a gracious gentleman of the Old School, rose to war-time demands with prompt and effective leadership. He immediately called able and patriotic leaders to comprise a Council of Defense, the first organization of the kind in the country. Immediate action was taken to protect property in the state and measures were inaugurated for the conservation of all possible resources.

An extra session of the legislature—the first such action in the Union—was called to convene in July, 1917, to enact measures to meet the emergencies of war. A tax on corporations was levied for a "Defense and Emergency Fund." A bond issue was authorized to prepare the state for defense and provide for the prosecution of the war. In July, 1917, the Governor mobilized the National Guard. The following month these troops, comprising 4,482 officers and men, largely equipped at state expense, were mustered into the federal service. Detachments of troops were placed on duty guarding important public utilities of the state, such as dams, reservoirs, tunnels and factories.

Since European war experience had proved the efficacy of the draft, the United States adopted the system within a month after our declaration of war. The machinery was immediately set in motion. John Evans, grandson of Colorado's second Territorial Governor, was appointed Provost Marshall for Colorado, and seventy-five local selective draft, or exemption, boards were created. On June 5, 1917, the first registration took place, to be followed in June and September, 1918, by second and third registrations. A total of 215,635 men between the ages of eighteen and forty-five were registered in Colorado. These men were all classified by the draft boards as to eligibility for war service. The first call under the selective draft came in July, 1917, and at frequent intervals thereafter additional calls were made. While a great army was being built up by means of the draft, active recruiting was being carried on, and many of Colorado's young men volunteered, enlisting in various branches of the army and navy.

It is practically impossible to trace the Colorado troops into the fighting lines and to detail their service. In the World War the nation at large was the fighting unit, and state lines were largely ignored. Colorado men were to be found in almost every camp and cantonment in the country. However, the 89th, the 40th, and the 34th Divisions contained more Colorado men than did any others, and the 341st Field Artillery, the 157th Infantry, the 115th Ammunition Train, and the 115th Engineers were composed almost entirely of Colorado men.

It was not merely an army, but a nation, that had to be prepared for war. The whole-hearted cooperation of

the people at home was one of the outstanding features of
that epochal period, the splendid response of Colorado being most praiseworthy. The State Council of Defense, under the able chairmanship of J. K. Mullen, devoted itself
energetically to the mobilization of the resources of the state
and to the carrying out of every phase of war activity. Members of the council were chairmen of important committees,
such as those of Finance, Food Conservation, War Relief,
Publicity and Information. A Woman's Council of Defense,
under the devoted leadership of Mrs. W. H. Kistler, was similarly organized, and consecrated itself to the promotion
and direction of war activity. The Denver County Councils of Defense were ably led by Ernest Morris and Mrs.
James H. Baker. Councils of Defense in the other counties
of the state were created and the organization was extended
to cities, towns, precincts and even to blocks, in a perfectly integrated machine for the conduct of every phase of
home mobilization. Scores of individuals put aside their
personal duties to assume positions of direction and service
in the war-work forces.

Throughout the country there was demand for increased production and for rigid conservation. The need
for wheat, meat, fats, and sugar was most urgent. "Wheat-
less" and "meatless" days were observed. Potatoes and beans
were substituted for other foods. Home grown products
were used to save transportation costs. The women of the
state were taught better methods of canning and drying
fruits and vegetables. Vacant lots in the cities were converted into gardens and untilled acres in the country were
planted to crops.

As an outstanding producer of sugar and wheat, Colorado was able to contribute these articles to the nation's
food supply. Potatoes and beans, also in great demand, she

furnished in large quantities. Cattle and sheep from her farms and ranges supplied meat for the army and hides and wool for the manufacture of shoes and army clothing. The steel mill at Pueblo, flour mills throughout the state, and various manufacturing plants contributed their part in producing articles needed by the nation.

With the diversion of effort to the work of prosecuting the war, general mining activity in the state diminished. The amount of gold, silver, lead, zinc, and copper produced in Colorado fell off during 1917 and 1918. But tungsten, needed in the making of steel, was actively mined in Boulder County, and the production of molybdenum, in demand for steel manufacturing, was developed in Lake County.

The war called for enormous sums of money, both to finance our own program and to bolster the depleted treasuries of our allies in Europe. Special taxes of many kinds were levied and five great bond issues were floated. The figures in the bond issues and Colorado's responses were as follows:

	Whole Country	Colorado's Quota	Colorado Subscriptions	No. of Colorado Subscribers
First	$2,000,000,000	$12,590,350	$18,284,750	65,853
Second	3,000,000,000	17,616,000	23,042,850	141,585
Third	3,000,000,000	20,333,900	31,050,500	177,937
Fourth	6,000,000,000	37,449,500	42,377,300	193,965
Victory	4,500,000,000	28,375,350	30,058,150	118,829

In addition to the bonds, the sale of War Saving Stamps amounted to a total of $13,800,000 in Colorado.

Nor was Colorado less generous in contributing to the various welfare funds. Drives to raise money for the American Red Cross, the Y. M. C. A., the Salvation Army, and similar welfare organizations were liberally supported.

Time as well as money was freely given. Many of the executives and directors of war work gave their services free. Four Minute men spoke in theaters and places of public meeting, advocating the purchase of bonds, the support of welfare work, and the conservation of food. Local Red Cross chapters became hives of industry, where women produced quantities of hospital supplies and clothes. Devoted mothers and sisters knit sweaters, helmets, and socks for the soldier boys, social gatherings often being turned into knitting bees.

Colorado's contribution to the military forces of the United States during the World War was approximately 43,000 men. Of this number, 1,009 were killed or died in service, and 1759 were wounded. The Colorado soldiers were excellent types of American manhood. They radiated the vigorous atmosphere of their home state; they embodied the spirit of the old West, its hardihood and courage. The war period in Colorado was one of unprecedented cooperation, of high resolve, and willing sacrifice.

With the war over, the nation and state were faced with the great task of transforming our industry and life to a peace-time basis. Reconstruction after a great war is always fraught with difficulties and the period following the World War was no exception. War industries ceased operations. Thousands of laborers in various lines of war-time work, as well as the soldiers themselves, had to be re-absorbed into our economic life and find employment in peace-time pursuits.

The production of tungsten and of molybdenum, which had been given extraordinary stimulation in Colorado by war needs, practically ceased for a time, with the close of hostilities. Copper fell nearly one-third in price from 1917 to 1919 and its production in the state diminished 70 per cent in the two-year interval. During the same period the price of zinc fell 27 per cent and the value of this metal mined in Colorado decreased from over $12,000,000 to less than $3,000,000 per annum. The total production in Colorado of gold, silver, copper, lead, and zinc in 1919 was but $21,679,614—just half of the value produced two years before. By 1921 it had fallen to the low figure of $14,000,-000. The abandonment of smelting operations at Denver and Salida in 1919 and at Pueblo in 1921 operated both as cause and as effect of the reduced production of the mines.

There had been such an increase during the war in the amount of money in circulation that the purchasing power of the dollar had decreased fully one-half—in other words, prices had doubled since the beginning of the war in Europe. There was not a decline in general prices immediately following the war as some had expected, in fact the cost of living continued to rise until 1920. Then a decline set in, rapid for certain commodities, gradual for others.

The prices of farm products were among the first to fall. Because of the huge crops in America in 1920 and the collapse of the European market, farmers had to sell at a figure below the cost of production, while the level of taxes, freight rates, and the prices paid for manufactured goods and for labor were still on a war-time scale. Many farmers went bankrupt, while others were forced to sustain heavy losses. In the grip of this unhappy situation the farmer lost much of his purchasing power, other industries soon felt the shock, and distress became widespread. Hard times continued through 1920 and 1921, when conditions began gradually to improve. Attempts were made by the national and the state government to improve the lot of the farmer, but the remedial measures fell short of the mark. General business conditions fluctuated during the ensuing years, but there was a gradual upward trend until the stock market crash of November, 1929.

In addition to other difficulties in Colorado, there came in 1921 the calamity of the Pueblo Flood. The swollen torrent of the Arkansas River rushed upon Pueblo and submerged the whole central portion of the city. It carried away bridges, wrecked houses, destroyed stocks of merchandise, and took a toll of human life. The people of the state and the Red Cross dispatched emergency relief to the disaster-stricken district. Other sections of the valley sustained property losses from the flood, but at no other points were misfortunes of such appalling proportions.

Pueblo bravely faced her disaster and evolved a plan intended to prevent the recurrence of such a calamity. In an extra session of the legislature (1922) a Conservancy District was created. Under its jurisdiction was built a new and adequate flood channel which has brought security to the metropolis of the Arkansas Valley. From the ruin of the flood has arisen a safer and a bigger Pueblo.

The special session of the General Assembly which enacted the flood-prevention measure for Pueblo passed another important measure intended as a great public improvement. Since the first settlement of Colorado the great wall of the Front Range of the Rockies had stood as a barrier to easy and direct transportation between eastern and western Colorado and had prevented Denver from securing direct transcontinental railroad communication. To overcome this natural barrier a great tunnel was conceived. It was a scheme long before visioned by Colorado state builders. The "Moffat Tunnel Improvement District" was created, comprising the counties of Denver, Grand, Moffat, and Routt, and portions of the counties of Eagle, Gilpin, Boulder, Adams, and

Jefferson—the area calculated to be benefited most by the building of the tunnel. A Moffat Tunnel Commission was chosen, bonds were sold on the credit of the District, and late in 1923 the project got under way.

A pioneer bore, intended for subsequent use as a water tunnel, was first constructed. Crosscuts from this bore to the line of the main tunnel were then run, to enable a number of crews to work simultaneously on the main tunnel and thus speed up the work. This great undertaking developed unexpected engineering difficulties. Where they had expected to find solid rock, a loose structure was encountered, necessitating a reenforced lining of steel and concrete, which entailed an enormous cost. The great bore, which was expected to be built for less than seven million dollars was to cost nearly eighteen millions before it was finally completed, thus placing a great tax burden on the property owners of the District.

The pioneer or water tunnel was "holed through" by eager workers on February 12, 1927, less than four years after the project was begun. The official celebration of the opening took place six days later, when the Governor of Colorado shook hands with the Mayor of Salt Lake City in the heart of the mountain, while by radio, speeches of congratulation by various officials were broadcast to the country. The railroad tunnel was not holed through until about five months later (July 7, 1927), and the first regular train went through the six-mile bore on February 26, 1928.

The immediate benefits of the tunnel were rather meager, inasmuch as the Moffat railroad, a local line, was the only road in a position to use the improvement. But in the fall of 1932 the federal Reconstruction Finance Corporation made a loan to the Denver and Rio Grande Railroad to enable it to begin construction of the Dotsero Cutoff. This

COLORADO GOVERNORS, 1915-1933
1. George A. Carlson.   2. Julius C. Gunter.   3. Oliver H. Shoup.
4. William E. Sweet.   5. Clarence J. Morley.   6. William H. Adams.

WRECKAGE OF PUEBLO FLOOD, JUNE, 1921

GOVERNOR ADAMS OF COLORADO GREETS MAYOR NELSEN
OF SALT LAKE CITY IN THE PIONEER BORE OF MOFFAT
TUNNEL, FEB. 18, 1927

forty-mile stretch of railroad along the Colorado River is to connect the Moffat road with the Denver and Rio Grande, create a much wider use for the Tunnel, and make possible the placing of Denver on a direct trans-continental route.

The past decade has witnessed considerable building activity in the cities of the state. Up until the 1890s solid masonry, with its strict limitations on the height and character of buildings, had been employed in all large structures. But the introduction of steel and concrete revolutionized building methods. A supporting skeleton of powerful steel now makes possible buildings of great height without undue massiveness of walls. Architectural beauty has also been an objective in the new buildings.

The skyline of Denver's business district has been greatly transformed since the World War. The most notable building activity occurred in 1926-7, when the Republic, the Security, the Midland Savings, the Cosmopolitan Hotel, and the Continental Oil buildings were erected. Prominent among more recent additions are the Telephone building completed in 1929 and the Municipal building completed in 1932.

Political fortunes in Colorado have fluctuated since the World War, but the Republican Party has usually controlled a majority of the political offices. In the election of 1918 the Republicans elected Lawrence C. Phipps to the Senate, Oliver H. Shoup to the Governorship, and Charles B. Timberlake, William N. Vaile, and Guy U. Hardy to Congress. Edward T. Taylor, Democrat, was returned to Congress.

The Non-Partisan League, which had originated in North Dakota, spread to Colorado and in 1920 secured partial control of the Democratic party. The Republicans were again successful. Governor Shoup was re-elected, S. D. Nicholson was chosen to succeed Senator C. S. Thomas;

while the rest of the Congressional delegation remained unchanged. The agricultural depression and the usual swing from the party in power enabled the Democrats to elect William E. Sweet Governor in 1922, but again the same Representatives in Congress were returned. Senator Nicholson's career was cut short by death in March, 1923, and Alva B. Adams was appointed to succeed him.

The Ku Klux Klan had a rapid rise in Colorado. In 1924 it controlled the election of Governor, Senator and a majority of the state legislature. But its ascendency was shortlived; it declined as rapidly as it had risen. In 1926 the Republicans elected their candidate, Charles W. Waterman, to the Senate, and won a majority of the General Assembly; but the Democratic candidate, W. H. ("Billy") Adams, was elected Governor. Governor Adams was re-elected in 1928, while the Republicans again obtained control of the legislature. W. R. Eaton, Republican, was sent to Congress from Denver in 1928, all of the other Congressmen being re-elected.

In Colorado, as in the nation at large, the Democratic Party made striking gains in 1930. Governor Adams was elected for a third term, the Democrats gained control of the lower house of the General Assembly, and materially decreased the Republican majority in the State Senate. The four Representatives to Congress were re-elected and Edward P. Costigan, Democrat, was sent to the United States Senate, succeeding Senator Phipps.

Governor Adams' administrations were characterized by economy and conservatism. One of the most difficult problems with which he was called upon to deal was a strike of coal miners in 1928. In this conflict the Industrial Workers of the World appeared as prominent partisans. A most unfortunate incident during these labor troubles was a clash in Boulder County between the strikers and state troops in which a number of lives were lost. The prison riot at Canon City in October, 1929, cost the lives of eight guards and five prisoners, and focused attention upon overcrowding, idleness and other unfortunate conditions existing at the state penitentiary. A fire at the same institution in the following February further emphasized the need for reform measures.

The stock market panic of November, 1929, initiated a period of general depression throughout the state and nation. The great drop in prices that ensued entailed heavy losses for merchants, manufacturers, farmers—in fact, for practically all industries and every line of activity. Lack of confidence and a feeling of financial insecurity further impeded the normal flow of business. A curtailment of production became necessary because of lack of markets and this in turn brought on a grave unemployment problem. The situation became so serious that organized drives were made to provide jobs and to raise funds to relieve distress. The general "Depression" has continued to the present (1933), though conditions in Colorado have been somewhat better than in the country at large.

The election of 1932 was a Democratic landslide in Colorado as in the nation. The Democrats won control of the legislature and secured all the elective state offices except the Secretary of State. Edwin C. Johnson, Lieutenant Governor and former State Senator, was elected Governor. All the Colorado Representatives to Congress—Lawrence Lewis, Edward T. Taylor, John A. Martin and Fred Cummings—were chosen from the Democratic ticket. To succeed Senator C. W. Waterman, who died in August, 1932, the Governor had appointed Walter Walker, who retained the title until December 7th. In the regular election Karl C. Schuyler, Republican, was elected to fill Waterman's unexpired term (to March 4, 1933) while Alva B. Adams, Democrat, won the full term designation. An act reapportioning Senators and Representatives of the General Assembly and an amendment to the State Constitution repealing State Prohibition were carried in the election of 1932.

❖ ❖ ❖

SELECTED REFERENCES FOR FURTHER READING

Baker and Hafen, History of Colorado, 947-956, 990-1013
E. C. McMechen, The Moffat Tunnel of Colorado (1927)
J. A. B. Scherer, The Nation at War (1918)
G. H. English, The History of the 89th Division (1920)
Colorado National Guard Year Book (1922)
History of the 341st Field Artillery
Denver Municipal Facts
Denver Post; Rocky Mountain News

CHAPTER XVII

COLORADO TODAY

Recent Changes and Innovations

THE twentieth century has witnessed great changes in the industries, productions, and living conditions of Colorado. One of the most important has been the shift of economic leadership from mining to agriculture. In the year 1900 the production of precious metals (amounting to $50,614,000) was three times the value of the farm crops of the state. But by 1930 conditions had been so reversed that the production of farm crops (totaling $126,174,000) was valued at more than nine times the output of the precious metals.

The change in the relative positions of mining and farming has been paralleled by a remarkable shifting of population. Mining towns and even counties, once the pride of Colorado and the mainstay of her prosperity, are now almost deserted. Crusted mine dumps, rusting shaft houses and forsaken miners' cabins dot the hills of Colorado. Mining camps, once bustling with life, now drowse silently in the sun. Ouray, Summit, Mineral, Clear Creek, Hinsdale, Lake, Pitkin, Gilpin, and Teller Counties suffered decreases in population ranging from 62 to 85 per cent in the three decades preceding 1930.

But the agricultural counties have made up the losses sustained by the mining counties. Population increases ranging from 100 to 200 per cent for the thirty-year period have taken place in Delta, Elbert, Huerfano, Jefferson, Larimer,

Mesa, Montezuma, Montrose, Otero, Rio Grande, Routt, Bent and Grand Counties. An even greater increase during the same period is shown by the Counties of Prowers, Phillips, Weld, Kiowa, Kit Carson, Morgan, Logan, Cheyenne, Washington, Yuma, Lincoln and Baca.

For the state as a whole the population increase was 92 per cent for the period 1900-1930. In general, the cities experienced a more rapid growth than the state at large, although Pueblo and Colorado Springs, with their previous dependence upon the mining and smelting industries, have had a smaller increase. The eight cities of the state having populations today in excess of 10,000, have for the three decades had increases as follows: Denver 115%, Pueblo 78%, Colorado Springs 58%, Greeley 303%, Trinidad 119%, Fort Collins 276%, Boulder 82%, and Grand Junction 192%.

From 1900 to 1930 the number of farms in Colorado more than doubled, while the total value of farm property during the period increased from $161,045,101 to $795,387,096. The principal field crops of the state in 1930, with the value of each, were as follows: Hay $28,247,000, Corn $23,028,000, Sugar Beets $22,895,000, Wheat $11,595,000, Potatoes $9,030,000, Barley $6,242,000, and Beans $5,301,000.

Colorado's horticultural production usually runs in excess of $5,000,000 annually, the principal fruits being apples, peaches, pears, cherries, and berries. During the past decade the floral industry in Colorado has shown a remarkable growth, of about 150 per cent, and now reaches $5,000,000 per year. Carnations, roses, sweet peas, gladioli, dahlias, baby breath, cyclamen, and seeds are the leading floriculture products.

COLORADO FIELD CROPS

Upper: Bean Field, Merino.   Middle: Corn Cribs.   Lower: Onion Production.

PLANT OF THE COLORADO FUEL AND IRON COMPANY, PUEBLO

The value of livestock in Colorado increased from $49,-
753,000 in 1900 to $152,936,000 in 1920 and then declined
to $88,746,000 in 1931, much of this later decrease being
due to a decline in market values. Cattle account for more
than half of the live stock value, with sheep, horses and
swine ranking in the order named. The raising of cattle
has shifted somewhat from the open range to the fenced
pasture, the forest ranges, and the feed lot. Feeding of cattle and sheep is promoted by the production of alfalfa hay
and of grain and by the available by-products from sugar
beet factories. In fact Colorado has become the leading lamb
feeding state in the Union, with over 2,000,000 lambs on
feed in January, 1930. While the number of cattle in Colorado has increased but slightly since 1910, the number of
sheep has more than doubled and the number of swine
trebled during this period. Horses, on the other hand (partially supplanted by automobiles and tractors), have decreased steadily.

Dairying ranks today among the state's leading industries, the total value of dairy products in 1930 being in excess of $28,000,000. Weld and El Paso lead all other coun-
ties in dairying. The industry has been promoted by the
construction of silos for the storage of winter feed, the number of silos in the state having increased to over 2,000 in
1929.

The poultry industry has had a marked development
in recent years. Formerly, chickens and eggs had to be
shipped into the state, but now local production not only
supplies the home market but provides a surplus for export.
The number of eggs produced has doubled in the past decade, being over 27,000,000 dozens in 1929. The number
of chickens and turkeys raised has had a substantial increase.

As noted above, mining, once the leading industry of

Colorado, has shown a marked decline in recent years. During the three decades since 1900 the production of the five principal metals (gold, silver, copper, lead and zinc) decreased from $50,614,000 to $13,129,693. In 1930 their values were as follows: gold $4,516,196, zinc $3,426,441, lead $2,321,592, silver $1,651,876, copper $1,213,588. This production is quite in contrast to that of 1900, when the value of the gold output alone was over $28,000,000, or to that of 1892 when the silver yield amounted to over $20,000,000. The high points of production for the other principal metals were as follows: Zinc, almost $18,000,000 in 1916; Lead, over $7,000,000 in 1900; and Copper, over $2,000,000 in 1917.

The decrease in the output of the more common metals has in part been made up in recent years by the finding of rare metals. Colorado has distinct leadership in the production of molybdenum and vanadium, and is capable of fair production of tungsten and fluorspar. Approximately 250 useful metallic and non-metallic minerals have been found in Colorado and about 30 metals have been produced commercially. Since 1917 the combined value of gold, silver, copper, lead, and zinc has been exceeded by the value of the other minerals produced in the state—such as coal, iron, cement, gypsum, lime, and petroleum.

The total mineral production of Colorado in 1928 was $58,594,688, of which by far the largest single item was coal. Since 1905 the production of coal has averaged over 10,000,000 tons annually, but a decrease has occurred in recent years due to the wider use of gas and oil and to adverse freight rates. The values of the total output of the seven principal minerals produced in the state up to the end of 1930 are as follows:

Coal	$735,121,708
Gold	715,477,000
Silver	518,489,000
Lead	217,175,237
Zinc	155,722,959
Copper	46,256,057
Petroleum	27,321,774

Manufacturing has assumed second rank among the industries of the state, with an increase of 242 per cent in the value of the product for the three decades preceding 1929. The five leading manufacturing industries of the state (in terms of the value of the product), in the order of their rank, are (for 1925): beet sugar production, slaughtering and meat packing, iron and steel manufacturing, printing and publishing, and the manufacture of flour and grain products.

In beet sugar production Colorado ranks first among the states of the Union. In 1930 the eighteen factories of the state produced 7,820,000 hundredweight of sugar. The most important single manufacturing institution in the state is the Colorado Fuel and Iron Company, located at Pueblo, which manufactures a line of products ranging from "nails to rails." An important and rather unique manufacturing plant for Colorado is that of the Gates Rubber Company of Denver, which manufactures a wide variety of rubber products, the annual value of which is in excess of $8,000,-000. The manufacturing plants of the state are far too great in number and variety to be enumerated here.

After the production of goods, one of our chief concerns is their distribution. Frequently there is as much time and effort employed in the sale of a commodity as in its production. There are over 2,000 wholesale establishments and more than 14,000 retail stores in Colorado. More than 19,000 full time employes are engaged in the retail trade of Denver alone. Many of the largest and most prosperous stores and business establishments of the state today had their humble beginnings in log cabins during pioneer times. A recent change in retail selling has been the rapid rise in the last decade or two of the "chain store." Another noticeable innovation has been the widely-adopted practice of installment buying.

The total sales from Colorado stores in 1929 amounted to approximately one-half billion dollars. It is interesting to note the relative positions of the ten groups into which the Census Bureau has divided the stores. For example, we spend in Colorado about as much for the purchase, care and operation of our automobiles as we do for food.

PRINCIPAL RETAIL GROUPS IN COLORADO (1929)

	No. of Stores	Net Sales	Per Cent
Automotive group	3,000	$116,028,283	23.30
Food group	3,493	115,857,617	23.28
General merchandise group	608	71,899,357	14.44
Lumber and building group	776	30,711,282	6.17
Apparel group	806	29,083,161	5.83
Furniture and household group	408	19,989,254	4.01
Restaurants and eating places	1,236	17,752,008	3.56
Country general stores	645	17,111,753	3.43
All other stores	2,819	76,812,818	15.44
Second hand stores	272	2,606,668	.54
	14,063	$497,852,191	100.00

Related to the general business development of the state, often supporting and frequently directing it, are the banking establishments of Colorado. There were 257 of these institutions in 1930, with combined assets of $380,-000,000. As noted previously, the first banks of the region were established in 1860, when one of the chief banking functions was the providing of currency in exchange for miners' gold dust. Some of those initial banking houses have become the largest financial institutions of the state.

Great changes in business methods and equipment have come in recent years. The typewriter, which was introduced at about the time when the telephone, electric light, and phonograph were given to the world, brought an important change in office methods. The past decade or two has witnessed the introduction of numerous new devices and methods. The adding machine, card filing systems, bookkeeping machines, mimeographs, dictaphones, etc., have effected great economies in time and effort.

Modern inventions and methods have also revolutionized work and conditions in the home. With factory-made clothes, canned goods, prepared package foods, and commercial bakeries and laundries, much of the labor once identified with the home is now done outside. Electrical equipment and devices such as vacuum sweepers, refrigerators, and automatic ovens have further reduced the physical labor of functions still remaining in the home.

The recent changes in the home and in the business world, together with the social changes that have accompanied them, have gone far toward taking women from the fireside and placing her beside man in the business world. In 1900, less than 15 per cent of the persons in Colorado engaged in gainful occupations (meaning outside the home) were women and girls. In 1930, female wage earners constituted over 25 per cent of all persons gainfully employed in this state. The financial independence of woman and her changed social attitude and status have resulted in her wider participation in political, social, and intellectual pursuits. Various types of woman's clubs and social activities have multiplied. Woman's new so-called free-dom is also reflected in the mounting numbers of divorces.

One of the most important changes in modern life has been brought about by the automobile and the good roads development, the introduction of which was discussed in a preceding chapter. During the early years, dependence had been upon the counties for practically all road improve-ments. But in 1900, prisoners from the state penitentiary were employed in highway construction, improving in that year seventy miles of road between Pueblo and Leadville. During the succeeding two decades much construction work in various parts of the state was accomplished with prison labor.

In 1914 a half mill state tax was voted by the people for highway construction and in 1919 an additional half mill was levied. In this latter year was introduced the gaso-line tax as a means of raising money for better roads. The first measure provided a one cent per gallon tax, but this has been successively raised to four cents (1933) and has replaced the mill levies for road building. A bond issue of $5,000,000 was voted by the state in 1920 and one of $6,000,000 in 1922, the proceeds to be expended on state roads. As early as 1916 the federal government began to distrib-ute money among the various states for road construction. This "federal aid" received by Colorado amounted to over a million dollars in 1919 and has generally been between one and two million dollars annually since that year. In addi-tion, government expenditures for road building in the Na-tional Forests and National Parks of the state amount to

approximately $500,000 per year. The proceeds from auto-
mobile licenses in Colorado has mounted annually from
slightly over $60,000 in 1913 to nearly $2,000,000 in 1932.
In the aggregate, the money expended in Colorado by county,
state, and nation for the construction and maintenance of
highways has well exceeded $10,000,000 per year during
the past decade.

During this period a remarkable transformation of the
roads of the state has taken place. Improved highways have
been built over many of the mountain passes. Paving has
been greatly extended and existing roads widened, straightened, and improved generally. Scores of substantial bridges
of steel and concrete have been built. Dangerous railroad
crossings have been eliminated. Roads have been taking on
a more substantial and permanent character. At the beginning of 1932 there were 72,456 miles of state and county
roads in Colorado. Of these, 447 miles were paved and 32,-
779 miles surfaced or graded. These excellent highways
constitute one of Colorado's most valued assets.

The important industry of building and maintaining
improved highways has been brought about largely by the
automobile. But road improvement is not the only innovation effected by this extraordinary vehicle. It has caused
the abandonment of various railroad lines and the development of bus and truck transportation on a large scale, has
stimulated the oil industry, has speeded up our economic life,
and changed conditions of living in both city and country.
Tractors have replaced horses on many farms, and trucks
have taken the place of farm and freight wagons. While
the automobile has increased accidents, caused heavy and
economically unproductive expenditures, and brought on
difficult traffic problems, it has at the same time made distant places accessible, resulted in marked economies in trans-

portation, multiplied tourist travel, and brought new opportunities for recreation and pleasure to the common people.

Thousands of men in Colorado are engaged in selling, assembling and repairing automobiles and in various related occupations. Near a half billion dollars is invested in automobiles, garages, automobile factories and salesrooms in Colorado; while the expenditure for gas and oil is nearly $40,000,000 annually, or more than four times the present value of the entire annual production of precious metals in the state.

The consumption of gasoline in Colorado has increased from less than 6,000,000 gallons in 1913 to over 176,000,000 in 1931. Approximately half of the amount consumed has come from Wyoming, and most of the remainder from Oklahoma, Texas, Colorado, and Kansas. During the eighteen-year period, Colorado has produced an amount varying from two to seventeen per cent of the total consumed. Although Colorado has been a producer of oil since 1862, her production was comparatively small prior to 1924. In November, 1923, a large well was brought in on the Wellington dome near Fort Collins and in the following March a good producer was announced south of Craig. The proving of these fields inaugurated important oil developments. In 1925 there were eighty producing wells in Colorado, and their total product was 1,211,702 barrels of crude oil. The output doubled in 1926 and in the succeeding three years amounted to nearly three million barrels annually. Oil refineries have been built at Florence, Craig, Rangely, and Denver. Oil was discovered in the Fort Morgan field in 1931.

In addition to the oil and gas to be tapped by wells, there is in Colorado an immense fuel resource of a related character—oil shale. This is found in extensive deposits covering thousands of acres on the western slope of the state. It has been officially estimated that fifty billion barrels of oil are recoverable from this great untapped reserve, which amount is more than fifty times the present annual production of the entire United States. At present, oil cannot be produced from shale at a cost sufficiently low to compete with oil from wells, but the potential oil is in Colorado and can be extracted when the need arises. The United States has already set aside two large shale areas as a reserve for the future needs of the navy.

What might be considered the acme of fast transportation has come with the modern airplane. Practical aviation had its inception at the beginning of the twentieth century. Wilbur and Orville Wright built a machine which made a flight of fifty-nine seconds in 1903. Improvements in structure and speed have continued since that time. Commercial flying has grown rapidly in the last decade, being given great impetus by the trans-Atlantic flight of Charles A. Lindberg in 1927.

Airplane development in Colorado has been a reflection of that in the country at large. Popular interest has mounted, flying schools have been established and at Colorado Springs the manufacture of airplanes has become an important industry. Denver opened her excellent airport in October, 1929. Other cities and towns of the state have provided landing fields, there being thirty-two airports in the state in 1931.

On May 31, 1926, was established the first air mail service for Colorado, the line running from Pueblo through Denver to Cheyenne, Wyoming. Extensions have since been made and new routes established. Regular lines provide passenger service by air from Denver to Kansas City, El Paso, Amarillo, and Casper.

Electricity has so revolutionized modern life that some have called the last half century the "Electric Age." For hundreds of years man had used water wheels and horse power as forces for propelling various grinding mills and other simple machines and devices. Then the introduction of the steam engine in the latter part of the 18th century brought on the "Industrial Revolution," with its great transformation of industrial and social life. When the settlement of Colorado began, the changes wrought by the steam engine were already commonplace. These engines, freighted across the plains by ox teams, were employed in running pioneer saw mills, stamp mills and similar machinery.

But when electricity came into use, even greater industrial changes were effected. Soon after Thomas A. Edison gave to the world a commercially-practical incandescent lamp, the Colorado Electric Company was organized, in February, 1881. It established at Denver what is said to be the first electric generating station west of the Mississippi River. The same year, July 16th, the Union Station was illuminated by arc lamps, and a number of similar installations lighted downtown street intersections soon afterward. The lighting of residences and business houses with incandescent bulbs followed shortly.

At the time, gas lights from the system installed in 1870, were being used for illumination in Denver. In 1883 street lighting by gas was supplemented by the erection of seven 150-foot towers, distributed through the suburbs, from the tops of which powerful arc lights flooded the surrounding area. In 1885, upon the expiration of the gas company's contract for street lighting, electric lights began generally to replace gas for street illumination.

At about the time of the introduction of the electric

light it was learned that the electricity-producing dynamo could, when reversed, become a motor, useable as a propelling force. This opened the way for the development of the modern street car and all types of electrically-driven machinery.

In 1885 S. H. Short, Professor of Physics at Denver University, built an electrically-driven street car. In that year a short electric line, employing the Professor's ideas, was built on Fifteenth Street, Denver. It is credited with being the second electric street car system to be commercially used in the United States. The electric power for these cars was carried by an under cable, reached through a slot between the tracks. Persons or animals making simultaneous contact with the cable and one track received a startling electric shock. This brought public objection and after a year's operation this first electric line reverted to the horse-car system. During the eighties extensive cable car lines were built, the street car being drawn by a long underground steel cable, the power being stationary steam engines. The cable system was soon given up and in the early 1890s improved electric street cars (similar to those of today), using overhead electric wires, displaced the horse-drawn and the cable cars.

The invention of the electric light and the electric motor created great demands for electric power plants. In the first plants in Colorado, steam engines, fed by coal, were used to turn the dynamos for generating electric current. Many plants are so operated today. Then hydro-electric plants were developed, the potential power of mountain streams being harnessed for man's uses. One of the first hydro-electric plants in the state was built at the then flourishing mining town of Aspen in 1887.

Before 1900 all the larger towns of the state were being furnished electric power, some plants municipally owned, others built by private companies. But it is since that date that the greatest electric development has occurred. Erection of a large hydro-electric plant was begun on the Colorado River near Glenwood Springs in 1906 and completed in 1919. The high tension line from this plant to Denver is 153 miles long and crosses three mountain passes, reaching an elevation of 13,700 feet. It supplies various towns enroute and carries a considerable part of the Denver load. The hydro-electric plant in Boulder Canyon, put into operation in 1910, has a generating capacity of 14,400 KW, equal to that of the Colorado River plant. The steam plant at Valmont is the state's largest electric generating station, having a capacity of 65,000 horse power.

While the introduction of electricity has caused the replacement of gas for illumination purposes, electricity has by no means eliminated the use of gas. Artificial gas, manufactured from native coal, continues to serve many of the larger cities and towns of the state, being especially convenient for use in cooking. An important innovation in this field came in June, 1928, when the natural gas pipeline from Amarillo, Texas, to Denver was completed. This great conduit, 340 miles long and costing about $23,000,-000, brought a new and flexible fuel to factory, kitchen and domestic furnace. A year later, the gas line was extended seventy-five miles north of Denver to Fort Collins, where it made connections with the Cheyenne, Wyoming, system.

There are less than a dozen companies supplying gas, natural and artificial, within Colorado's boundaries, while more than thirty utility companies furnish electricity. Of these, the Public Service Company of Colorado is the largest, supplying approximately sixty-five per cent of the state's electricity, and an even larger proportion of the gas. This

THE "MILLION DOLLAR HIGHWAY," OURAY TO
RED MOUNTAIN

1. THE VALMONT ELECTRIC POWER PLANT NEAR BOULDER
2. UNITED STATES PORTLAND CEMENT PLANT AT CONCRETE

organization, a consolidation of many pioneer gas and electric concerns, operates in a wide territory in the Rocky
Mountain region. It employs about 2,000 men and women
and disburses over $3,000,000 annually in payrolls.
During the year 1930, 573,341,000 kilowatt hours
were distributed to customers by all of Colorado's electric
utilities. Of this total, 235,843,000 kwh were generated by
water power and 337,498,000 kwh by fuel power.

Only a comparatively small part of the water power
of the state has yet been utilized. More than 100,000 horse
power is being developed, whereas there is over 2,000,000
horse power available. The federal government has set aside
over 400,000 acres of land in Colorado as power site re-
serves. The presence of large deposits of coal has encouraged the use of this fuel in generating electric power. For
although the cost of operation of coal-steam plants is greater
than for those using water power, the initial cost of hydro-
electric installation exceeds that of the steam plants.

Transportation and electrical progress has been paralleled by development in modes of communication. As noted
in a previous chapter, the first telegraph line in Colorado,
running from Julesburg to Denver, was built in early Territorial days (1863). Lines were continued into other parts
of the state and the telegraph became the chief reliance for
rapid communication. It has continued as an important
agency in Colorado's development, though being somewhat
overshadowed in later years by the telephone. In 1930 there
were four telegraph companies in the state, operating 27,394
miles of wire (compared to 478,850 miles of telephone wire),
the lines valued at almost $3,000,000.

In the very year that Colorado became a state (1876),
Alexander Graham Bell gave us the first practical telephone

in America. Within two years thereafter telephone development was begun in Colorado. The Colorado Coal and
Iron Company (predecessor of the present C. F. & I.) built
a private line from office to coal yard. The great Prairie
Cattle Company and the J. J. Cattle Company, with their
extensive ranges in southeastern Colorado, quickly saw the
advantage of telephone communication and built private
lines.

Frederick O. Vaille might properly be called the father
of the telephone system in Colorado. He began soliciting
subscribers for a telephone system in Denver late in 1878.
Within three months a list of 161 subscribers assured success to the enterprise. A switchboard was installed over
Frick's shoe store, on Larimer Street, and on Feb. 24, 1879,
the telephones began to ring. The instrument was rather
crude and imperfect. One piece served both as receiver and
transmitter. A person put it to his ear to listen and then
to his mouth to reply, passing it from ear to mouth as the
conversation progressed. The early type instruments were
continually getting out of order, breaking off the conversation at the most unhappy moment and emitting exasperating
hummings and wailings. But mechanical improvements
came and the telephone took its high place in our modern
world. Booming Leadville established a telephone exchange
in 1879 and extensions from Denver reached Golden, Idaho
Springs, and Central City the same year. A line was run to
Boulder in 1881 and one to Colorado Springs and Pueblo in
1884. Rapid extension continued, until telephone wires
soon connected all parts of the state. Telephone progress
has been marked by great and frequent innovations, involv-
ing great outlays of capital. Today the Mountain States
Telephone and Telegraph Company, operating in seven western states, has a capital of $48,000,000. It has 3,300 em-

ployes in Colorado and operates about 180,000 telephones, or over 90 per cent of those in the state. Its magnificent 15-story, $3,000,000 building, completed in 1929, is the out-standing business structure in Denver.

In December, 1901, Marconi sent his first wireless message across the Atlantic. Other scientists and inventors carried forward the work which resulted in the development of our modern radio. At Colorado Springs in 1920, Dr. W. D. Reynolds established "the pioneer broadcasting sta-tion" in Colorado, moving it the following year to Denver, where it became Station KLZ. In December, 1924, KOA, the powerful General Electric Station, was established at Denver. By 1932 thirteen broadcasting stations in the state were giving regular programs and numerous amateurs were experimenting with private sets. Of the 268,531 families in Colorado in 1930, 37.8 per cent had radios. There were 325 radio dealers in Colorado in 1930 and their annual sales amounted to about $2,000,000. The past decade has wit-nessed a remarkable development in radio. What the wiz-ardry of the future will reveal no one can foretell.

In the years immediately following 1900 the moving picture was introduced to the American public. From hum-ble and crude beginnings it rose to first rank in the world of popular entertainment. Recently, the silent drama has been largely pushed aside by the "talking picture." In 1931 there were 298 motion picture theaters located in 214 cities and towns of Colorado. All the larger theaters, and approximately half of the total number, present sound pic-tures. Several millions of dollars are invested in these the-aters, some of which are handsome structures with most elaborate and beautiful appointments.

Opportunities for outdoor recreation have increased in

recent years. All the larger cities of the state have parks and playgrounds and some have provided tennis courts, golf links, swimming pools or beaches, and such facilities for physical recreation. A number of the larger municipalities have undertaken a new and unique development, going beyond their boundaries to establish parks and playgrounds in the nearby mountains. In 1911 Denver inaugurated her Mountain Parks System, which had grown to include over 10,000 acres and upon which expenditures had exceeded $2,000,000 by 1930. Excellent highways connect these parks. Water systems, fireplaces, shelter houses and similar conveniences are provided. The mountain parks of other Colorado cities are similar in character.

In the National Forests, which comprise approximately 20 per cent of the total area of the state, roads and trails have been built, camping facilities provided, and measures taken to safeguard the natural beauty of the area for the enjoyment of the people.

Game, once the principal resource of Colorado, has naturally diminished as settlement proceeded, but it is comparatively abundant still. A census of large game animals in the National Forests of the state in 1930 reported 10,500 elk, 3,450 mountain sheep, 36,300 deer, and 2,717 bears. Small game, such as sage hens, grouse, ducks, and rabbits also are numerous. Twenty-two state game refuges, where game may not be killed at any time, have been established in Colorado and comprise over 3,000,000 acres. Outside of these refuges practically all varieties of game may be killed during specified "open seasons."

Today, hunting is overshadowed by the fishing opportunities in the state. Numerous streams and lakes are regularly stocked with fish, 30,000,000 trout being planted annually in Colorado during recent years. A quarter million dollars, all of which is obtained from hunting and fishing licenses, permits, fines, etc., is expended annually by the Game and Fish Department of Colorado in the protection and propagation of fish and game. Over 120,000 fishing and hunting licenses, many of them obtained by visitors to the state, are issued annually.

Colorado has been called "the nation's playground." High rugged mountains, gem-like lakes in conifer settings, glacier-fed streams tumbling down rocky canyons, endless stretches of piled-up hills bright with aspens or dark with evergreens, make the mountain region of the state one vast area of natural beauty. From the crowded cities and the baked farms of the East and South, throngs of summer visitors come for a few days or weeks of recreation in the refreshing out-of-doors. The invigorating low-pressure atmosphere of the high altitudes, the days of warm sunshine and the cool refreshing nights are attractive features for relaxation.

The scenic beauty and the numberless tourist attractions of the state we shall not attempt to describe or enumerate. The national government has recognized their importance and extent by the creation of two National Parks, four National Monuments, and fifteen National Forests in the state. These are made accessible by good automobile roads and by trails. Plant and animal life and the primeval beauty of the natural landscape are safeguarded for the enjoyment of successive generations by these federal agencies.

Considered from the financial standpoint the tourist business is of great value to the state. Figures show that 1,390,000 visitors came to Colorado in 1931, approximately two-thirds coming by automobile and one-third by train.

Their total expenditures in the state in 1931 were over $90,000,000, making the tourist business rank after agriculture and manufacturing as the third industry of the state. Colorado ranks well among the states in educational facilities. The school system is continually expanding, the most notable growth in recent years being in the High Schools and Colleges of the state. In 1876 the first class was graduated from a Colorado High School. By 1900 the enrollment in secondary schools was 6,744 and by 1930 this had increased to 64,577 (including Junior High Schools). In the same year the regular enrollment in Colleges and Universities was 12,072, which is an increase of more than 400 per cent over the enrollment for 1900. The summer schools conducted by institutions of higher learning have gained greatly in favor of late. The type of work offered and the cool summers and attractive recreational features of Colorado bring many students from other states. Three institutions in 1930 had larger enrollments for the summer than for the winter term.

In 1930 there were 252,718 public school students in Colorado, being taught by 9,745 teachers, the total expenditures amounting to over $26,000,000. In addition, 61 parochial and private schools, with 526 teachers, reported an enrollment of 12,853. There were 3,208 school houses in the state in 1930, the value of buildings, equipment, and grounds being approximately $90,000,000.

Education is being promoted by over 100 public libraries in the state, containing one and one-half million volumes. A number of museums, with exhibits of historical, archaeological, natural history, and art collections are open to the public. Citizens of the state as well as thousands of visitors to Colorado are enlightened and entertained through their visits to these free institutions.

TYPES OF MODERN COLORADO SCHOOL BUILDINGS
1. Central High School, Pueblo.   2. East High School, Denver.
3. Byers Junior High School, Denver.

GOVERNOR EDWIN C. JOHNSON, 1933

The State Historical Society, created by the legislature
in 1879, gathers historical and archaeological materials; pre-
serves and exhibits these collections in the State Museum
(facing the Capitol); and disseminates historical information
through its publication, the *Colorado Magazine*.

The various arts have received deserved attention in
Colorado during recent years. Outstanding schools of music
and of art are exerting their influence on the cultural tone
of the state. "Music Week" has received general attention.
Art is manifesting itself in the architecture of business and
school buildings as well as in home planning and decoration.
The Civic Theater in Denver and the Little Theater movement in the state have won active support. A rather notable
group of writers also has developed in Colorado. Denver
has become a recognized center for authors of the West.

The power of the press in the field of popular education can scarcely be over estimated. Almost from the very
founding of the principal towns of the state the newspaper
has been an established institution, mirroring and aiding the
growth of the community. Today, twenty-one daily and over
100 weekly newspapers are published regularly; reaching
practically every home in the state. Upon the information
carried in these papers the people chiefly rely for the facts
upon which to form their opinions and base their actions
concerning public questions. A number of magazines and
books also are published in Colorado. Altogether, the printing and publishing business ranks fourth among the manufacturing industries of the state from the standpoint of financial return from the product. The educational value of
these publications can not be measured.

The Church has paralleled and supplemented the school
in furthering the educational and spiritual welfare of Colorado's citizens. Church establishments began to function in

Colorado during the 1850s and from those pioneer beginnings have continued to spread as settlement expanded. Today, 77 religious bodies are reported in the state, with over
1600 church organizations owning property valued at $25,-
000,000. Welfare agencies have arisen to care for the unfortunate. Community Chests or other forms of organized char-
ity function in the larger towns and cities to relieve immediate distress, while orphanages, day nurseries, homes for the
aged, and similar institutions are devoted to the care of the
dependent. The Parent-Teacher organization, the State
Child Welfare Bureau, and various service clubs promote
the welfare of children. Social legislation has recognized the
interest of society in the well-being of the individual. Factory and mine inspection is provided to safeguard the lives
of workers. The State Workmen's Compensation Law, enacted in 1915, provides compensation for dependents in case
of accident or death of the wage earner. Laws have been
passed fixing maximum hours of labor and minimum wages
for certain classes of workers and in certain industries.
Widow and old age pension laws have been enacted.

In safeguarding health the agencies of city, state, and
nation have joined hands. Food inspection, sanitary regulations, control of communicable diseases and numerous similar
measures are being taken to insure health and safeguard
society.

Important aids in health work and in the care of the
sick are the excellent hospitals and sanitariums maintained
in Colorado. Thirty-three Colorado hospitals in 1930 had
the approval of the American College of Surgeons, meeting
that organization's requirements as to character of staff,
equipment and general conduct. Together, these institutions
have a capacity for over 7,000 patients. In addition there

are private sanitariums and smaller hospitals in various towns and cities of the state. The Fitzsimons General Hospital is not only the largest hospital in Colorado but is the largest United States army hospital and the largest tuberculosis hospital in the nation, having a capacity of over 1800 beds. Another large institution maintained by the federal government is the United States Veterans Hospital at Fort Lyon. Certain institutions in Colorado, devoting themselves exclusively to the treatment of tuberculosis, have won nation-wide fame.

Our survey of Colorado's development has no doubt impressed us with the remarkable changes that have taken place since the beginnings of permanent settlement here. Truly, life in Colorado today is in striking contrast to that of pioneer times. The ox team, prairie schooner and Indian travois have been replaced by the automobile and airplane; the Pony Express, by the telephone and radio. The buffalo, antelope and wild Indian are gone; the open prairie is fenced. Texas longhorns have given way to Shorthorns, Herefords, and dairy cattle. River beds are nearly dry while reservoirs and man-made ditches run full. The steep, narrow toll road is a broad, free highway; pole bridges have become spans of steel and concrete. Eldorados and bonanzas lie buried beneath crusted mounds of mining dumps. Sleepy burros drowse unclaimed in mountain valleys, and trim Forest Rangers are met more often than grizzled prospectors. Recreation-seekers have taken summer possession of the mountains.

And what seems most remarkable is the fact that all these changes have come within the span of one man's life. A child who came to the Pike's Peak country before there was a Colorado sees, in the evening of his life, our Colorado of today.

SELECTED REFERENCES FOR FURTHER READING

Baker and Hafen, History of Colorado, 711-734, 739-755, 1231-1285
W. F. Stone, History of Colorado, 317-324, 449-477, 546-562, 877-890
J. Henderson et al, Colorado: Short Studies of Its Past and Present (1927), 122-202
State Board of Immigration, Year Book of the State of Colorado (1918-1931)
Denver Municipal Facts
Colorado Magazine: "Early Days of the Telephone in Colorado" (Aug., 1928); "Brief History of National Jewish Hospital at Denver" (Oct., 1928); "The Counties of Colorado, Their Origin and Their Names" (Mar., 1931); "Colorado Cities, Their Founding and the Origin of Their Names" (Sept., 1932); "Origin of the Denver Mountain Parks" (Jan., 1932)

APPENDIX

GOVERNORS OF COLORADO

Robert W. Steele, "Jefferson Territory," 1859-61

TERRITORIAL

William Gilpin, 1861-62
John Evans, 1862-65
Alexander Cummings, 1865-67
A. Cameron Hunt, 1867-69
Edward McCook, 1869-73
Samuel H. Elbert, 1873-74
Edward McCook, 1874-75
John L. Routt, 1875-76

STATE

John L. Routt (R), 1876-79
Frederick W. Pitkin (R), 1879-83
James B. Grant (D), 1883-85
Benjamin H. Eaton (R), 1885-87
Alva Adams (D), 1887-89
Job A. Cooper (R), 1889-91
John L. Routt (R), 1891-93
Davis H. Waite (P), 1893-95
Albert W. McIntyre (R), 1895-97
Alva Adams (D), 1897-99
Charles S. Thomas (D), 1899-1901
James B. Orman (D), 1901-03
James H. Peabody (R), 1903-05
Jesse F. McDonald (R), 1905-07
Henry A. Buchtel (R), 1907-09
John F. Shafroth (D), 1909-13
Elias M. Ammons (D), 1913-15
George A. Carlson (R), 1915-17
Julius C. Gunter (D), 1917-19
Oliver H. Shoup (R), 1919-23
William E. Sweet (D), 1923-25
Clarence J. Morley (R), 1925-27
Williams H. Adams (D), 1927-33
Edwin C. Johnson (D), 1933-

DELEGATES AND REPRESENTATIVES TO CONGRESS

Hiram J. Graham (Delegate for people of Pike's Peak), 1858-59
Beverly D. Williams (Delegate from "Jefferson Territory"), 1859-60

COLORADO TERRITORY

Hiram P. Bennet, 1861-65
Allen A. Bradford, 1865-67
George M. Chilcott, 1867-69
Allen A. Bradford, 1869-71
Jerome B. Chaffee, 1871-75

STATE OF COLORADO

James B. Belford (R), 1876-77
Thomas M. Patterson (D), 1877-79
James B. Belford (R), 1879-85
George G. Symes (R), 1885-89
Hosea Townsend (R), 1889-93
John C. Bell (P & D), 1893-1903
Lafe Pence (P), 1893-95
John F. Shafroth (R & D), 1895-1903
Robert W. Bonynge (R), 1903-09
Herschel M. Hogg (R), 1903-07
Franklin E. Brooks (R), 1903-07
George W. Cook (R), 1907-09
Warren A. Haggot (R), 1907-09
Edward T. Taylor (D), 1909-
Atterson W. Rucker (D), 1909-13
John A. Martin (D), 1909-13
Edward Keating (D), 1913-19
George J. Kindel (D), 1913-15
H. H. Seldomridge (D), 1913-15
B. C. Hilliard (D), 1915-19
Charles B. Timberlake (R), 1915-33
William N. Vaile (R), 1919-27
Guy U. Hardy (R), 1919-33
S. Harrison White (D), 1927-28
William R. Eaton (R), 1928-33
Lawrence Lewis (D), 1933-
John A. Martin (D), 1933-
Fred Cummings (D), 1933-

UNITED STATES SENATORS FROM COLORADO

Henry M. Teller (R), 1876-82
Jerome B. Chaffee (R), 1876-79
Nathaniel P. Hill (R), 1879-85
George M. Chilcott (R), 1882
Horace A. W. Tabor (R), 1883
Thomas M. Bowen (R), 1883-89
Henry M. Teller (R & D), 1885-1909
Edward O. Wolcott (R), 1889-1901
Thomas M. Patterson (D), 1901-07
Simon Guggenheim (R), 1907-13
Charles J. Hughes, Jr. (D), 1909-11
Charles S. Thomas (D), 1913-21
John F. Shafroth (D), 1913-19
Lawrence C. Phipps (R), 1919-31
S. D. Nicholson (R), 1921-23
Alva B. Adams (D), 1923-25
Rice W. Means (R), 1925-27
Charles W. Waterman (R), 1927-32
Edward P. Costigan (D), 1931-
Walter Walker (D), 1932
Karl C. Schuyler (R), 1932-33
Alva B. Adams (D), 1933-

Colorado Delevolpment and Production by Decades

	1930	1920	1910	1900	1890	1880	1870
Population	1,035,791	939,629	799,024	539,700	413,249	194,327	39,864
Population per square mile	10.0	9.06	7.71	5.21	3.99	1.87	0.38
Total assessed value	$1,586,462,903	$1,590,268,000⁸	$414,885,770	$216,776,356	$220,544,064	$73,698,746	$43,453,946†
Miles of railroad	4,928	5,389	5,532	4,587	4,176	1,570	157
Bank Deposits³	$ 309,991,117	$ 296,209,000					
Value of all farm property	795,387,096	1,076,794,749	$491,471,806	$161,045,101	$117,439,558	$ 41,991,650	$ 5,223,563
Number of farms	59,956	59,934	46,170	24,700	16,389	4,506	1,738
Improved land in farms	$ 8,448,684	7,744,757	4,302,101	2,273,968	1,823,520	616,169	95,594
Average value of all farm property per farm	13,266	17,983	10,645	6,520	7,166	9,319	3,006
Number of farms irrigated	31,288	28,756	25,857	17,613	8,227	*	*
Acreage irrigated	$ 3,393,619	$ 3,348,385	2,792,032	1,611,271	890,735	*	*
Investment in irrigation works	$ 87,603,240	$ 88,302,442	56,636,443	11,758,703	6,368,755	5,039,228	2,335,106
Value of agricultural products	126,174,000	149,687,000	50,110,627	16,970,588	13,136,810	8,703,342	2,871,102
Value of livestock on farms	116,920,000	152,936,000	68,620,000	49,753,000	22,594,010	2,157,495	*
Acres of patented land	37,163,043	29,462,000	17,648,322	13,837,973	9,980,172		
Acreage of homestead land	8,027,468	8,985,820	21,726,192	39,650,247			
Number of manufacturing establishments	1,545	2,631	2,034	1,323	1,518	599	256
Number of persons engaged in manufacturing	38,932	44,729	34,115	22,768	17,067	5,074	876
Capital invested in manufacturing	$ 304,654,661	$ 243,827,000	$162,668,000	$ 58,173,000	$ 26,651,840	$ 4,311,714	$ 2,835,605
Value of output of factories	$ 8,238,094	$ 275,622,000	130,044,000	89,068,000	42,480,205	14,260,159	2,852,820
Coal (long tons)	4,517,619	12,514,693	12,104,887	5,495,734	3,075,781	375,000	69,977⁵
Gold, value	$ 1,687,398	$ 7,576,000	$ 20,506,000	$ 28,762,000	$ 4,151,132	$ 3,253,000	$ 3,015,000⁶
Silver, value	1,366,820	5,896,000	4,595,000	12,609,000	19,740,000	16,557,000	660,000⁶
Copper, value	2,213,000	744,000	1,062,000	1,299,000	559,000	184,000	39,000⁶
Lead, value	3,480,864	3,730,000	3,347,000	7,228,000	4,914,000	3,567,000	15,000⁶
Zinc, value	1,627,987	3,952,000	4,163,000	716,000	16,500		
Petroleum, barrels		111,000	240,000	317,000	369,000		

NOTE—In this compilation census figures have been used exclusively, where applicable, so that they may be comparable. Figures indicate only the amount or number reported for the census year, and do not indicate 10-year totals. Colorado was not a state until 1876, hence much of the information prior to that time is not available.

¹ The figure shown here is the first state assessment, that for 1877.
² Data concerning deposits of both state and national banks prior to 1920 are not available.
³ No census figure published for the year indicated.
⁴ Prior to 1900 much of the public domain in Colorado was unsurveyed, and there was no record of its approximate area.
⁵ Production for 1873, the first year of which there is a record.
⁶ Total value of the product from beginning of the industry to 1870.
⁷ Prior to 1886 the production of petroleum from 1862 averaged about 15,000 barrels annually.
⁸ In 1913 Colorado's assessment system was changed from that of a valuation on a basis of one-third the actual value to full value, thus accounting for the large increase between 1910 and 1920.

(Prepared by the State Board of Immigration)

INDEX